ADOBE ACROBAT 9
HOW-TOs
125 ESSENTIAL TECHNIQUES

DONNA L. BAKER

Adobe

Adobe Acrobat 9 How-Tos
125 Essential Techniques

Donna L. Baker

This Adobe Press book is published by
Peachpit

For information on Adobe Press books, contact:
Peachpit
1249 Eighth Street
Berkeley, CA 94710
510/524-2178
510/524-2221 (fax)

To report errors, please send a note to errata@peachpit.com
Peachpit is a division of Pearson Education

For the latest on Adobe Press books, go to
www.adobe.com/adobepress

Editors: Becky Morgan, Valerie Witte
Production Editor: Tracey Croom
Copyeditor: Elizabeth Welch
Proofreader: Elissa Rabellino
Compositor: ICC Macmillan Inc.
Indexer: Rebecca Plunkett
Cover design: Mimi Heft
Interior design: Mimi Heft

ISBN 13: 978-0-321-55294-5

ISBN 10:   0-321-55294-6

9 8 7 6 5 4 3 2

Printed and bound in the United States of America

Dedication

For Pippi

Acknowledgments

Thanks to the folks at Adobe. It's been terrific to work with Acrobat all these years and watch it grow into such a robust and—dare I say it—cool piece of software.

Thanks to the folks at Peachpit, especially my diligent editor, Valerie Witte, and the all-seeing, all-knowing Becky Morgan.

Thanks to the folks at home who offer me support and fresh coffee: my dear hubby, Terry; my girls, Erin and Deena; and my goofy dogs.

Finally, as always, thanks to Tom Waits for bringing on the music.

Contents

Chapter One: Getting Started, Staying Organized 1

  #1:   Getting Around the Interface 2

  #2:   Helping Yourself 4

  #3:   Customizing What You See on the Screen 5

  #4:   What Do You Prefer? 7

  #5:   Getting Organized 10

  #6:   Conducting Searches 12

  #7:   Searching for Specifics 15

  #8:   Building and Applying an Index 17

Chapter Two: Creating PDF Files Outside Acrobat 21

  #9:   Printing with the Adobe PDF Printer 22

  #10:   Using PDFMaker in Microsoft Word 25

  #11:   Merging Word Files to PDF 29

  #12:   Producing PDF Files in Excel, Access, and Project 31

  #13:   Generating PDF Documents in PowerPoint 33

  #14:   Adding Specialized Media Content 35

  #15:   Making PDF Documents from Web Pages 38

  #16:   Archiving E-mail Messages 40

Chapter Three: Creating PDF Files in Distiller and Acrobat 43

  #17:   Working with Acrobat Distiller and Job Options 44

  #18:   Watching Folders via Distiller 48

  #19:   Starting a PDF File from a Blank Page 50

  #20:   Merging Multiple Files into a Single PDF Document 52

  #21:   Creating a PDF from Web Pages in Acrobat 54

  #22:   Creating a PDF from a Scan in Acrobat 56

  #23:   Creating a PDF from a Clipboard Image 59

  #24:   Attaching Source Files to a PDF 61

Chapter Four: Producing a PDF Portfolio....................................**65**

#25: PDF Portfolio Building 101.....................................66

#26: Customizing the Appearance..................................68

#27: Branding a PDF Portfolio 70

#28: Organizing and Modifying Contents..........................73

#29: Applying Acrobat Commands 75

#30: Managing and Distributing a Portfolio 77

Chapter Five: Creating Output: Saving, Exporting, and Printing **79**

#31: Finding Information about Your Document 80

#32: Using the Examine PDF Process...............................83

#33: Optimizing a PDF Document 85

#34: Exporting PDF Documents in Other Formats..................88

#35: Saving Image PDF Files.......................................91

#36: Choosing Settings for Basic and Production Printing 93

#37: Choosing and Using Fonts....................................96

#38: Print Troubleshooting 101 98

Chapter Six: Complying with PDF and Accessibility Standards **101**

#39: Testing and Fixing a Document with Preflight................102

#40: Ensuring Standards Compliance 104

#41: Fixing Print and File Issues Automatically 106

#42: Making Preflight Work for You 108

#43: Creating and Using a Printing Droplet 110

#44: Examining a Document's Output 112

#45: Navigating a Document 114

#46: Specifying Accessibility Requirements 117

#47: Basic Document Tagging 119

#48: Reporting On and Repairing a Document....................121

#49: Enhancing PDF Accessibility.................................123

Chapter Seven: Transforming Document Pages **127**

#50: Changing Pages and Their Contents 128

#51: Cropping and Rotating Pages. 132

#52: Applying Page and Bates Numbering 134

#53: Inserting Headers and Footers. 137

#54: Adding Watermarks and Backgrounds 139

#55: Batching Tasks to Save Time 141

Chapter Eight: Touching Up and Modifying a PDF Document. **145**

#56: Selecting and Editing Text in a PDF 146

#57: Editing Text and Modifying Attributes 148

#58: Object TouchUps. 151

#59: Reusing Images 153

#60: Round-trip Editing an Image 155

#61: Extracting Active Text from an Image 157

#62: Redacting Content 160

Chapter Nine: Building Content with Adobe Presenter. **163**

#63: Creating a Presenter Publication. 164

#64: Specifying a Theme 167

#65: Recording and Using Audio and Video 170

#66: Including Attachments 173

#67: Working in the Quiz Manager. 176

#68: Writing a Quiz. 178

#69: Previewing and Publishing 182

Chapter Ten: Commenting in a PDF Document **185**

#70: Adding Sticky Notes and Highlighting Comments. 186

#71: Setting Commenting Preferences. 188

#72: Working with Text Edit Comments. 190

#73: Using and Managing Stamp Tools 192

#74: Drawing and Marking Up Shapes in Acrobat 195

#75: Working with the Comments List 197

#76: Exporting Comments to a Word Document (Windows) 200

#77: Setting Comment Status and Creating Summaries 204

Chapter Eleven: Live Reviewing and Collaboration **207**

#78: Collaborating Live on Acrobat.com 208

#79: Starting a Shared Review 211

#80: Using an E-mail Review. 214

#81: Participating Online 216

#82: Moving to a ConnectNow Meeting Room 219

#83: Working in Buzzword. 222

#84: Comparing Documents 225

#85: Tracking a Review 228

Chapter Twelve: Creating and Handling Forms **231**

#86: Letting the Form Wizard Guide You 232

#87: Working in Form Edit Mode 234

#88: Drawing and Customizing Form Fields. 237

#89: Adding Calculations and Field Behaviors. 241

#90: Organizing and Ordering a Form 244

#91: Simplifying a Visually Complex Form. 247

#92: Distributing Forms 249

#93: Tracking Forms. 253

#94: Handling Form Returns. 255

Chapter Thirteen: Using Flash Video and 3D Media **259**

#95: Inserting Flash Media in a PDF File. 260

#96: Inserting SWF in a PDF File 263

#97: Inserting Movies and Legacy Versions 265

#98: Working with 3D Content 268

#99: Editing in Adobe 3D Reviewer 270

#100: Measuring 3D Objects. 272

#101: Inserting Multimedia Comments 274

#102: Using Actions to Show Multimedia Views 277

Chapter Fourteen: Using Drawings, Maps, and Layers **279**

#103: Converting Visio, InDesign, and Illustrator Documents 280

#104: Working with a Layered Document 283

#105: Adding New Layers. 285

#106: Using Data Embedded in a Document 287

#107: Applying Positioning Features 288

#108: Measuring Objects 290

#109: Commenting and Measuring on a PDF Map. 293

#110: Bookmarking Drawings, Maps, or Layers .296

Chapter Fifteen: Controlling Action and Interaction **299**

#111: Linking Content in a Document 300

#112: Creating Bookmarks in a Source Document. 303

#113: Adding Bookmarks in Acrobat 305

#114: Naming Destinations. 307

#115: Drawing a Simple Button 309

#116: Building a Batch of Buttons 311

#117: Configuring a Push Button 313

#118: Editing Actions. 315

Chapter Sixteen: Making Your Documents Secure. **317**

#119: Using Security Levels and Passwords for a Document 318

#120: Creating a Digital ID Profile 321

#121: Signing a Document 325

#122: Tracking Changes 328

#123: Creating and Managing Security Policies. .332

#124: Managing Multimedia and Security Trusts 334

#125: Using Secure ePaper 338

Index **341**

CHAPTER ONE

Getting Started, Staying Organized

Microsoft Word—Adobe Photoshop—Firefox—when you think of a piece of software, it's generally easy to figure out what to do with it. Adobe Acrobat, however, is unique in that it has many functional areas utilized by a diverse range of users. A print designer uses Acrobat to display page proofs and run preflight checks; an engineer or architect uses Acrobat to hold and organize models, as well as product or project documentation; a dentist uses Acrobat to store patient records and scanned x-rays.

The scope and depth of Acrobat is amazing, but it boils down to the fact that fundamentally you are handling information. If you are dealing with information on an ongoing basis, Acrobat can assist you with its wide range of tools.

Rather than trying to qualify the program in a single word, let's consider the ways in which Acrobat functions. Acrobat is designed to create PDF content using material from a wide range of sources; combine content from source files or selected subsegments of existing PDF files; collaborate with others using commenting and review; add interactive content and multimedia using Flash; and so much more.

In this book, I have assembled techniques that I use and experiment with on a regular basis. My goal is to show you what Acrobat can do, and how to find tools and use processes that can help you work smarter and faster.

In this first chapter, you'll see what makes up the program's interface, learn how to look at your document, and discover ways to organize your PDF files and their contents.

#1 Getting Around the Interface

When you open Acrobat 9 Pro, the default program includes several elements (**Figure 1**). You can configure the Acrobat layout in a variety of ways by adjusting the panel groupings and settings:

- **Menu items.** The Main menu across the top of the program contains common menu items like File and Edit, as well as Acrobat 9 Pro menu items such as Advanced and Document.

- **Toolbars.** Acrobat contains a variety of toolbars; most items found in toolbars are available as menu commands as well.

- **Task buttons.** You can access a variety of tasks and functions for a specific type of work, such as creating a PDF or signing a document, using the task buttons.

- **Document message bar.** Look for a message bar that lets you know if the document contains certain types of content, such as form fields or signatures, below the toolbars.

- **Navigation pane.** The icons along the left side of the program window make up the Navigation pane. The functions available from the Navigation pane let you manage and control the content of your PDF document.

- **Document pane.** An open PDF document displays in the Document pane. The document's page size and scroll bars frame the bottom and right sides of the Document pane.

Look Before You Touch

You can modify the screen display—toolbars, Navigation panel tabs, and so on. But before you do, familiarize yourself with the contents. Click the down arrows to see what's in a pop-up menu, for example. Click an icon in the Navigation pane to see its contents. Click its Options menu to learn what you can do in the pane. Checking out Acrobat's default offerings may help you as you learn how to work with the program.

Navigation pane

Menu items   Task buttons

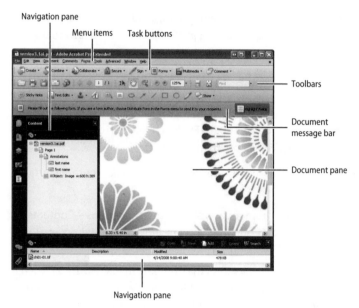

Toolbars

Document
message bar

Document pane

Navigation pane

Figure 1 The Acrobat 9 Pro interface is made up of several components.

Note
Throughout this book, the Windows command is given first, followed by the Mac command in parentheses.

#2 Helping Yourself

Acrobat 9 offers a Web-based Help system. In addition to the usual sorts of information you'd expect to find in a Help file, such as how to use the program features and where to find shortcuts, the Help system includes links to online resources such as Adobe Video Workshop, where you can view videos on Acrobat and other Adobe software.

For in-depth information, use the main Help feature:

- Choose Help > Adobe Acrobat 9 Pro Extended Help or press the F1 key. The Adobe Help Viewer opens in a browser window.

- Use the navigation menu in the left frame to make your way through the files.

- You can choose from two types of search options—Contents or Search—depending on what you are looking for and on your preferred method of working.

The Adobe Help Viewer shows the Contents menu (**Figure 2**) when it opens. The content is arranged in a hierarchy. Each plus sign (+) next to a topic means subtopics are available: Click the + to open a nested item list. If a topic name displays a minus sign (–), it has nested content already displayed. Click an item to display its contents in the main frame of the browser window.

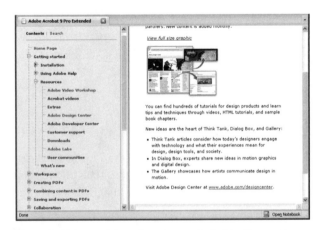

Figure 2 Click one of the main topic areas in the How To panel to open a list of topics.

Get Around

Unlike with Help systems in the "old" days, you won't find navigation or print buttons in Acrobat 9. The Acrobat 9 Help system uses the browser tools for common functions like printing and navigating, thus leaving a minimal, streamlined Help interface.

Help Is Close at Hand

Sometimes you need to refer to a page in the Help file repeatedly. Instead of closing the window and then reopening and finding the page again, set a bookmark for the page and add it to your browser bookmarks.

Help Using Help

Pay attention to the way you work. If you are a systematic person, the Contents menu in the Adobe Help Viewer will guide you from general to specific topics. Use the Search menu if you are familiar with the program and want to locate a specific topic.

#3 Customizing What You See on the Screen

One of the best ways to save space, and your eyesight, is to control what tools you display on the screen. It is possible to open enough toolbars to fill a good portion of the screen, leaving little room for the actual document. These techniques help you "de-clutter" your screen:

- If you have opened a number of toolbars and want to return to the default set, choose View > Toolbars > Reset Toolbars. Acrobat closes the extras and the layout reverts to the default toolbars in the default locations.

- Even using only the default toolbars and task buttons, you may find it confusing to figure out what you have to work with. Move your pointer over the hatched vertical line at the left edge of a toolbar to display the toolbar's name; move your pointer over a tool to view its name and a description of how to use it in a tooltip (**Figure 3a**).

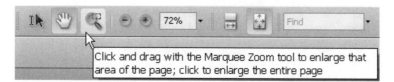

Figure 3a Display a description and name of the button in a tooltip.

- Move your pointer over the hatched vertical line and drag to pull a toolbar from its docked position. When you release the mouse, the toolbar is floating on the screen. Drag the toolbar back to the toolbar area and release the mouse to dock it again.

- You can further control your use of screen real estate by setting how the labels are displayed. Choose View > Toolbars > Show Button Labels and then select the Default, All, or No button label option.

- Task buttons work slightly differently. You can't drag an individual task button off the taskbar (as you can with individual tools on toolbars); if you try, you'll remove the entire taskbar. As with other toolbars, add and remove Task buttons in the More Tools dialog.

- Rather than using the Main menu, save one step when changing toolbars. Right-click (Control-click) the toolbar well to display the same options available from the menus.

(continued on next page)

Returning to Default Settings

If you return to the default toolbar settings, any tools you removed from a default toolbar, as well as any that you added, are returned to their original locations. Unlike other programs in Adobe Creative Suites, Acrobat 9 has no ability to save a workspace, including custom toolbars and arrangements.

Locking Toolbars

When you close and reopen a program, the arrangement of toolbars and task buttons is maintained. If you like a particular arrangement of toolbars, you can lock it. When you get to the point where you are "one with the program," select tools and keep working without searching for a tool. Choose View > Toolbars > Lock Toolbars. The separator bars between the individual toolbars disappear. Floating toolbars don't lock, and they can't be docked with a locked toolbar.

- Right-click (Control-click) the toolbar well and choose More Tools to open the More Tools dialog (**Figure 3b**).

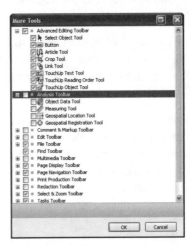

Figure 3b Select tools to display and hide in the More Tools dialog.

#4 What Do You Prefer?

You can define a number of preferences that help you get to work faster. Some preferences get you into the program faster; others show you what you are working with more quickly.

Choose Edit > Preferences (Acrobat > Preferences) to open the Preferences dialog. You see a long Categories list in the left pane of the dialog; clicking an option displays a range of settings in the right pane of the dialog. Click Documents in the Categories list to display the Startup options in the right pane of the dialog (**Figure 4a**).

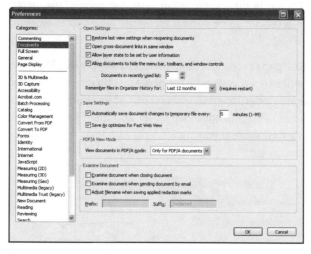

Figure 4a Configure settings to help you get into the document quicker.

The Open Settings preferences are listed at the top of the window, followed by Save Settings, PDF/A View Mode, and Examine Document preferences.

Here are a few hints for selecting options:

- Do you like to see the same thing each time you open a file? Select the "Restore last view settings when reopening documents" check box.

- If you work with more than five documents on a regular basis, change the value shown in "Documents in recently used list" from its default of 5. Click the File menu heading to see the list at the bottom of the menu and quickly select the document you want to open.

(continued on next page)

More and More Windows

Acrobat 9 is different from previous versions in that it has been reengineered to comply with Windows Vista issues. Each PDF file you open—either via Acrobat or through a browser window—opens a new instance of Acrobat. Fortunately, each instance shares memory and resources, so it isn't like running full multiple copies of the program. On the upside, you can always access each PDF you have open without having to select from a list, and crashing one file won't crash the whole program and lose your work.

Settings for All Seasons

The settings you choose are not specific to a particular document but apply to the program in general. Each time you open Acrobat 9, the program uses your preferences until you change them again.

Set Your Autosave

Set an autosave time in the "Automatically save document changes to temporary file" field. By default, Acrobat saves document changes every five minutes. If you are working on a large document, the autosave can take some time away from your work; you may want to increase the duration between autosaves.

How Smooth Is Smooth?

Experiment with the Rendering options in the Page Display preferences for different displays. Click the Smooth Text pull-down arrow and specify either Laptop/LCD or Monitor. If you work with both a desktop and a laptop, for example, you may find smoothing options necessary for clear viewing on one monitor that you won't need on another.

- If your workflow involves preparing files for archival purposes, choose Only for PDF/A mode from the "View documents in PDF/A mode" pop-up menu. Your files are automatically evaluated and tested.

- If your workflow involves sensitive material such as legal documents, choose the Examine Document options to evaluate the content of a file for hidden and other sensitive material before closing or before e-mailing documents.

Click Page Display in the options listed in the left pane of the Preferences dialog. You can set some page preferences to get up to working speed faster:

- Leave the "Use page cache" check box selected (**Figure 4b**). The page cache is a buffer area. If you cache the pages, as you display one page the next page in a document is read and placed in a buffer area until you are ready to view it. Pages load faster, and the faster load time is particularly noticeable if you are working with image-intensive or interactive documents.

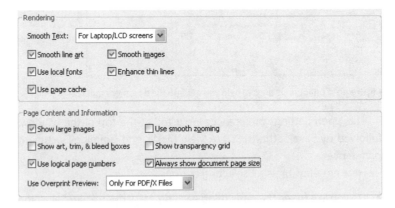

Figure 4b Speed up page display by choosing settings that draw content and display pages faster.

- Deselect the "Show large images" option if your computer has a slow redraw speed. On older computers, images take a lot of time to draw on the screen. Each time you move the image means more time waiting for the image to redraw again.

Getting Started, Staying Organized

- Deselect the Rendering preferences—text, line art, and images—if your computer is particularly slow. Deselecting the smoothing may save some time in displaying your documents, although you sacrifice some of the clarity and crispness of the content for display speed.

- If you work with different-sized pages often and need to know the page sizes, choose "Always show document page size" in the Page Content and Information settings.

When you have completed setting and changing the preferences, click OK to close the Preferences dialog and apply your settings.

#5 Getting Organized

Acrobat 9 contains a nifty feature called the Organizer. Use the Organizer to—you guessed it—organize your PDF files. Click the Organizer button on the File toolbar or choose File > Organizer > Open Organizer.

The Organizer opens in a separate window and displays three panes (**Figure 5**). You can drag the splitter bars between the panes to resize each one as you are working. Click an option in the Categories pane to display its list of PDF files in the Files pane; click a file in the Files pane to display its content in the Pages pane.

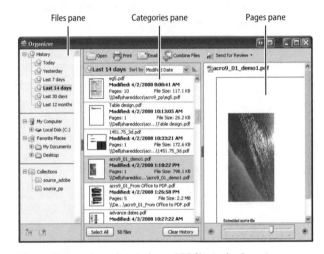

Figure 5 Organize and control your PDF files in the Organizer.

The Categories pane uses a hierarchy of folders. There are three types of categories: History, your computer's folders (to which you can add favorites), and Collections.

- History works like the History function in your Web browser. Select a time frame from the History listing to show the PDF files you have opened during that time frame in the Files pane. To clear the history, select the item in the History listing and click the Clear History button at the bottom of the Files pane.

- To add a Favorite Place, click Add a Favorite Place at the bottom of the Organizer window. Locate the folder you want to add in the resulting dialog, and click OK.

Repeating History

Take care when clearing the History. If you choose a History setting such as Last 12 Months or Last Week, all history listings of shorter duration, such as Today or Yesterday, are also cleared.

Things to Do in the Organizer

Above the Pages pane are several commands in a toolbar you can use to work with the selected file or files. For example, you can open, print, e-mail, or start a document containing multiple PDF files, or even start a review cycle right from the Organizer.

- To add a collection, right-click (Control-click) the Collections label and choose options to name the collection and add files. Right-click (Control-click) an existing collection to add or delete files.

In the Files pane, information displayed about each listed document includes basic details. An unprotected document shows a thumbnail; a document containing security or one opened from a Web browser shows only a PDF document icon. The default listing is by filename; you can click the Sort by down arrow to choose other sorting options, such as keywords, the document's title, or the author.

- The file selected in the Files pane is shown in the Pages pane. Use the – and + buttons to change the magnification of the view, or drag the slider to show the file's content.

- Name your collections to keep track of your work, and delete a collection when you are finished with a project.

- Choose File > Organizer > Collections to access your collections' contents from the main program menu.

- The History contents are also available in the File menu. Choose File > History and one of the date options. The History command is conveniently listed above the last documents opened in the File menu.

Collecting Logically

Use collections to organize your content in ways you find logical. For example, if you are working with a set of files that are to become a single PDF at some point in your workflow, add them to a collection. Right-click (Control-click) the Collection label in the Organizer and choose Add Files. Locate and select the files you want to add in the Browse for Folder dialog and click OK. Click the collection's name to view your working files.

#6 Conducting Searches

One feature we all use at one time or another is the dependable Search function. Acrobat 9 offers different methods to search, including through the Find toolbar or using the Search window.

Use the Find toolbar to quickly search an open document. To access the toolbar, use the Ctrl+F (Command+F) shortcut keys; or right-click (Control-click) the toolbar well and choose Find. Type the word or phrase in the field. To customize the search term, click the pull-down arrow and choose one or more options from the list (**Figure 6a**). Then, press Enter (Return) to show the first match on the visible page. Click Find Next to highlight the next match; click Find Previous to return to a prior result.

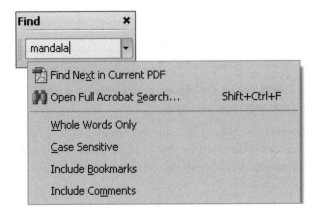

Figure 6a The Find toolbar is a convenient way to search an open file.

If you need to track down content in multiple folders, or are searching for a particular phrase or group of words for redaction (described in #62, "Redacting Content"), use the Search function. Choose Edit > Search or use the Shift+Ctrl+F (Shift+Command+F) shortcut keys to open the Search window (**Figure 6b**).

Figure 6b The Search window offers several ways to search for content.

Taking a Shortcut

Shortcut keys allow you to work quickly through a long list of search results in the Search window. In Windows, open the first document, and then press F3 to jump to the next and subsequent hits. Press Ctrl+] to go to the next document; press Ctrl+[to go to the previous document. In a document, press Ctrl+G to go to the next result; press Ctrl+Shift+G to go to the previous result.

Tip
Click Arrange Windows at the top of the Search window to lock the Search and Acrobat windows into place.

Follow these steps to conduct a search:

1. Type the word or words you want to find in the first field. You can't search using wildcards such as (*) or (?).

2. Select the file or folder you want to search by clicking the appropriate radio button. Choose from the currently active or selected document or all the files in a specified folder.

3. Choose search options by selecting the check boxes. You can select whole words, request case-sensitive results, and include bookmarks and comments.

(continued on next page)

4. Click Search. When the search is finished, the results and their locations appear by filename in the Results area of the Search window (**Figure 6c**).

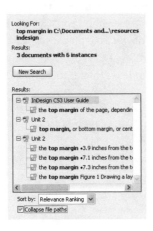

Figure 6c The results are ranked by relevance and listed in the Results area of the Search window.

You can see the number of instances of the word occurring in the set of files you searched, along with the number of documents containing the word. Click the box to the left of the file path to open a list of the results' locations, and then hover your mouse over a result listing to display the document page number.

Click a result in the Results area. Acrobat obligingly loads the document you selected (if it is not already displayed in the Document pane) and highlights the term on the document for you.

Sorting by filename isn't the only way to view results. To reorder the results, choose a sort method from the Sort by pop-up menu. You can choose from Modification Date, Location, and Relevance Ranking.

#7 Searching for Specifics

You can fine-tune a search using the Advanced Search options, or search for content such as keywords or metadata. Click the Use Advanced Search Options link at the bottom of the basic Search window to display additional searching parameters. To search the text in the document, type the word or words in the "What word or phrase would you like to search for?" field. Search using any combination of words or phrases, or you can use a Boolean query. Search using content other than a document's text, including bookmarks, attachments, and indexes. (Refer to #8, "Building and Applying an Index," to see how indexes are used.) A search can be conducted in a folder, a PDF Portfolio, or even a PDF Portfolio's attachments (check out Chapter 4 to learn about Portfolio creation).

Figure 7a shows the Search window for a search based on keywords rather than text in the document. You can use up to three additional search parameters.

Figure 7a Rather than using simple words or phrases, search for files using combinations of criteria such as keywords or dates.

Use the pop-up menus below the "Use these additional criteria" label. Click the pop-up menu on the left to display a list of options, as shown in the figure. Select the search option you desire, and then click the pop-up menu on the right and select a modifier. Finally, type the search term in the field, such as the keyword you wish to search for. A green check mark displays in the check box to the left of the criteria's fields.

Searching in the Neighborhood

Use proximity searching along with the "Match Exact word or phrase" option in the Advanced Search window to find occurrences of search terms within 900 words of each other. Increase or decrease the range of words for searching in the Search preferences.

Develop a System

If you are working with hundreds of documents or PDF images, developing a system before embarking on a document properties adventure is the smart thing to do. Decide if a term is used as a subject or a keyword, not both. If you search using a subject term and have used it as a keyword in some documents, your search results are limited.

If you want to use an author's name, decide beforehand if the first name, first name and initial, or full name of the author is to be used. This way, anyone working with the files understands your properties system. Unless you create a naming and description system that is understandable to all using the documents, it's a waste of time to make the effort to include additional descriptions.

Click the Search button to search the document properties for the files in the selected folder. Acrobat returns results that contain **all** additional search criteria only. You can remove criteria by clicking the green check mark to deselect it.

When you create a PDF, technical data that is part of the source document is converted along with the text and images you see on the page. You can add more types of data from within Acrobat by modifying the Document Properties.

Open the document you want to alter, and then choose File > Properties, or use the shortcut Ctrl+D (Command+D) (**Figure 7b**).

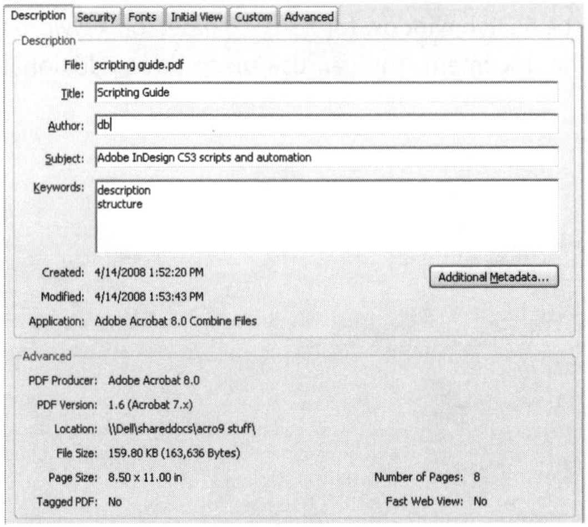

Figure 7b Add search terms and categories in the Properties dialog.

Enter the additional information you want to use for searching and organizing in the appropriate fields. If you are working with images, clicking the Additional Metadata button opens the Document Metadata for [*filename*] dialog to add further information about the image.

Click OK to close the Properties dialog. Then, save the document to save the information you added in the dialog.

#8 Building and Applying an Index

For a large collection of documents, save searching time by building an index and attaching it to the files. Once your files are collected in a single location, follow these steps:

1. Choose Advanced > Document Processing > Full Text Index with Catalog to open the Catalog dialog, and click New Index. The Index Definition dialog opens (**Figure 8a**).

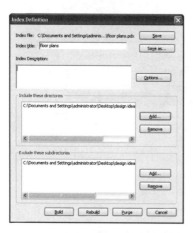

Figure 8a Configure the content for your index.

2. Add information to the dialog to name and describe the index, and specify the folders you want to include.

Fixing Indexes

You need to rerun the Catalog process if you make changes to the content of the documents contained within the index, or move or rename the documents. Instead of building from scratch, choose Advanced > Full Text Index with Catalog and click Open Index in the Catalog dialog. Locate and select the index you want to modify, and click Open to load the file into the Index Definition dialog (shown in Figure 8a). Click Rebuild to repair and reconfigure the index. If you want to delete the index, click Purge.

Power Indexing

Save time by setting preferences for indexing. Choose Edit > Preferences (Acrobat > Preferences) and click Catalog in the left column. In the Catalog preferences, choose the same options as those shown in Figure 8b in the Options dialog and click OK to close the Preferences dialog. The next time you build an index, any options you chose in the Preferences, such as stop words, are automatically applied to the index.

3. Click Options to display ways to either add or remove content from the index in the Options dialog (**Figure 8b**). Choose to exclude numbers, add custom properties, use stop words, or specify the tags to include, described in the sidebar "Getting Ready for Indexing."

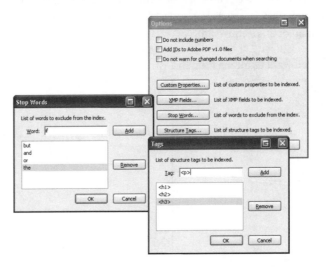

Figure 8b Specify the options you want to include—or exclude— in the index.

4. Click OK to dismiss the Options dialog, and then click the Build button at the bottom of the Index Definition dialog. The collection is processed and the results displayed in the Build dialog. Click Close to dismiss the Build dialog.

Note
Several files are added to the index's folder, including a log file and the index.pdx file, which is the index's database file. There is also a folder containing two more indexing files. Don't delete or move any of the indexing folders or files, or you will corrupt the index.

To see your index in action, follow these steps:

1. Choose Edit > Search to open the Search window, and click Use Advanced Search Options.

2. Choose Select Index from the Look in pop-up menu. The Index selection dialog opens.

3. Click Add to locate and select indexes from your computer. Choose the index you want to attach from the list.

4. Click OK to attach the index or indexes to your PDF.

Getting Ready for Indexing

Here are some tips to make indexing smoother:

- Move or copy the files you want to use into a separate folder. Acrobat adds indexing to files and folders. Keeping everything all in one place prevents indexing errors.

- Break a large document into chunks. For example, create PDF files from individual chapters of a manual. The indexed searches will be faster.

- Make sure all the information required in the individual documents is complete, including bookmarks, links, keywords, and so on. Information added after the index is generated isn't included.

- If your documents are tagged, you can specify the content to include in the index by listing the appropriate tags, shown in Figure 8b.

- Consider using stop words—words that are excluded from the index, such as "and," "if," "or," and so on by clicking Stop Words in the Options dialog to open a Stop Words dialog, also shown in Figure 8b. You can exclude up to 500 case-sensitive words, which can result in faster search returns.

- If you are designing an index using stop words, include a read-me text file so your users understand what they can search for and how to use the index.

CHAPTER TWO

Creating PDF Files Outside Acrobat

Acrobat lets you choose among several ways to create a PDF file from within other applications, and these capabilities expand with each revision of Acrobat. After you install Acrobat, you'll find new menus and toolbars in most Microsoft Office programs, such as Word, Excel, PowerPoint, and Outlook. The menus and toolbars make up PDFMaker 9, which you can use to configure settings and create PDF content right from your Office program. Acrobat also installs the Adobe PDF printer driver, which lets you print PDF documents from many programs, as well as Adobe Distiller, a program that converts PostScript or Encapsulated PostScript (EPS) files, such as those created in Adobe Illustrator, to PDF format. Read about creating PDF files with Distiller in Chapter 3 "Creating PDF Files in Distiller and Acrobat."

Note

In Acrobat 9, the PDFMaker feature is no longer included in Mac systems. Because of differences in system architectures, the Mac PDFMaker doesn't have the functionality of the Windows PDFMaker; converting to PDF in Mac can be done using system tools. Also, Acrobat no longer supports PDFMaker in Office 2000 and earlier.

Conversions can be controlled by PDFMaker settings, by Acrobat Distiller, and by source programs that export PDF-formatted files directly. You configure conversion settings according to the material you are working with—and according to what you intend to do with it. Preparing information for print use, for example, is different than preparing information for online use. You have a lot of choices!

#9 Printing with the Adobe PDF Printer

If you can print a file in a program, you can usually generate a PDF file. The key is the Adobe PDF printer driver included as part of the Acrobat 9 installation process. For convenience, the Adobe PDF printer is included in your system's printer list and is available through your Print dialog.

To create a PDF file from a source program in Windows, follow these steps:

1. Open your program and the document you want to convert to a PDF. Choose File > Print to open the Print dialog.

2. Choose Adobe PDF from the Printer Name menu.

3. Select from a number of options for printing using the Print what radio buttons at the lower left of the dialog. Printing choices include the entire document, or you can specify components based on the type of document you are converting.

4. Click Options at the bottom left of the Print dialog to open a list of different print options (such as field codes, XML, and document properties) that vary according to the type of file you are converting. When you've made selections, click OK to dismiss the dialog and return to the main Print dialog.

5. Click OK to process the file, choose a name and storage location depending on the program's print command process, and click Save. The file saves to PDF, rather than to your printer, and you have a PDF version of the source file.

More Printer Settings

You can modify preferences and settings for the Adobe PDF printer driver. In the Print dialog, click Properties to open the Adobe PDF Document Properties dialog. Review the check boxes at the lower part of the Adobe PDF Document Properties dialog:

- If you are printing to save the document for future use, deselect "View Adobe PDF results" to prevent the file from opening in Acrobat.

- Leave the "Add document information" option selected; the information can be later used in Acrobat for searching, indexing, and identification.

- Deselect the "Rely on system fonts only; do not use document fonts" option if you are planning to use the document later in Acrobat or Acrobat Distiller. Distiller requires embedded fonts, and you often use font embedding to prepare a document for distribution.

(continued on next page)

6. Click Properties in the Print dialog to open the Adobe PDF Document Properties dialog, which displays the Adobe PDF Settings tab by default. Here you can choose additional print options that vary according to the type of file you are converting (**Figure 9**):

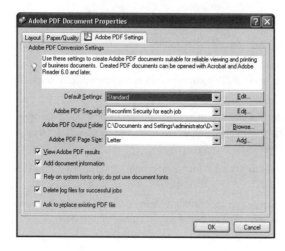

Figure 9 Choose from a number of options to configure the print driver and PDF output.

- Use the four settings at the top of the dialog to save time. If you always produce basic PDF conversions, leave the Standard Default Settings, or choose an alternate from the pull-down list.

- Automatically attach password protection to all your files at conversion using an option from the Adobe PDF Security pull-down list. Choose from either "Reconfirm Security for each job" or "Use the last known settings."

- Click Browse and locate a consistent output folder, displayed in the Adobe PDF Output Folder setting. This is a great timesaver if you routinely convert files and leave them in a staging area before further work.

(continued on next page)

- Leave the "Delete log files for successful jobs" option selected. You don't need to trouble-shoot a document that converts successfully.

- The "Ask to replace existing PDF file" option is deselected by default. If you are indeed replacing an existing file, the Save As dialog asks you about replacement, so you don't have to duplicate the function.

Converting a Group of Documents

If you are converting a large number of documents, convert one and check that it meets your needs before converting the others. This will save you valuable error-checking time.

Convenient File Naming

Get into the habit of setting up a system of filenames when you are converting files from one format to another. When you print or generate a PDF using the Adobe PDF printer driver or other PDF conversion methods, by default the folder containing the source document opens and the file is assigned the source document's name and the .pdf extension. Using the same naming structure saves time, and you can track which documents have been converted to PDF more easily.

- Choose an alternate page size from the Adobe PDF Page Size dropdown list if your work requires it.

  Click OK to dismiss the secondary dialog and return to the Print dialog.

Preparing for Conversions

Before you convert a document to PDF format, be sure to complete these steps:

- Check spelling and grammar, and make sure the finished content is how you want it to appear in the PDF format. It is easier to ensure that the original document is complete than to edit it in Acrobat.

- Decide how the document is to be used. You choose different conversion settings for an online document, for example, than for one intended for high-quality printing.

- Check links and other content such as comments if you plan to convert them for PDF use.

- Check the conversion option's settings. For example, you may choose a Standard conversion option but require changes in the graphic conversion settings.

#10 Using PDFMaker in Microsoft Word

One of the most common programs used with Acrobat is Microsoft Word. You can use the PDFMaker that Acrobat automatically installs into Word on Windows to quickly generate a PDF version of the document. If your workflow includes merging documents on a regular basis, try out the Mail Merge to Adobe PDF feature, which not only merges database content with a Word file but also converts the merged documents to PDF.

The Standard conversion setting, the default used by PDFMaker, produces a PDF file that is both suitable for printing and small enough for easy distribution. Once you specify the settings, they remain until you adjust them again. Converting a Word document to PDF is a one-click process.

When your document is ready for conversion, save it and then click Convert to PDF 📄 on the PDFMaker 9.0 toolbar in Windows or choose Adobe PDF > Convert to Adobe PDF. Using the default PDFMaker settings, a Save As dialog opens displaying the same name as your Word document; change the filename and location if necessary and then click Save to close the dialog and convert the file.

To view the settings, choose Adobe PDF > Change Conversion Settings to open the dialog (**Figure 10a**).

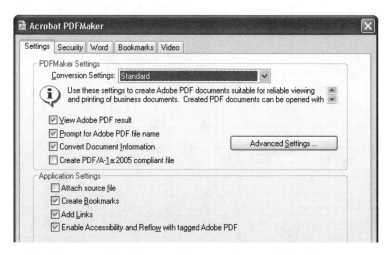

Figure 10a The Acrobat PDFMaker dialog contains different numbers of tabs depending on the program, but always includes the Settings and Security tabs.

The dialog displays five tabs: Settings, Security, Word, Bookmarks, and Video (read about inserting video and 3D in #14, "Adding Specialized Media Content"). Choose an alternate group of settings from the Conversion Settings pop-up menu. Regardless of the conversion setting you select, the Settings tab selections remain much the same. Most of the PDFMaker Settings are common in all PDFMakers (see the sidebar "Simple Settings"); the Application Settings vary among programs, as described in the sidebar "Application Settings for Conversions."

Each PDFMaker installed into Microsoft Office programs on Windows includes settings specific to the program, either in separate tabs or as options in the Settings tab. In Word, you can convert content such as bookmarks and comments, as well as text. Select the Word tab to display Word-specific options:

- To preserve comments in your converted Word documents, select "Convert displayed comments to notes in Adobe PDF." (See Chapter 10 "Commenting in a PDF Document," to learn about using comments.) Comments in the source document are listed in the Word tab (**Figure 10b**). Use the options to configure the comment appearance.

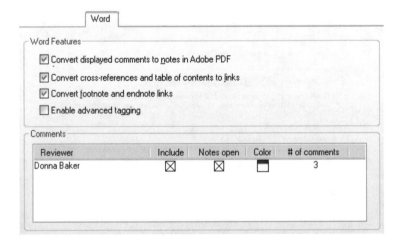

Figure 10b Choose options for converting Word-specific content such as footnotes and comments.

- Preserve referencing work you have done, such as cross-references, a table of contents, footnotes, and endnotes, by choosing one of the convert options. Click "Enable advanced tagging" to integrate the tags for selected features into the converted PDF file. Read about using tags in #46, "Basic Document Tagging."

The Word PDFMaker in Windows gives you three choices for generating bookmarks, depending on your document's structure. Bookmarks are created from document styles or from headings you select from the default template. If you have added bookmarks to the document, you can use them in the PDF document automatically. Open the Conversion Settings dialog and select the Bookmarks tab (**Figure 10c**).

Figure 10c Specify the styles or headings to use as bookmarks.

The options on this tab let you do the following:

- Convert bookmarks you created in Word to PDF bookmarks.

- Convert Word headings by selecting/deselecting heading levels in the list.

- Convert specific styles by selecting them in the list.

- If you make changes to PDFMaker settings and want to revert, click Restore Defaults at the lower left of the dialog.

- The "Create PDF/A-1a: 2005 compliant file" option isn't found in all programs' PDFMakers, and isn't necessary except in those cases where you want to produce a file for long-term archival storage.

Application Settings for Conversions

The lower part of the Settings dialog varies according to the PDFMaker; most programs include the following options for Application Settings:

- Select "Attach source file" to attach the source file automatically to the converted PDF document.

- The Create Bookmarks option converts elements to PDF bookmarks, such as headings in Word, worksheet names in Excel, and slide titles in PowerPoint.

- Add Links converts active links and hypertext in the document to PDF links.

- The "Enable Accessibility and Reflow with tagged Adobe PDF" option embeds specialized tags in the file used by devices like screen readers to control how the document is described and read. (Read about accessible PDF documents in #48, "Complying with Accessibility Standards.")

If you use styles or headings, it's much quicker to scroll through the list to check off the specific styles or headings you want to convert rather than selecting a check box at the top of the dialog and then deselecting the elements you want to exclude.

Note
If you make custom bookmark assignments in the Bookmarks tab of the Conversion Settings dialog, your settings are overridden if you choose Add Bookmarks to Adobe PDF in the Settings tab.

Pick What You Want

All Office PDFMakers in Windows now offer an option to create a PDF from subsets of the file as well as the entire document. If you want to share information on a particular table on one page of your annual report, for example, select the content on the page and follow these steps:

1. Choose Adobe PDF > Convert to Adobe PDF to open the Save PDF File As dialog.

2. Name the file, and click Options to display a dialog where you choose the content for conversion, including the selection, a page range, or the entire document.

3. Choose the page features from the available options. The choices depend on the content you are converting. For example, you can't use bookmarks if you are converting a selection.

4. Click OK to close the dialog; then click Save to convert and save the PDF content.

What About Security?

The Acrobat PDFMaker dialog contains the Security tab, used to add password protection to a file. If your document is being converted for further use in Acrobat, don't add security at this point. Wait until the document is processed in Acrobat and then apply security settings. Otherwise, each time you open the converted PDF document, you have to input passwords. Chapter 16 discusses using passwords and other forms of security.

#11 Merging Word Files to PDF

The Word PDFMaker in Windows also produces merged documents. This feature, first introduced in Acrobat 8, can attach the merged PDF files to e-mail messages. Be sure your source data and the merge document containing the merge fields are ready first (**Figure 11a**). When you're ready, test the merge first before running the PDFMaker process. If you don't have the Word source files prepared properly, you'll see an Acrobat PDFMaker message outlining the error of your ways, and the merge won't proceed.

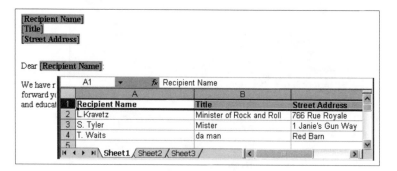

Figure 11a Be sure to test your merge functions before starting.

Take the Time to Save Time

Be sure to test the appearance of the merge in Word before starting the PDF-Maker conversion process. You don't want to run a batch of hundreds of documents to find out there's a space missing between merge fields. Although Acrobat PDFMaker shows a message if your mail merge components aren't configured properly, checking spelling, punctuation, and the like isn't part of its function.

Keeping Names in Order

When you use the PDFMaker to produce merged documents, the PDF file is named using the text you type in the "Specify PDF file name" field ("PDFMailer" is used in the example). The merged documents are named using the text, an underscore, and a numerical seven-digit suffix in the order in which the files are converted. In the example, the files are named PDFMailer_0000101.pdf, PDFMailer_0000102.pdf, and so on.

Once the documents are ready and you have tested the merge, follow these steps:

1. Choose Adobe PDF > Mail Merge To Adobe PDF to open the Acrobat PDFMaker—Mail Merge dialog (**Figure 11b**).

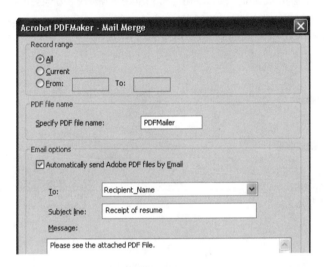

Figure 11b Choose the settings for the mail merge to PDF process, and choose e-mail settings if desired.

2. Choose the records to use for the merge, as well as a name in the "Specify PDF file name" field.

3. To create merged PDF files and attach them to e-mail messages, select "Automatically send Adobe PDF files by Email" to activate the remaining fields in the dialog and specify the e-mail options.

4. Click OK to close the dialog. The data is processed, and a Browse For Folder dialog opens. Locate and select the folder where you want to save the finished files, and click OK to close the dialog.

5. When the files are processed, the Choose Profile dialog opens. Select your e-mail profile and click OK. The dialog closes, and the e-mail messages are created and sent. On completion, a message dialog opens, explaining that the process was successful. Click OK to close the dialog. The job is done!

#12 Producing PDF Files in Excel, Access, and Project

The data-oriented programs in Microsoft Office in Windows, including Excel, Access, and Project, offer only the Settings and Security tabs in the Acrobat PDFMaker dialog.

Choose Adobe PDF > Change Conversion Settings in Excel to open the Conversion Settings dialog. The Settings tab includes the options described in the sidebar "Simple Settings" in #10.

Figure 12 shows the Application settings in the Settings tab of Excel's Conversion Settings dialog. Select the Fit Worksheet to a single page option to rescale the contents of your Excel worksheet to fit one page. You can also convert Comments and add Links if you select those options.

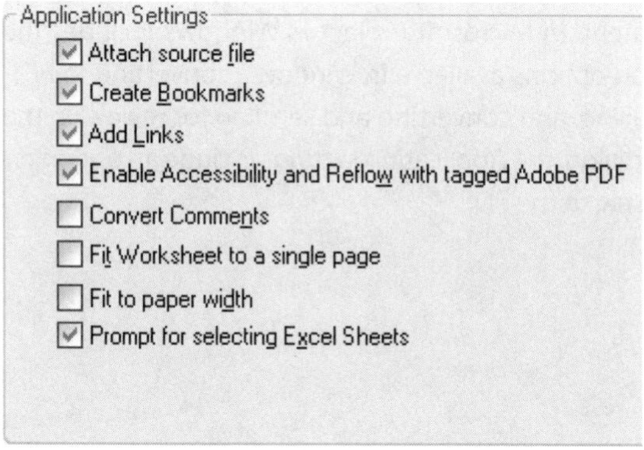

Figure 12 Specify options such as fitting content to pages or picking selected worksheets.

Note

The Excel PDFMaker in Windows also allows you to insert a 3D model into a spreadsheet. Read about using 3D models in Office programs in #14, "Adding Specialized Media Content."

Pick a Report

In Access, choose Adobe PDF > Convert Multiple Reports to Single Adobe PDF to open the reports listing in the Acrobat PDFMaker dialog. Select the reports in Access you want to convert, and click Add Report(s). When all the reports you want to convert are included in the Reports In Adobe PDF list, click Convert to start creating the PDF.

Getting Your Worksheets in Order

The Acrobat 9 PDFMaker for Excel lets you specify the organization of the worksheets in the PDF document. If you want to choose a group of worksheets in a custom order, select "Prompt for selecting Excel Sheets" in the dialog shown in Figure 12. As the document is converted, you are asked about each worksheet.

In Access, the conversion options depend on whether the file is an Access 2002–2003-format file, or an Access 2000-format file:

- In an Access 2002, 2003, or newer file, select the reports, tables, queries, or forms for conversion, and then choose a command from the Adobe PDF menu. Access 2000 files only convert reports to PDF.

- Bookmarks can be created from report titles. Select Add Bookmarks to Adobe PDF on the Settings tab of the Acrobat PDFMaker dialog.

- The Adobe PDF menu in Access includes one report option used to combine a selection of reports into a single PDF document automatically (read more in the sidebar "Pick a Report").

The Adobe PDF menu in Microsoft Project in Windows includes the three basic conversion options available in Windows: converting to PDF, converting and e-mailing, and converting and sending for review. In the Conversion Settings dialog, the Application settings include an option for attaching the source file to the PDF.

#13 Generating PDF Documents in PowerPoint

How would you like to distribute a PowerPoint slide show—complete with slide transitions and animation—without having to pack the files and add a player?

PowerPoint's PDFMaker in Word has several options you can configure for converting a presentation to a PDF document (**Figure 13**).

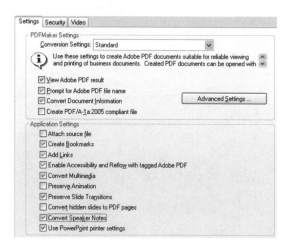

Figure 13 PowerPoint's PDFMaker includes a number of options for converting media and animations added to the slides.

Like a Word document, a PowerPoint document allows for comment, tag, and bookmark conversions. These options include the following:

- Convert Multimedia adds any linked audio or video files to the PDF file. Read about using different media in Acrobat in Chapter 13, and see how to use video in PowerPoint in #14.

- Preserve Animation converts animations in the presentation to PDF animations. The settings allow for overlapping shapes and graphics, Action Buttons, and Action Settings.

- Preserve Slide Transitions converts the PowerPoint transition effects to PDF transition effects.

- "Convert hidden slides to PDF pages" converts any slides designated as hidden (they don't play in the regular presentation) to pages in the PDF file.

(continued on next page)

Using Print Settings

Using Print Settings

If you want your slides to be included as part of a larger PDF file that uses standard-sized pages, use the PDF layout based on PowerPoint print settings in the Application Settings of the PDF-Maker Settings dialog. The default layout for a presentation uses Landscape orientation and often a full-color background; printing a presentation as part of a larger document can take a lot of time and consume a lot of ink if you simply convert the presentation itself. Of course, using the print settings option depends on the content of your presentation. Bullet lists, for example, will display properly in a Portrait orientation; images or charts may not.

- Convert Speaker Notes converts the notes added to your slides to text note comments in the PDF. Read about text notes and other types of comments in Chapter 10.

- "Use PowerPoint printer settings" uses the same printer settings in the PDF document as in the original file. Read more about printer settings in the sidebar "Using Print Settings."

Slides—Without the Backgrounds

If you don't remember to use a print setting to convert your PowerPoint presentation to PDF, don't worry. You aren't stuck with redoing it to remove the backgrounds. Acrobat 9 offers a new feature that lets you remove the background only from your converted slides. Read about using and modifying backgrounds in #54, "Adding Watermarks and Backgrounds."

#14 Adding Specialized Media Content

The ability to use and manipulate media increases with every new version of Acrobat, and Acrobat 9 is certainly no exception. If you are working with Acrobat 9 Pro Extended in Windows, the PDFMakers in Word and PowerPoint contain new commands that allow you to embed a Flash movie in FLV (Flash video) format. As part of the installation, Acrobat also installs 3D ActiveX controls in Word, PowerPoint, and Excel that let you insert a 3D model into your source file.

To embed a movie in a source Office file, follow these steps:

1. Display the page or slide where you want to embed the movie.

2. Choose Adobe PDF > Embed Video and Convert to Flash Format, or click Video to Flash 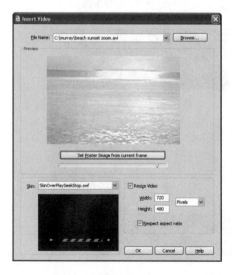 on the Acrobat PDFMaker toolbar to display the Insert Video dialog.

3. Click Browse to locate and select the video you want to use. You'll see the video in the Preview area (**Figure 14a**).

Figure 14a Specify the appearance and function for the embedded video.

(continued on next page)

Specify Video Settings

The settings used for embedding the file specify how the content is displayed on the page. Choose Adobe PDF > Change Conversion Settings and click the Video tab to define how the Flash Video movie is used in the PDF file:

- Define a storage location, or leave the default, which is the same location as the source document's folder.

- Choose one of five video qualities, or leave the default, which is Good @400kbps.

- Choose Encode Audio and select a Data Rate value. You can choose one of five rates from the pull-down list or use the default value, Good @160kbps.

4. Choose settings for the movie playback that include the following:

- Select a poster frame, which is shown on the page when the movie isn't playing. To choose, drag the slider below the preview until you see the desired frame display, and then click Set Poster Image from Current Frame.

- Click the Skin pull-down arrow and choose an option from the list. The list offers different sets of playback tools that are displayed on the finished PDF document.

- To reset the size of the movie, click Resize Video to activate the settings, and make width and height changes in either percentage or pixel values.

5. Click OK to close the dialog. You see the video object on the page or slide.

6. Convert the file to PDF to view the page (**Figure 14b**).

Figure 14b The video sizes itself appropriately on the slide with the controller as an overlay.

Creating PDF Files Outside Acrobat

Note

In addition to the new menu and toolbar commands, both the Word and PowerPoint PDFMakers now include a separate tab in the Acrobat PDFMaker settings dialog you use to set video settings. Read about the settings in the sidebar "Specify Video Settings."

To insert a 3D model, click Insert Acrobat 3D Model 🔲 or choose Adobe PDF > Insert Acrobat 3D Model to open the dialog. Click Browse for Model to locate a 3D file (choose from many major CAD formats); click Browse for Script to locate a JavaScript for the model if required, and click OK to place the model on the page (**Figure 14c**). When you convert the document to PDF, the PDFMaker uses your settings to generate a 3D PDF document.

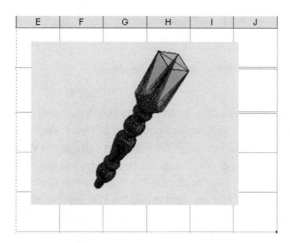

Figure 14c Insert a 3D model in a file, like a spreadsheet.

Both 3D models and Flash video (inserted as FLV format) can be inserted either in the source files or after a file has been converted to PDF. There are many more options for configuration in Acrobat—check them out in Chapter 13 "Using Flash Video and 3D Media."

#15 Making PDF Documents from Web Pages

A PDFMaker is installed in Internet Explorer when you install Acrobat 9 in Windows. To create a PDF file from a Web page displayed in Internet Explorer, click the down arrow on the Adobe PDF toolbar to display the menu and choose Convert Web Page to PDF (**Figure 15a**). If the page includes frames, all the content is flattened into one PDF document page.

Quick Conversions

If you convert a fair number of Web pages to PDF documents, save yourself some mouse-clicks and time with easy preference changes. Click the down arrow on the Adobe PDF toolbar and choose Preferences to open a small dialog. Select or deselect the options shown in the dialog:

- Choose a file type, either HTML or text, and click Settings to select configuration options from a dialog, such as page size, encoding, colors, and fonts.

- Choose PDF settings, including bookmarks, tags, headers, and footers.

- Define page size, margins, orientation, and page scaling.

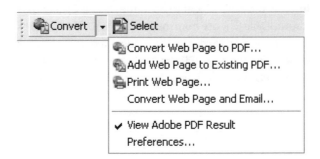

Figure 15a The Internet Explorer PDFMaker includes several ways to create PDF files.

To attach the displayed Web page to an existing PDF document, click Add Web Page to Existing PDF. A dialog opens that lets you select the document to use for the attached page. Click Save to convert the Web page and append it to the end of the selected document. You can also right-click (Control-click) the page to display the shortcut menu, which includes both the Convert to PDF and Add to Existing PDF commands.

Have you ever spent time converting Web pages to PDF, and then spent more time in Acrobat selecting objects like navigation buttons and ads to remove them? Well, wait until you see the new PDFMaker feature for Internet Explorer. Click Select Object on the PDFMaker toolbar, and then click to select all the items you want to convert (**Figure 15b**). Each item you click is framed in blue; the active area under the tool is outlined with a red hatched box.

When you've made your selections, right-click (Control-click) and choose either Convert to PDF or Add to Existing PDF options. Very slick!

Figure 15b Select only the objects you want on the page for conversion to PDF.

Browsers Behaving Badly

So you've selected bits of several Web pages and constructed your PDF files, and now you find you can't work in the browser properly. There's no mystery—check to be sure you have deselected the Select Object tool on the PDFMaker. Now try again.

#16 Archiving E-mail Messages

Acrobat 9 Pro lets you archive your Outlook e-mail messages, which you can then index and search or add to other PDF documents. There are several ways to archive your e-mail messages manually:

- You can select individual e-mails in Outlook and then click "Create Adobe PDF From selected messages" ▣. The Save Adobe PDF File As dialog opens. Browse to the location where you want to save the file. Type a name for the file, and click Save.

- To convert all the e-mails in a folder at once, select the folder in Outlook and click "Create Adobe PDF from folders" ▣. Name the file, specify the storage location in the Save Adobe PDF File As dialog, and click Save to save the file.

- You can add files to existing archives by selecting the file you want to add from the Outlook messages, selecting Adobe PDF > Convert and Append to Existing PDF Messages, and choosing either Selected Messages or Selected Folders. Again the Save Adobe PDF File As dialog opens. Select the file you want to add the additional document to. Click Save to process the file(s).

Acrobat 9 offers an automatic archival process that automatically converts e-mail to PDF in the background, letting you continue to work. You can choose specifics such as real e-mail addresses from mailto data; embed header information as metadata; include fields like To, CC, and BCC; or even download images via PDFMaker and hide them in Outlook.

To set up the archives, follow these steps:

1. Select Adobe PDF > Setup Automatic Archival to open the Acrobat PDFMaker dialog with the Automatic Archival tab active.

2. Choose the settings for your requirements:

   - Select Enable Automatic Archival to activate the options; specify the frequency, the time, a log file, and whether to embed an index.

   - Click Add to open a dialog listing the Outlook folders and select the folder or folders to include in an archive. Click OK to dismiss the dialog, and open the Save PDF Archive As dialog.

Bring It Forward

If you have "old" PDF files archived in Acrobat 7 or earlier (which were built in the pre-PDF Package/Portfolio days), choose Adobe PDF > Upgrade Acrobat 7 PDF Archive to open a dialog. Locate and select the file or files and click Open. The files are processed and reconfigured as a PDF Portfolio.

Automating Lotus Notes E-mail Conversions

Acrobat installs an Acrobat PDFMaker toolbar in Lotus Notes, which shares most of the same features as the Outlook PDFMaker, including automatic archival. Content can be converted to PDF as single messages or folders, as well as capturing additional e-mail fields.

- Specify a name and location for the archive, and click Open to dismiss the dialog and return to the Acrobat PDFMaker. You see the Outlook folder as well as the PDF Archive File listed in the dialog (**Figure 16a**).

- Continue adding folders and archive files as required; if you want to create archives immediately, click Run Archival Now. Otherwise, click OK to close the dialog and PDFMaker will process the files according to your schedule.

Figure 16a Specify conditions for e-mail message and folder archival.

Automatic Attachments, Anyone?

Here's a nifty timesaver for those of us who like to send PDF attachments with e-mail messages but don't like to take the time to convert the files first. Choose Adobe PDF > Change Conversion Settings to open the Acrobat PDFMaker dialog and look for this option at the bottom of the dialog: Show "Attach as PDF" button. Select the check box and click OK to close the dialog. When you start a new e-mail message, notice that there are two Attachment icons on the toolbar—the regular one, and a new Attach as Adobe PDF icon 📎 🔲 Attach as Adobe PDF.

Planning Archival Names

Some organizations such as governments require that all e-mails be saved. Archiving e-mails using PDF is a terrific way to organize material for storage. Regardless of why you need to archive e-mail, it pays to take a few minutes to organize a method for naming the archives.

For a graphic designer, consultant, or engineer, it may be useful to archive according to project name, for instance. In other circumstances, it may be useful to archive by sender's name; you might want to select files and track correspondence regarding purchases by product name if you are involved in a retail business.

Whether you archive e-mail messages manually or using the automatic archiving, the files are combined into a PDF Portfolio, named using the folder's name (**Figure 16b**). You can locate the contents of the archive based on folder location for the source file, sender, date, subject, and whether there are file attachments. Read about constructing a PDF Portfolio in Chapter 4, "Producing a PDF Portfolio."

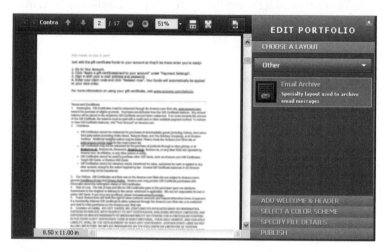

Figure 16b The e-mail messages are combined into a PDF Portfolio.

CHAPTER THREE

Creating PDF Files in Distiller and Acrobat

Only a limited number of programs have a PDFMaker installed with Acrobat 9, and not all programs have internal PDF-generating options for export. In many applications—illustration programs, for example—you can generate other file formats that can then be processed using Acrobat Distiller 9. Distiller is a separate program installed with the Acrobat 9 installation process and is used to convert EPS (Encapsulated PostScript), PS (PostScript), and a specialized Windows format called PRN to the PDF format. You can use either PS or PRN files in Distiller. The PS file format uses the PostScript language. Some programs produce PRN files instead of PS files; other programs generate PRN files if you choose Print to File as a printing option. Both file formats are based on the printer drivers installed on your computer.

Most programs allow printing, and if you can print a file, you can create a PDF file using the Adobe PDF printer (read how in #9, "Printing with the Adobe PDF Printer"). In addition to the files you may have handy on your hard drive, Acrobat converts content from other sources, including scanners, Web pages, your system clipboard—or starts from a blank page.

Many common file types can be converted to PDF from within Acrobat. In Acrobat 9 you can combine files of different types, convert them all to PDF, and either merge them into a single PDF file or produce a PDF Portfolio, which collects the contents and combines them as subsets of a new interface document (read about PDF Portfolios in Chapter 4, "Producing a PDF Portfolio").

#17 Working with Acrobat Distiller and Job Options

Controlling Joboptions Files

You may create a number of custom joboptions files over time. To keep track of their use or purpose, name them according to client name, project name, or anything else that is meaningful. For example, highquality(1). joboptions doesn't mean as much as bigdog_tools. joboptions.

You can share the settings files with others. E-mail the joboptions file as you would any other type of file. Your recipients add the file to the storage folder. The next time they access the custom settings dialog from a PDFMaker, Acrobat, or Distiller, the shared settings are ready to use.

Acrobat Distiller is installed as a separate program you access from the desktop, or in Acrobat 9 Professional, by choosing Advanced > Print Production > Acrobat Distiller.

To distill a file, choose File > Open. In the Open dialog, locate the file you want to convert, select it, and click Open. The file is opened and processed. Information about the processed files, such as numbers of pages, length of job, and whether it was a successful process, is shown in the log at the bottom of the dialog (**Figure 17a**).

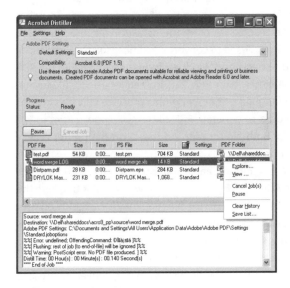

Figure 17a Acrobat Distiller displays an activity log showing details about the processed files.

In the example shown in the figure, the second file shows a different icon from the first two, indicating the file wasn't processed and the PDF file wasn't generated. The second file is an Excel spreadsheet, not one of Distiller's processing formats.

You can manage the files in your Distiller session from the program's dialog. Right-click (Control-click) a distilled file from the list to display the shortcut menu (also shown in Figure 17a) and choose from the options on the list. The History is maintained for each Distiller session; when you close and reopen the program again, the list is cleared.

When converting files to PDF, Acrobat uses several settings known as *joboptions*. You can create custom conversion settings for your own work by modifying one of the default options, or you can start from scratch.

Creating PDF Files in Distiller and Acrobat

In Distiller, choose Settings > Edit Adobe PDF Settings to open the Adobe PDF Settings dialog (**Figure 17b**). The dialog shows a list of headings for each joboptions file. Select a conversion option, such as Standard, to display a list of six categories (each joboptions file contains the same six categories). Click a heading, such as Standard, to open its set of categories, and then click a category to display the settings in the right pane of the dialog. By default, the settings shown in the dialog are the same as those available from any joboptions file's General category.

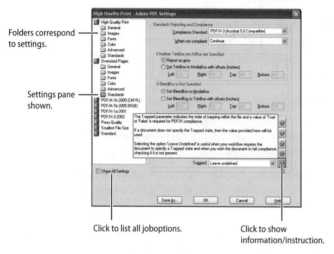

Folders correspond to settings.

Settings pane shown.

Click to list all joboptions.

Click to show information/instruction.

Figure 17b Each folder listed for a setting in the left column displays as a collection of options at the right side of the dialog.

In the default dialog, shown when the settings open (and shown when you click the joboption's General heading in the left column), are several settings you may want to modify (see sidebars in this technique for descriptions of additional settings):

- **Compatibility.** The default is Acrobat 6.0 (PDF 1.5). Depending on your users' needs, you can choose an option as far back as Acrobat 4. Older versions of the program have fewer options for features such as transparency or font embedding.

- **Object Level Compression.** Choose either Off or Tags. Compression of objects combines small objects such as bookmarks into compressible

(continued on next page)

Consider a Few Advanced Settings

Unless you are familiar with Document Structuring Conventions and the like, you won't have to change many options in the Advanced dialog. The settings in this dialog describe how the conversion from PostScript to PDF is performed. Let's look at three default options:

- The "Convert gradients to smooth shades" option converts gradients from a range of programs, including Adobe FreeHand, QuarkXPress, Adobe Illustrator, and Microsoft PowerPoint. This option produces a smaller PDF file size and often results in improved output.

- The "Save Adobe PDF settings inside PDF file" option embeds a copy of the joboptions file as an attachment. Including the file is handy if you're working on a project remotely and want to send the PDF and settings files to your colleague.

- The other option of note, "Save original JPEG images in PDF if possible," processes JPEG images (which are compressed) without compressing them again, resulting in faster file processing.

Don't Use Page Ranges

The General tab includes an option for selecting a specific range of pages. Don't enable this option unless you're sure the custom settings are for onetime use. If you specify a range of pages when you create the job options and then reuse the settings another time, you convert only those pages specified in the General tab. This can lead to time-consuming troubleshooting when you use your custom settings and can't figure out where your pages have gone!

content. Off leaves the document's structure as is; the Tags Only option compresses structural information in the PDF document. Compressed information is viewable only in Acrobat 6 and newer; leaving the option set to Off allows structure and tagging information to be usable in Acrobat 5 as well.

- **Resolution.** You can set this option to emulate the resolution of a printer for PostScript files. A higher resolution usually produces higher-quality but larger files.

- **Embed thumbnails.** Thumbnail previews are used for navigation, and have been created dynamically since Acrobat 5. Don't enable this option unless you are using very old versions of Acrobat; it adds to the file size unnecessarily.

- **Optimize for fast Web view.** Choose this setting if the file is intended for online use, or distribution via e-mail or a server. An optimized file byte serves the content, breaking it up into chunks a page at a time, letting the user read as the file is loaded rather than waiting for the entire file.

In the Images dialog, you may need to adjust and test setting changes several times for converting files with complex images. Consider these options:

- **Downsample.** Pixels in images with a resolution above a specified amount are combined to reduce the resolution. You may want to increase or decrease the downsampling level. For images such as maps (where the user zooms in to a high magnification), a high resolution is much more legible.

- **Compression/Image Quality.** Select options depending on the file's color, or if you have grayscale or monochromatic images.

- **Anti-aliasing.** Smooth jagged edges in monochrome images by turning on anti-aliasing.

- **Policy button.** Click this button in order to specify how to process images when they are below the resolution you define. You can specify whether to ignore, warn, or cancel a job based on the resolution of color, grayscale, and monochrome images. Setting policies can save you processing and reprocessing time in the event the images in a file don't use the correct resolutions.

In the Fonts dialog, specify whether you want to embed fonts or sub-set embedded fonts when the percentage of characters used falls below a value you enter. If you're using unusual fonts, or your layout is highly dependent on the fonts, be sure to embed them. Choose the Subset option when you want to embed a portion of a font's characters. Don't use a low value if you expect to change any characters in the page. Read about using fonts in Chapter 5, "Creating Output: Saving, Exporting, and Printing."

In the Color dialog, choose settings that correspond with files used in your source applications, such as Adobe Photoshop or Illustrator. The options available depend on the color settings you choose. If you are sending files to a press, you often receive settings from the printer. Read more about printing in Chapter 5.

In the Standards dialog, you can include an Acrobat 5.0 Compatible standard for High Quality Print and Press Quality joboptions. Read more in the sidebar "Meeting the Standards."

When you have finished designing your custom settings, choose Save As to open the Save Adobe PDF Settings As dialog. Name the file and click Save. The custom conversion settings file is saved with the extension .joboptions.

Meeting the Standards

The Standard, Oversized Pages, and Smallest File Size default settings don't include options to select an option in the Standards dialog. In these cases, not enough information is stored in the file to comply with the standards' requirements.

If you're constructing settings that comply with standards, you can choose options in the Standards dialog that check document contents against standards before creating the PDF document. The options displayed in the tab vary according to the standard you select from the Compliance Standard menu. Read more about standards in Chapter 6, "Complying with PDF and Accessibility Standards."

#18 Watching Folders via Distiller

It Isn't Polite to Share

You can use up to a maximum of 100 watched folders. But don't set up watched folders to act as a service for other users on your system. Everyone who creates Adobe PDF documents needs a separate Acrobat license.

Develop a System

Instead of generating PDF files on a file-by-file basis—very time-consuming when you work with a large number of files—set up a folder for each joboptions file you need to use. As you finish working with a file, drop it in the appropriate watched folder. Distiller checks the folder and processes the files according to your settings. Use logical folder names; instead of *watched_5*, name it *Bob's Takeout Menu* if you use the folder to process documents for Bob's Pizza Emporium.

Another way to take advantage of the many profiles and tools at your disposal is to use the watched folder system in Acrobat Distiller 9. Distiller can be programmed to automatically look for PostScript files in an In folder, convert them to PDF according to specified settings, and send the finished documents to an Out folder. In some workflows, an automated process like this could save you a lot of time.

Add a folder you want to use as a watched folder to your hard drive. Then open Distiller and follow these steps to set up watched folders:

1. In Distiller, choose Settings > Watched Folders; the Watched Folders dialog opens (**Figure 18**).

Figure 18 Set up the watched folders in Distiller and add conversion settings and security if required.

2. Click Add Folder, and locate and select the folder you want to use (you can't create a new folder with this dialog). Distiller adds In and Out subfolders automatically.

3. You can add security, custom settings, or both to a folder. Distiller adds an icon to the left of folders you have customized, as shown in Figure 18. Fortunately, a key at the bottom right of the dialog identifies the icons used for the folders. If you want to change settings, first select a folder and then do the following:

- Click Edit Settings or Load Settings to open the Settings dialog. Modify the default range of conversion settings if desired and click OK. The file is saved to the individual folder as folder.joboptions.

- Back in the Watched Folders dialog, click Edit Security to add password protection to the folder; if you change your mind, click Clear Security.

- Click Load Settings to locate and attach joboptions files from your system.

4. Choose options to manage your set of watched folders:

- Specify how often to check the folders in seconds. You can check every 1 to 9,999 seconds; 1 hour is 3,600 seconds.

- Specify what to do with the original PostScript file. It can be moved to the Out folder with the PDF document or deleted. Log files are copied to the Out folder.

- Specify how many days (up to 999) to keep the PDF documents in the folder. You can also specify to delete the PostScript and log files.

5. Click OK to close the dialog.

Which Is More Secure?

Be aware of the settings applied to a folder and the settings used in Distiller. If you specify security in Distiller's settings, the settings may or may not be the same after the file is processed. In fact, the file may not be processed at all. If a folder's joboptions file is read-only, Distiller won't convert the file. If Distiller's settings include security options and the watched folder doesn't, the file is processed and the security settings are in place.

When Files Go Missing

You can delete a folder from the Watched Folders list by clicking Delete in the Watched Folders dialog. Deleting a watched folder does not delete the In and Out folders, the contents, or the folder's joboptions files from your computer; you'll need to remove them manually. If you delete or move a folder from your computer that you have designated as a watched folder in Distiller, the next time you open the dialog, you'll get a Watched Folder Alert. Click Open List to show the Watched Folders dialog, where you see the Missing Folder icon to the left of the folder's name.

#**19** Starting a PDF File from a Blank Page

Before the release of Acrobat 8, the only way to start a blank PDF document was to use a workaround, such as saving a blank document as a PDF page, or adding a blank page to an existing file before converting to PDF. At long last you can start a new PDF file from within Acrobat.

Unlike with the other file creation types, you don't find the command in the Create PDF task button menu. Instead, follow these steps to start a new PDF file:

1. Choose File > Create PDF > From Blank Page. The New Document Editor is initialized, loads a blank page in the Document pane, and opens a new toolbar (**Figure 19a**).

   • Notice that guidelines identify the margins and a blinking cursor displays at the upper left of the page.

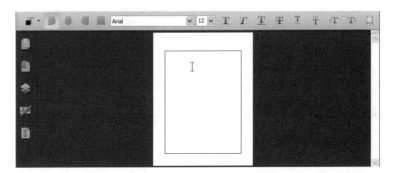

Figure 19a A blank page and the New Document toolbar display for you to enter content into the PDF.

2. Type the content you wish to add to the page. Groups of tools on the toolbar offer configuration settings, including the text color, alignment, font, and font size, and styles such as bold, italic, and superscript.

3. Click Page Setup 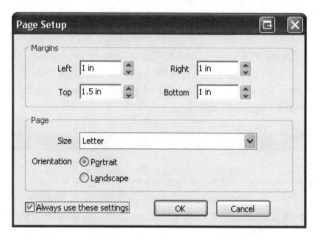 to configure the page's appearance. Specify the margins, page size, and orientation in the Page Setup dialog (**Figure 19b**), and click OK.

Figure 19b Specify the margins and layout for a new PDF file in the dialog.

4. Choose File > Save As, and save the file. The next time you open it, choose Document > Resume Editing. The New Document toolbar and the page's margins display.

5. To prevent making changes to the text, choose Document > Prevent Further Edits. A dialog opens asking if you are sure, and states that the saved document won't have editable text. Click Prevent Further Edits and save the file. Or click Keep Text Editable to allow changes.

The specialized features of the New Document Editor, including the toolbar, the page margin guides, and the commands in the Document menu, are available only when the document is created with the New Document command and isn't locked for editing.

Pick What You Prefer

Rather than using the program defaults for new pages, choose your own. If you have a font you use for all your business communications, for example, make sure the new pages use your fonts automatically by setting the preference. Choose Edit > Preferences > New Document (Acrobat > Preferences > New Document) in the left pane to display the settings. You can choose the following preferences:

- **A font and size.** The default is Arial at 12 pt.

- **Margins.** The default is 1.5 inch left and right and 1 inch top and bottom.

- **Page type.** The default is letter-sized pages with a portrait orientation. Choose a size, and specify whether to use Portrait or Landscape as the default orientation.

Make it even quicker—the next time you choose settings manually, select "Always use these settings" in the Page Setup dialog (Figure 19b). The settings become your defaults.

#20 Merging Multiple Files into a Single PDF Document

Converting from the Inside

Not all files can be converted to a PDF from within Acrobat. The formats you can use include the following: AutoDesk AutoCAD, AutoDesk Inventor, BMP, GIF, HTML, Adobe InDesign, JDF Job Definition, JPEG 2000, Microsoft Access, Microsoft Word, Microsoft Excel, Microsoft PowerPoint, RTF (Rich Text Format), Microsoft Project, Microsoft Publisher, Microsoft Visio, PCX, PNG, PostScript, EPS, Text, and TIFF.

Don't bother with opening programs, converting various types of files to PDF, and then laboriously combining the content in Acrobat. Instead, in Acrobat 9 bring all the content together, and let the program do the conversions and create the single combined PDF document for you. It's a true time-saver! Creating a combined file works in both Acrobat 9 Standard and Pro versions; however, Standard can't convert Visio, Project, or AutoCAD files.

1. Click the Create PDF task button to display the menu options. Then click Merge Files into a Single PDF to open the Combine Files dialog (**Figure 20a**). Notice that the Single PDF option is selected at the top right of the dialog.

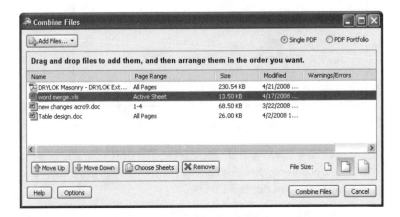

Figure 20a Specify the files to use for combining in the dialog.

Converting from the Inside

State Your Options

There are several options that Acrobat can apply automatically to the PDF you create in the Combine Files wizard. These include the following:

- Adding tags for accessibility and reflow

- Adding bookmarks

- Continuing the process whether or not errors occur

- Converting all the files to PDF

All choices except for adding tags are selected by default.

Note
A combined PDF file is different from a PDF Portfolio—read about creating and using portfolios in Chapter 4, "Producing a PDF Portfolio."

2. Click Add Files to open a drop-down list and choose an option to locate your content. Use these features to get the files you want in the order you want:

- Click Add Files to display the Add Files dialog and locate the first file you want to add to the wizard (you can select multiple files from the same folder), and then click Add.

- Click Add Folders. Locate and select the folder you want to include in the Browse for Folders dialog, and click OK.

- If there are open files in Acrobat, click Add Open Files to include the files in the list.

- To reorganize the files you add in the dialog, select a file in the list, and then click the arrow buttons at the bottom of the window to move a file up or down in the stacking order. You can also click Delete to delete a file from the collection.

- If you want to include part of a file, select the file in the list and click Choose Pages to open the Preview and Select Page Range dialog (**Figure 20b**). The name of the dialog varies according to the type of file you are viewing. Preview by selecting the pages or slides in the dialog. Type the numbers as ranges or individual numbers and click OK.

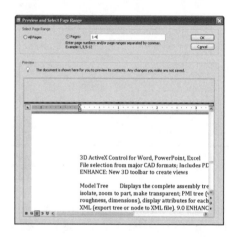

Figure 20b Preview and select pages from a document in this dialog.

Conversion Clues

Should you convert a document in the source program or in Acrobat? The short answer is: It depends. If you are working in a program and know you will need a PDF version of a file, generate the file then. If you are working in Acrobat and realize you need another file, generate the file from Acrobat.

Even if you are working in Acrobat, if you plan to generate files from PDFMaker-governed programs and either can't remember the settings you last left for the PDFMaker or know you need to change the settings, you should work through the program instead of Acrobat. That approach is preferable to generating a file that is converted using the incorrect settings and then having to redo it.

3. When your files are assembled, click the appropriate File Size button [icon] at the bottom right of the Combine Files dialog. Select the smallest button for a lower quality/smaller file size, the center button default for medium quality/file size settings, and the right button for a better quality/larger file size option.

4. Click Combine Files to start processing the list of items. Each file is processed separately, and any files in the list that are not PDFs are converted to PDFs.

5. When the conversion is complete, the Save As dialog opens, showing the filename as Binder1.pdf by default. Type a filename, choose a location, and then click Save. Your merged file is complete.

#21 Creating a PDF from Web Pages in Acrobat

Although you can easily download a page from a Web site using the PDF-Maker that installs in Microsoft Internet Explorer, you can also download a Web site from within Acrobat and control its content and how it is displayed in the resulting PDF file.

Click the Create PDF task button and click PDF from Web Page, or choose File > Create PDF > From Web Page to open the Create PDF from Web Page dialog (**Figure 21a**). Click Capture Multiple Levels  to display more settings in the dialog; you can then specify the number of levels to download and other criteria, such as the path or server.

Figure 21a Specify the location and define the settings for converting a Web page to PDF in Acrobat.

Access the file you want to convert in one of three ways, depending on the location and type of file. You can type the URL for the file if it's on the Internet, click the arrow to the right of the URL field to work with Web files that have been opened previously in Acrobat, or click Browse to open the Select File to Open dialog to locate a file that's on a local disk.

Click Create to start the conversion process. The Download Status dialog shows you the number of connections active in the downloaded material, as well as the names, sizes, and locations of the files. When the download is complete, Acrobat displays the new PDF file in the Document pane and adds a document structure to the Bookmarks tab. Choose File > Save to save the converted Web pages.

As You Like It

Click Settings in the Create PDF from Web Page dialog to open the Web Page Conversion Settings dialog. In the General tab, choose file type and PDF options, such as including bookmarks, headers and footers, and PDF tags, and saving refresh data. Specify file formats, fonts, and encoding for HTML or Plain Text formats. The second tab of the dialog contains page layout options, including page size, orientation, and margins. Changing the page settings to coincide with other documents you may later use in a PDF Package or combined document provides consistency throughout the document. Click OK and return to the Create PDF from Web Page dialog, and click Create to process the Web page and create the PDF document.

As you scroll through the document, notice that both a header and footer are added to the pages (**Figure 21b**). The header is the Web page's name; the footer contains the URL for the page, the number of pages, and the download date and time.

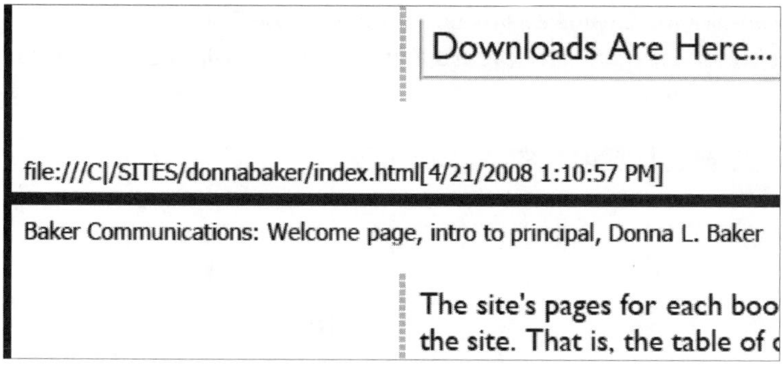

Figure 21b Headers and footers are added to the pages automatically as they are converted.

Acrobat captures Web pages using default settings for both file formats and page layouts. You can configure some formats and modify the page to your requirements (see the sidebar "As You Like It").

Adding On

Although it is simpler and safer to leave the default level 1 setting, what do you do if you import the page and realize you need additional pages? Luckily, you can easily add more. Choose Advanced > Web Capture > Create PDF From/Append Web Page to open the Add to PDF from Web Page dialog, identical to the original Create PDF from Web Page dialog. Select another level, and the additional pages are added to those already in the document.

So Many Pages, So Little Time

In the Create PDF from Web Page dialog, you can specify how many levels of the Web site you want to download. The default level is 1. Don't change this number without careful thought. Level 1 refers to the first set of pages for a Web site, the actual pages that you see if you type the URL in a browser address bar. Additional levels attach more sets of pages. If you choose Get Entire Site, you'll download the entire site, whether that consists of 10 pages or 1,000 pages.

#22 Creating a PDF from a Scan in Acrobat

Use your scanner to capture a digital copy of a document or image. Not only can you scan directly into Acrobat 9, but you can also specify the type of scan you want, as well as adjust the settings for a better scan.

Click the Create PDF task button and select From Scanner to open the Configure Presets dialog (**Figure 22a**). If you are working in Windows, you can click the Create PDF task button, and choose From Scanner and one of several text or image presets. Your selection is reflected in the dialog once it opens.

Figure 22a Choose preset options to scan a document directly into Acrobat.

You have four preset configuration decisions to make prior to scanning:

1. Select your scanner and a preset. If you make any changes in the dialog, you'll see the Save button next to the Presets activate—click to save your settings using the Preset name. Click Scanner Options to pick a data transfer method, and specify whether or not to view your scanner's interface.

2. The configuration settings that appear depend on your scanner. In the Input section of the dialog, specify whether to scan the front or both sides of the document. Choose scan characteristics, including the color mode, resolution, and paper size. If you want to scan several files and need to change settings during the scan process, select "Prompt for scanning more pages."

The Art of Scanning

Acrobat offers several optimizing filters to adjust or correct your scan results:

- Deskew rotates a skewed page so that it's vertical. The default setting is Automatic.

- Background removal is used with grayscale and color pages to make nearly white areas white, resulting in clearer scans. The default is Low; you can also choose Medium and High options.

- "Edge shadow removal" gets rid of the black edges sometimes seen from scanned pages. The default is Cautious; an aggressive option is also available.

- Despeckle removes black marks from the page. Low is the default; you can also choose Medium and High.

- Descreen removes halftone dots, like those from a scanned newspaper. The default is Automatic: Acrobat applies the filter automatically for grayscale and RGB images of 300 ppi or higher.

- Halo Removal removes high-contrast edges from color pages. The default setting is On.

3. To optimize the document's content, particularly for images, drag the Optimization slider left (to decrease) or right (to increase) file size and quality. Click Options and set compression and filter settings in the Optimization Options dialog (**Figure 22b**). Click Custom Settings to activate the Compression and Filtering settings, make the desired adjustments, and click OK to dismiss the dialog and return to the Configure Presets dialog. (You can read more about filters in the sidebar "The Art of Scanning.")

Figure 22b Specify different ways to improve the appearance of a scanned page or image.

4. Finally, choose options in the Text Recognition and Metadata section of the dialog. The default option for a text preset is to create a searchable document, meaning the contents of the document are converted to words and images. Image presets, on the other hand, don't use any default selections. Click Options and then change the conversion options. (See #61, "Extracting Active Text from an Image" to learn how that's done.)

When you have finished, click OK and Acrobat automatically starts the scan. The scanned page opens as a PDF file in Acrobat. Select the command again to scan the next image, and so on.

Checking Your Scan Results

Many of the files you convert to PDF are composed of text and images that you can manipulate using a variety of tools. PDF files created by scans using older versions of Acrobat or from some programs, such as Photoshop, are images only; you can't make any changes to the file's contents. Here's a quick way to tell the difference.

Click the Select tool on the Select & Zoom toolbar. Then click an area of text on the document. If you see the flashing insertion point, you know the page contains text. If you click a text area on the document and the entire page is selected, you have an image PDF.

Make Mine Custom (Windows)

Acrobat offers an opportunity to create custom scan presets. Click the Create PDF task button and choose PDF from Scanner > Custom Scan to open a dialog containing the settings shown in Figure 22a, as well as the options shown in Figure 22b. For a custom scan preset, along with choosing configuration settings for the actual scan, you specify a destination for the scanned page, either to a new file or appended to the active document displayed in the program window. If you prefer, click Browse to open a Select File dialog and locate and select a file to which you want the scan attached. As with the standard presets, choose configuration and document options such as Add Metadata and Make Searchable.

Starting and Stopping

When you have configured or chosen a scan preset in Acrobat, the settings remain as is until you change them again. Not only that, but once you have made a preset, the next time you start a scan—whether you are in your current Acrobat session or have reopened the program another time—all you have to do is choose the command from the Create drop-down menu and the scan is started automatically.

#**23** Creating a PDF from a Clipboard Image

Your computer's operating system maintains a storage area called a *clipboard*. Content you select and copy or cut from a document is placed on the clipboard, and you can then paste it into another location or another document. You have two ways of using the clipboard contents in Acrobat: creating a new file or adding the clipboard contents to an existing file.

Creating a new document is a simple process. Select and copy the image or text you want to use for a PDF document in your source program. In Acrobat, click the Create task button and choose PDF from Clipboard from the menu. The image is converted to PDF and opens in Acrobat.

You can use the image in an existing PDF document as an image stamp rather than making a separate PDF file for an image. Copy the image to your system clipboard and follow these steps:

1. Open the PDF document you want to work with in Acrobat and then choose Tools > Comment & Markup > Paste Clipboard Image as Stamp Tool.

2. Move your mouse over the document. You see the pointer changes to a stamp pointer ⬢. Click the page where you would like to insert the image, and the image is pasted to the page. The location on the page where you click determines the center location of the pasted image.

3. The stamp pointer changes to the Hand tool. If you want to make adjustments, move the pointer over the stamp and click the image on the page to select it (**Figure 23**). You can drag the image to move it, or drag a resize handle to change the size of the image. Save the file with the added image.

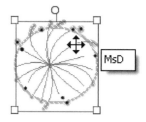

Figure 23 Resize or move the pasted image on the page as you like.

Make It Snappy

Acrobat includes the Snapshot tool, which lets you capture some of the content on a page to reuse. Choose Tools > Select & Zoom > Snapshot tool, or choose the Snapshot tool 📷 from the Select & Zoom toolbar.

Resize the page, the Document pane, or the program window to show what you want to capture, and click anywhere on the Document pane to capture everything visible.

Drag a marquee with the Snapshot tool anywhere on the page to capture the content within the marquee.

You see the colors invert when you capture the content, which is copied to the clipboard and is then ready to use in another PDF file or another application. By the way, anything you capture on the page is used as an image, whether it started out as text or an image.

You can copy and paste content as well as images within a PDF document—see how that's done in Chapter 8, "Touching Up and Modifying a PDF Document." If you have content in a PDF document that you'd like to use again (and don't want to take the time to export the file or its elements), use the Snapshot tool. Read about using snapshots in the sidebar "Make It Snappy."

#24 Attaching Source Files to a PDF

Acrobat 9 provides a feature for attaching source files to a converted document (except for open files), and offers a pane for managing attachments.

If you are working in a source program that contains a PDFMaker (such as Word in Windows), choose Adobe PDF > Change Conversion Settings to open the Acrobat PDFMaker dialog. Click "Attach source file to Adobe PDF" in the Application Settings area of the Settings tab, shown in Figure 10a in #10, "Using PDFMaker in Microsoft Word." Then click OK.

You can attach any type of file from within Acrobat, and use an icon placed anywhere on your page that your users click to view the attachment.

1. Choose Comments > Comment & Markup Tools > Attach a File as a Comment.

2. Move the pointer, which looks like a pushpin, over the document to where you want to display the attachment icon and click to place the icon.

3. Locate and select the file in the Browse for Attachment dialog, and click Select.

4. Choose an alternate icon, color, or opacity in the File Attachment Properties dialog (**Figure 24a**). Select the General tab to display fields where you can modify the attachment's name, your name, and a description of the attachment. Click Close.

Tools, Tools, and More Tools

The tools for attaching a file to a document aren't shown on the default Acrobat 9 toolbars. You can add the tools if you intend to work with attached files during a session. It's not worth the time to locate and attach the tools for attaching (get it?) if you are likely to reset the toolbars. Instead, use the command from the menu.

Right-click (Control-click) the toolbar well and choose More Tools. You can select the Attach a File tool from the File toolbar list, or the Attach a File as a Comment tool from the Comment & Markup toolbar list in the More Tools dialog.

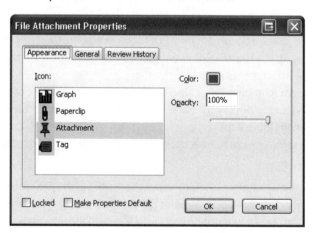

Figure 24a You can customize the appearance of the icon in the dialog.

Voilà! The attachment icon displays where you clicked earlier, and if you move the pointer over the icon, you can see information about the attachment in the form of a tooltip as well as in the Attachments pane (**Figure 24b**).

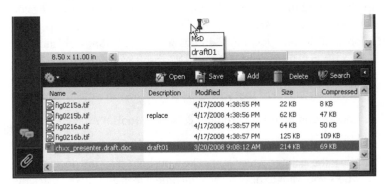

Figure 24b Move the pointer over the icon to see information about the attachment, or read basic information about the item in the Attachments pane.

5. Save the document. Files attached using the Attach a File as a Comment tool are listed in both the Attachments and Comments panes (see Chapter 10, "Commenting in a PDF Document," for information about adding comments and #75, "Working with the Comments List," for working with the Comments pane).

Managing Attached Files

Whether you attach a document from PDFMaker or embed it within Acrobat using the Attach File as a Comment tool, you can manage the attachments in the Attachments pane.

Click the Attachments icon in the Navigation pane at the left of the program window to display the pane horizontally below the Document pane (shown in Figure 24b).

Here are some ways to handle attachments and attaching files to PDF documents:

- You can add descriptive labels to any of the listings in the pane. Select the listing, click the Options menu ⚙ to open it, and choose Edit Description. Type a description and click OK to add the information to the Description column of the attachment.

- To open an attached file, double-click a listing in the Attachments pane, and click Open on the pane's toolbar or choose the command from the Options menu. If the attachment is a PDF document, it opens automatically. If it is another file format, you see a warning dialog that describes the hazards of opening documents that may contain macros, viruses, and so on. Click Open to proceed, or click Do Not Open to stop the process.

- You can save a file independently from the PDF document to which it is attached. Select the attachment and either click Save on the Attachment pane's toolbar or select the Save command from the Options menu. In the Save Attachment dialog, choose the storage location for the file and name it if necessary (it uses the name shown in the Attachments pane), and click Save.

- You can add another attachment to the document itself by clicking the Attach File button on the File toolbar, clicking Add on the Attachments pane's toolbar, or selecting Add from the Options menu. Locate the file you want to attach in the Add Attachment dialog, and click Attach.

- Click Delete to delete an attachment.

Please Read Attachments

Don't leave the discovery of attached files to chance. Before saving the file, change the way Acrobat and Adobe Reader open to display attachments.

In the Attachments pane, choose "Show Attachments by default" from the Options menu. Save the file. When it opens, the document displays in the Document pane and the attachments display in the pane at the bottom of the program window.

Why Bother with Attachments?

Consider your workflow when deciding whether it is necessary to use attachments:

- If you move the PDF document on your hard drive, the attached files or pages automatically move with it, saving you time in moving documents.

- You can attach more information about content in your PDF without having to convert the entire document. For example, create a PDF executive summary and attach detailed documents, spreadsheets, and so on.

- You can search attached files using the Acrobat Search function, a significant time-saver when you're trying to locate information in a big project.

- You can attach a great deal of accessory material to one PDF document, great for large projects containing multiple information sources.

- You can quickly see information about the attachment in the Attachments pane.

- You can protect attached information when e-mailing it by using a Security Envelope (see #125, "Using Secure ePaper," to learn how to use this special type of security).

CHAPTER FOUR

Producing a PDF Portfolio

Do you have to collect the correspondence for a contract negotiation? Or maybe you need to pull together material for a presentation to a potential customer? An Acrobat portfolio may fit the bill perfectly.

Acrobat 9 takes the idea of packages—the method used to bring together multiple PDF files within a parent file in Acrobat 8—to a new Flash-fed feature called Portfolio. In Acrobat 9 Portfolio, available in Acrobat 9 Standard and up, not only can you gather multiple files into a parent file, but you can also configure the interface used to present your files and explore other new features. For example, you can establish a folder hierarchy, search in a portfolio, apply program commands to the portfolio's contents and the overall portfolio, and use both PDF and non-PDF files in the portfolio. Each file retains its own original features and elements, such as pagination, security, forms, digital signature, and default views.

Since Portfolio is a way to bring together content from different sources, and then manage and edit the component parts in different ways, this chapter includes dozens of references to specific topics mentioned elsewhere in the book.

#25 PDF Portfolio Building 101

Acrobat 9 offers two methods for combining multiple files. Instead of merging the content of a number of files into a single PDF file (described in #20, "Merging Multiple Files into a Single PDF Document"), you can use the Combine Files dialog to build a PDF portfolio.

A portfolio is a great way to bring all the material for a project or a task together, while maintaining the features of the component files and including navigation controls. Follow these steps to compile a basic portfolio:

1. Click the Combine task button and choose Assemble PDF Portfolio (Assemble Files into a Portfolio). Your Acrobat window is renamed the *Portfolio[#].pdf* window.

2. Click Add Files at the bottom left of the window to display the Add Files dialog. Locate and select the files you want to use, and click Open.

   - The dialog closes, and the selected files are listed at the left of the Edit window (**Figure 25**).

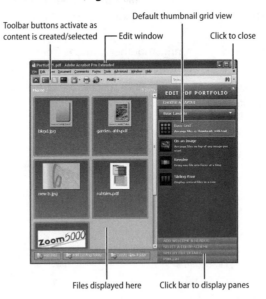

Figure 25 The selected files are listed in the Portfolio Edit window.

3. Select appearance and display options:

   - Select a layout from the Choose a Layout pane options at the right of the Portfolio window. The default uses a basic thumbnail grid (read about the other options in #26, "Customizing the Appearance").

- Click the Add Welcome & Header bar to display the Welcome Page and Header panes. (For more on designing the Welcome Page, skip ahead to #27, "Branding a PDF Portfolio.")

- Click the Select a Color Scheme bar to show some color scheme options, or design your own (see how that's done in #26, "Customizing the Appearance").

4. Click the Specify File Details bar to display the files in a list view; configure the list columns in Details mode using the options in the Specify File Details pane (read more in #28, "Organizing and Modifying Contents").

5. Click Home 🏠 on the toolbar to return to the original layout mode.

6. Click the Publish bar to display options for managing the PDF portfolio. You can save, e-mail, or share the portfolio (see Chapter 11, "Reviewing and Collaboration," for information on sharing a portfolio on Acrobat.com).

7. Choose File > Save (File > Save Portfolio) from the Acrobat menu and save the portfolio file.

8. To close the portfolio and return to Acrobat, click the "X" at the upper right of the menu bar in the Portfolio window.

The finished package provides its own interface for controlling the view of the package and its contents. Read about the different views in the sidebar "The View's the Thing."

Pack Your Portfolio

Not sure where you may want to use a portfolio? Here are some ideas:

- Collect information to keep a set of files together for future reference. For example, during discussions with a new client, archive information to retain for future discussions and negotiations.

- Rather than sending a zip file containing several types of files, along with an e-mail explaining the files in the zip, combine them into a portfolio and add descriptions to the files' page in the portfolio.

- Presentations of all kinds look professional when distributed as a portfolio. You could use a portfolio presentation for making a proposal, distributing product documentation, or sending materials to prospective clients.

Check It Out

If you aren't quite sure if you have the right file in your portfolio collection, click a PDF file to see a preview of the file. The same goes for a non-PDF file in a PDF portfolio, with one caveat—the source program that created the non-PDF file must be installed. Microsoft Office files can be previewed only on Windows systems using Office 2007 and/or Windows Vista; on the Mac, you have to use Quick Look.

#26 Customizing the Appearance

Pick a Picture

One of the layout choices offers an image background. Once your portfolio is started, follow these steps to use an image:

1. Select On an Image from the Choose a Layout pane. The files selected for the portfolio move to the bottom of the preview area as thumbnails.

2. Click Pick an Image to locate and select the background image, which can be a JPEG, GIF, or PNG file.

3. Once the image loads into the portfolio, drag the thumbnails from the preview to any location you'd like on the background image.

The Portfolio interface uses an SWF template, called the *Navigator*. Use the Navigator feature to enhance the portfolio's appearance and functionality.

You can customize the appearance of a portfolio by configuring the layout and color. Start a portfolio as described in the previous technique, and select and add the files or folders you want to use.

Choose a layout. Select one of these options:

- Basic Grid is the default view (shown in Figure 25) that arranges content based on a thumbnail grid.

- The On an Image option displays your portfolio content with an image as the background. Click the thumbnails placed on the background image to display their contents. For details on building this layout, see the sidebar "Pick a Picture."

- Revolve presents the content as a sequence where one file comes into focus at a time, great for displaying images or other highly visual content. You can include a description on the pages; click page icons to navigate.

- Sliding Row presents the content on a horizontal slider with the central three files in focus, ideal for displaying visual sequences of images and content that needs descriptions. Click page icons below the slider to navigate.

As you see in **Figure 26a**, the layouts are significantly different.

Figure 26a Pick a layout that suits your content, such as the image background (left), Revolve layout (center), or Sliding Row (right) layout.

Select a color scheme. Click the Select a Color Scheme bar to display the default color schemes. Click Customize Color Scheme to open a list of the colors used in a scheme. Click an item (such as Background Color or Primary Text Color) to open a color picker that lets you choose a custom color (**Figure 26b**).

Figure 26b Choose an alternate color scheme or customize the colors used for editing and in the finished portfolio.

Bring Your Colors Along

You can customize the portfolio colors to use your corporate or team colors. Unfortunately, Acrobat 9 doesn't offer a method to import color swatches from other programs, such as Photoshop or Illustrator. However, you can make a list of the Hex values for the colors you want to use in the portfolio, and then type them into the appropriate display elements' fields in the Custom Color Scheme list.

A Picture's Worth a Thousand Words

If you plan carefully, the image background can greatly enhance your portfolio. For example:

- Show scenery as the image background in a portfolio describing convention and tourist venues in that scenic location.

- If you use a suite of business materials, coordinate the portfolio with your other pieces by using an image of the background used for PowerPoint presentations.

- For educational pieces, use an image of the subject of study—say, a windmill—and place files corresponding to discussions on the blades, the grindstones, and so on, at the appropriate locations on the image.

#27 Branding a PDF Portfolio

A PDF portfolio offers numerous ways in which to customize the display in accordance with your corporate or business requirements. You can construct a welcome page using different types of content, and insert a header that offers different text and image options. If branding is vital, use both a welcome page (as the initial introduction) and a header (to maintain your identity as the user navigates through the portfolio).

Tip

For more identity maintenance, add a background/watermark or header/footer to your component PDF files using the Acrobat menu. Read about using program commands in a portfolio in #29, "Applying Acrobat Commands"; check out #53, "Inserting Headers and Footers," and #54, "Adding Watermarks and Backgrounds," for particulars on using the document features.

A welcome page introduces your portfolio. In some cases, there's no need to include an introduction. However, if you are designing a PDF brochure for your mountain resort, or want to include a list of instructions for participants in a shared portfolio, turn to a welcome page.

With your portfolio under way, follow these steps:

1. Click the Add Welcome & Header bar to display the pane. Click Welcome Page to open a list of options, including Text Only, Image Only, Image & Text, or Flash Movie content.

2. Choose an option to display the appropriate text or graphic frames on the preview area, and resize them as desired.

3. Insert text or an image in the frames accordingly:

   - To insert an image, click the image frame to open the Browse for Image dialog. Locate and select the image to display, and click Open. The image is inserted, the dialog closes, and the Image toolbar is activated. On the toolbar, select a background color, and set the Scale and Opacity values by dragging the sliders.

- Click the Text field and type in your text. When you input text, the Text toolbar—which lets you specify font size, color, alignment, and background color—displays. If you want to use different font styles, such as the underline shown in **Figure 27a**, select the text on the text frame first.

Figure 27a Select options, and configure text and an image for the welcome page.

Tip
Although you can resize the frame, you can't drag it to another position on the page. What you can do is change the size of the image/text frames to reconfigure them on the page's layout, "resizing" them from one area of the page to another.

Maintain your identity by using a header that displays at the top of your portfolio by following these steps:

1. Click the Add Welcome & Header bar to display the pane. Click Header to open a list of options, including text and image options.

2. Select the option for the text you want, such as an e-mail address or URL.

(continued on next page)

72

More Personalization

The features available in the Navigator are simplistic. That is, you are limited in the number of images you can use, the text display, and background choices.

Plan ahead: If you want to customize the Portfolio interface more extensively than what is allowed by the program, compose a custom image containing the fonts, colors, logo, and other features on your desired layout, and add it as a single image to the welcome page.

The same planning advice applies to the header display.

There Are Differences

While a portfolio can be designed in all Acrobat 9 versions, not all offer the same customizations:

- Acrobat 9 Standard includes one default Navigator, while Acrobat 9 Pro versions offer five Navigators.

- Acrobat 9 Standard doesn't include multiple or custom color schemes.

- Adobe Reader 9 can view all Navigators.

3. Insert an image if you've selected an image option; insert and config-ure text in the fields inserted on the page.

4. Click Home ⌂ to return to the default mode, where you see your header displayed above the presentation content (**Figure 27b**).

Figure 27b Use combinations of image and text displays for the portfolio header.

#28 Organizing and Modifying Contents

One important feature of Portfolio is the ability to arrange the files in logical and meaningful ways. You can coordinate the portfolio files using a folder system, organize and sort the file details, and view an individual file to manage its content.

Here are some tips for organizing your Portfolio component files:

- If you import a folder, its contents—including any subfolders—are preserved in the portfolio.

- You can't select more than one folder at a time from the Browse for Folder dialog to add them to the portfolio. Either locate and select the parent folder (and then delete any subfolders you don't want to maintain), or repeat the Browse for Folder process until you have the folders you want.

- The folder hierarchy in a portfolio is shown as a breadcrumb menu (**Figure 28a**). In the example shown in the figure, there are three nested levels of folders from the Home mode.

Figure 28a Use the menu to move through folder levels.

Add Your Own Columns

If you need to track data other than that offered in the default list in Details mode, add your own column. Here are some tips for working with custom columns:

- To add another column, type the label in the "Add a column" field, choose Text/ Date/Number from the pop-up menu, and click Add 🔲 to move the new column to the list.

- Double-click the name of an added column to activate the text to change it—the default columns can't be renamed.

- Like the default columns, deselect the check box to hide your custom column in Details mode.

Make Your Own Folders

To add a folder to your portfolio, click Create New Folder in the Edit Portfolio mode to display a pop-up field. Type a name for the folder in the field and click OK. Once the folder is added to the interface, you can drag and drop files and other folders into it.

Do It Manually

Selecting files and folders over and over got you down? No problem. Open a Browse window and locate the files and folders you want to use in the portfolio. Simply select and drag the whole works into the Portfolio window. Your content is added, and any preexisting folder structures are maintained.

Acrobat Portfolio lets you manage existing information about each component of the portfolio and add custom data. To check details, click the Specify File Details bar in the Edit pane. You'll see the Columns to Display settings in the Edit pane, and the folders listed in Details mode (**Figure 28b**).

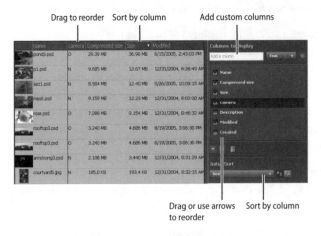

Figure 28b Edit content using Details mode.

Keep these ideas in mind as you organize, sort, and rearrange columns and data:

- You can choose the settings in the Edit pane, or directly on the list in Details mode. Changes made in one area automatically display in the other.

- Drag the vertical separator between columns in Details mode to change a column's width.

- To sort the contents, choose a column name from the Initial Sort pop-up menu. You can sort by any of the active columns in Ascending A_Z or Descending Z_A order.

- To add content or change values, such as a file's name, click the label in Details mode and type the new value when the text is activated.

- Select the check boxes for each column you want to display—deselect those you don't want to use.

- Custom columns can be configured and used in the same ways as the default columns; read how in the sidebar "Add Your Own Columns."

#29 Applying Acrobat Commands

Files added to a portfolio aren't static. That is, you can open a file from the portfolio, make changes (such as Reader-enabling the file or adding a digital signature), and save the revised file. Some commands can be applied directly in the Portfolio window.

Opening files for editing. Although not every file type can be edited from within your portfolio, a great many file types can. Check out the sidebar "Update These Files …" for a list of formats.

Follow these steps to edit a PDF file:

1. Select the file to work with from the Home or List mode, and then click Preview  on the Portfolio toolbar to display the files in the Preview Portfolio window (**Figure 29**).

Figure 29 Select and review component files in the preview.

2. Click Open to display the file in Acrobat. You can access all the Acrobat menus and tools.

3. Make your changes as necessary and save; the portfolio file is automatically updated.

Note

The same process applies to non-PDF files, although the files open in their native program.

Editing in portfolio. Some commands can be applied directly in the Portfolio window to a selected file or files, such as Reduce File Size, Run the PDF Optimizer, and others. Select the file or files in Home or List mode, and then choose the menu item. A sampling of the commands you can use in Portfolio are listed in the sidebar "Command Your Portfolio."

Scanning into a Portfolio

You can't append a scanned PDF to an existing file in your portfolio. Instead, the scanned file is added as a new PDF.

Update These Files …

Not all files from every program can be updated from within Portfolio, but the list of program formats that allow updating is impressive:

- Microsoft Office XP, 2003, 2007, 2008
- Adobe CS2 and CS3 formats
- Other Adobe formats, including those generated by Adobe Flash, Adobe Premiere, Adobe Fireworks, and Adobe FrameMaker
- AutoCAD 2007 and 2008
- Files generated by OS applications such as WordPad, Notepad, and so on

Command Your Portfolio

PDF Portfolio includes a number of commands you can access from within the Portfolio window. Many of these commands are applicable to individual files as well as the overall portfolio file. Here's a list of some commands, and where to look for techniques and sidebars elsewhere in the book:

- Convert multiple selected non-PDF files to PDF in one step (#20, "Merging Multiple Files into a Single PDF Document")
- Reduce File Size and PDF Optimizer (#33, "Optimizing a PDF Document")
- Print (#36, "Choosing Settings for Basic and Production Printing")
- Bates Numbering (#52, "Applying Page and Bates Numbering")
- Insert Header/Footer (#53, "Inserting Headers and Footers")
- Apply Watermark/Background (#54, "Adding Watermarks and Backgrounds")
- Batch Processing (#55, "Batching Tasks to Save Time")
- OCR (#61, "Extracting Active Text from an Image")
- Extend features to Adobe Reader (#79, "Starting a Shared Review")
- Secure the Portfolio (#119, "Using Security Levels and Passwords for a Document")

Control the Action with Buttons

You can assemble all the content for your portfolio, and then add buttons for actions, such as opening a file from a list of ancillary documents in an annual report. To do that, select the file and click Open 📄 on the Portfolio toolbar to open the file in a regular Acrobat window. Once the file opens, you can access all the usual tools and menus. (Read about using buttons in Chapter 15, "Controlling Action and Interaction.")

Linking Portfolio Files

Here's an interesting fact: Linking relationships aren't maintained when files are added to a portfolio, but can only be created within the portfolio.

To add a link, double-click a file in Home or Details mode to open it in Preview mode. Choose Tools > Advanced Editing> Link tool 🖉 and define the link. Be sure to use the "Go to page view" action to display another page in the portfolio, rather than the "Open a file" action that you'd usually use when linking two documents. (For more on links, see #111, "Linking Content in a Document.")

#30 Managing and Distributing a Portfolio

The portfolio is a PDF file, and Acrobat offers some portfolio-specific commands. Here are a few:

- From the Home mode, click Modify on the Portfolio toolbar and choose Secure Portfolio from the pop-up menu—or choose File > Modify PDF Portfolio > Secure Portfolio on the program menu—to specify restrictions and set a password. (See #119 for more information.)

- From the Home mode, choose File > Export > Export Multiple Files to extract the component files of your portfolio in a selected file format. In the Export Multiple Files dialog, click Add Files > Add Open Files to specify the portfolio and click OK. In the Output Options dialog, select a target folder, specify a naming system, and choose an export format. Click OK to process the files. (See #34, "Exporting PDF Documents in Other Formats.")

- From any viewing mode, choose File > Portfolio Properties to open the Document Properties dialog, where you can add descriptions, specify security, and so on. (See #31, "Finding Information about Your Document.")

- From any viewing mode, select an imported movie file, and choose Modify > Convert to Flash Movie to change the file's format. (See #96, "Inserting SWF in a PDF File.")

Sometimes a portfolio can become very large, and it's not always easy to keep track of your content. Fortunately, Acrobat offers a customized search feature for Portfolio that lets you search everything in your portfolio, including the information listed in Details mode, and in non-PDF files.

To search the files in a portfolio, follow these steps:

1. Type the terms in the Search field and click Search ⚙.

- You can set some criteria from the pop-up menu, including Whole Words Only and Case Sensitive. The Search Entire Portfolio option is selected by default, and can't be deselected.

(continued on next page)

Managing Forms Using a Portfolio

One super feature in Acrobat 9 is the ability to use a portfolio for handling forms. Once a form is designed and distributed, forms results can be compiled and stored in a portfolio. See #94, "Handling Form Returns." Aggregating the form data can be handled by both Acrobat 9 Standard and Pro versions.

How Reader Gets In on the Act

You can update files in a PDF portfolio using Adobe Reader if the file is Reader-enabled. In a portfolio, each file must be enabled separately—there isn't an overriding command to apply to all the portfolio contents. See #79 for details on enabled files.

2. Review the returns shown in the Search Results dialog (**Figure 30**).

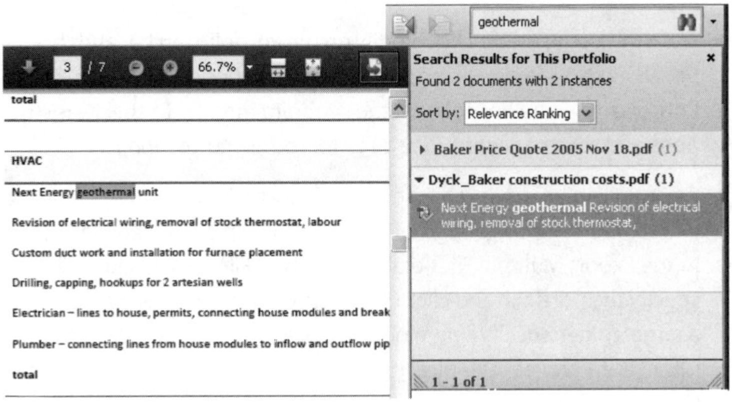

Figure 30 Search returns are listed and highlighted in the portfolio's files.

3. Click a return to read the file's details. If you are in Details mode, the file is highlighted in the list; if you are in Preview mode, the result is highlighted on the page, as you see in Figure 30.

4. Click Previous ⬅ or Next ➡ to review the results.

5. Close the Search Results pane when you have finished.

CHAPTER FIVE

Creating Output: Saving, Exporting, and Printing

You know that you can print any PDF document and it retains the integrity of your original document—that's one of the big attractions of the Portable Document Format, after all.

However, in addition to providing a variety of printing methods and options, Acrobat 9 Pro includes a suite of preflight tools, which are used to evaluate and prepare documents. Preflight has been used for testing files for compliance to certain printers or standards. In Acrobat 9, professional preflight goes further than ever before, offering a wide range of fix-ups and checks for all manner of standards and features.

#31 Finding Information about Your Document

Crafting Your Readers' Viewing Experience— Part 1: Navigation

To offer your viewers clues to the navigation included in your document, choose File > Properties, and select the Initial View tab to display the document view settings. Choose a Navigation tab option based on the document's contents and how the reader uses the document:

- In a long document, you often use a bookmark structure as a way to link content in various locations. For such documents, choose the Bookmarks Panel and Page view.

- In an image-based document, such as a slide show, use the Pages Panel and Page view. That way, your reader can easily browse the document using the thumbnail views of the pages.

- In a short document with multiple attachments, choose the Attachments Panel and Page view.

- In a layered document, choose the Layers Panel and Page view; your readers can make their way through the layers in the document.

There is a lot more to a document than what you see on the screen or printed page. Use the Document Properties dialog when you want to find or modify information about your documents. Choose File > Properties (or press Ctrl+D [Command+D]) to open this dialog. It opens to the Description tab by default. If you have modified settings in the dialog, the last tab you worked with displays instead.

The dialog contains six tabs:

- The Description tab contains information about a document (**Figure 31**)—how much information depends on the source program that created the original document. Use this tab to add keywords for searching. Click to activate a field and add content to any description element.

Figure 31 Add information about the document, such as author and keywords, in the Description tab.

- The Security tab describes what level of security has been added to the document, and lists permissions granted to users of the document. If you are the author, use either the document's password or a security certificate to change the security settings, depending on how they are applied. You can read more about security in Chapter 16, "Making Your Documents Secure."

- The Fonts tab lists the fonts, font types, and encoding information used in the original document. Having this information at hand can be a real time-saver. Read about fonts in #37, "Choosing and Using Fonts."

- Click Initial View to display information that defines how the PDF document looks when it is opened. A range of options related to the document, user interface, and window are available:

  - See the sidebar "Crafting Your Readers' Viewing Experience—Part 1: Navigation" for information on controlling the visible panes.

  - For information about choosing a magnification option, see the sidebar "Crafting Your Readers' Viewing Experience—Part 2: Magnification."

  - The sidebar "Crafting Your Readers' Viewing Experience—Part 3: Window Displays" describes when to use different window options.

- The Custom tab lets you add properties and values that identify the content in the document according to your own criteria, such as corporate or government keyword or nomenclature structures.

Crafting Your Readers' Viewing Experience—Part 2: Magnification

Along with choosing the navigation pane that best suits your document's presentation, don't forget about the page magnification. Choose File > Properties > Initial View and select an option from the Magnification pop-up menu. Keep these ideas in mind:

- As with the page layouts, the reader can control magnification in the document using the controls on the Page Display toolbar.

- Choose a zoom option depending on the document's content. Fit Width is common for text documents, for example—the reader sees the entire width of the document and can scroll through vertically to see the rest.

- Use magnifications carefully. A large image is often best presented at full size, and the reader can zoom in for a closer look.

Crafting Your Readers' Viewing Experience—Part 3: Window Displays

Match the Window Options settings to your document:

- If you are using a full-page layout, for example, click the "Resize window to initial page" option to show your entire page with the document window fitted around it. This produces the most professional-looking layouts.

- Choose "Center window on screen" for special types of content, like movies where the movie and window sizes match.

- Choose "Open in Full Screen mode" if you are playing a slide show.

- The Advanced tab shows PDF settings and reading options. Normally, you won't often change this information, aside from attaching an index to a document. Click Browse to open an Attach Index dialog and locate an index on your hard drive. Click Open and attach the selected index to the document.

When you have finished making changes to the document's properties, click OK. Save the file to apply the modified properties.

Font Information to the Rescue

In situations where you need to expand an original body of work but don't have a template, for example, you can quickly check in the generated PDF and see the fonts in the Fonts tab of the Document Properties dialog. Click the plus icon (+) to the left of the font name to open a list with more information. For each font, you see the name and font type used in the original document; the list displays the font, font type, and encoding used to display the document in Acrobat.

#32 Using the Examine PDF Process

Acrobat 8 introduced the opportunity to examine the contents of a document and remove features such as hidden text or metadata based on the idea that sensitive material in a PDF file may not be suitable for sharing with your readers, or may be unnecessary for saving the file long-term. Acrobat 9 Pro takes the Examine PDF process a step further by looking for more types of content, displaying the results in a navigation pane, and listing the numbers of items found.

Follow these steps to evaluate and change a document:

1. Choose Document > Examine Document. The file is evaluated, and the Examine Document navigation pane opens. Items identified are indicated by check marks; the number of each item found is shown in brackets following the item name. Click Expand to show the values and preview options for the list; click Collapse to return the list to its default view (**Figure 32a**).

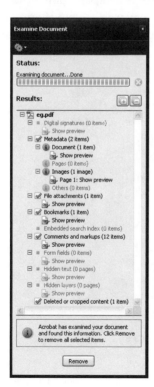

Figure 32a Make sure that the check boxes are selected only for the items that you want to remove from the document.

(continued on next page)

84

Watch Out When Deleting!

Other program items are automatically removed when you delete content using the Examine Document process. Digital signatures, for example, are a type of form logic. After the deleting process? Gone. Document information from other applications and plugins? Ditto. Files enabled for Adobe Reader users to allow for review, sign, and fill-in forms? Removed.

Auto-examinations

Some workflows include examining each PDF for hidden content before sending it by e-mail or filing it. You don't have to test manually or remember to do it at all if you set a program preference.

Choose Edit > Preferences > Documents (Acrobat > Preferences > Documents). Select either (or both) "Examine document when closing document" or "Examine document when sending document by email."

2. Check through the features identified. If you want to see the entire list of items that Examine Document looks for (shown in pale gray text in Figure 32a), click Options ⚙ and select Show All items. To select items you want to remove from the document, you can do any of the following:

- Click Info ⓘ to open a metadata dialog listing the types and values of metadata included for the file.

- Click Preview 🗐 to display the listed content. Acrobat opens navigation panes, such as Comments or Bookmarks, or a Hidden Text dialog, depending on the item you are evaluating.

- Click to select or deselect items checked ✅ in the Examine Document pane.

3. Click Remove to process the file, after reading and dismissing an information dialog that explains how removing content affects your document. After the file is processed, a list of the items removed displays in the pane (**Figure 32b**).

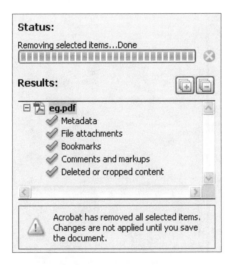

Figure 32b Items removed from the document are listed in the Examine Document pane.

4. Save the document to preserve the changes; if you need to save the original format, be sure to save the file with another name.

#**33** Optimizing a PDF Document

Some projects are quite involved, and the finished document reflects that complexity. There may be all sorts of nonoptimized content, such as images with overly high resolutions, multimedia renditions added and deleted, or pages inserted and removed. Acrobat Professional has included the PDF Optimizer in the last few versions; Acrobat 9 Pro includes new enhancements.

For removing "regular" types of extra content, such as comments and hidden text, run the Examine Document process, described in #32, "Using the Examine PDF Process." For making a document the most efficient without sacrificing its quality, turn to the PDF Optimizer in Acrobat 9 Pro.

Choose Advanced > PDF Optimizer. The first step is to analyze the document to see its contents. Click "Audit space usage" at the upper right of the PDF Optimizer dialog. Acrobat examines the document and displays a report (**Figure 33a**).

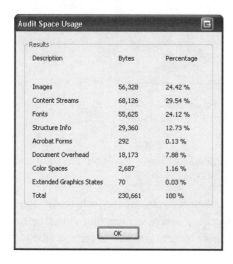

Figure 33a See what is contained within a document before deciding how to optimize it.

Depending on the document's contents, you see listings for such elements as fonts, comments, and images; each is defined both in percentages of the entire document size and in bytes. Click OK.

The default settings in the PDF Optimizer are the same as those of the document. If you select another program version from the "Make

Easy Optimizing

Do you need to apply the same optimization settings to a number of files? Once in a while or on a regular basis? Do you have a number of files that need optimizing right now? Customize a collection of settings in the PDF Optimizer and click Save in the dialog to name and save the settings. The next time you need to optimize a file using the same settings, you'll find that the custom settings are included in the Preset menu for you to select. You can remove your custom settings as well. Simply select the setting's name from the Preset menu and click Delete.

If you find you are optimizing files on a regular basis, include output options in a batch sequence instead. Read about batch sequences in #55, "Batching Tasks to Save Time."

compatible with" menu, the Settings name in the upper left of the dialog changes from Standard to Custom. The options available in the different panes of the dialog vary according to the selected program version.

Click a label in the left column of the dialog to display settings (**Figure 33b**).

Figure 33b You can customize dozens of settings in the PDF Optimizer to precisely balance the quality of the document against the file's size.

As you look through the list, deselect items that you don't want to optimize; look for optimizing in these areas:

- **Images.** Define settings for color, grayscale, and monochrome images. Choose compression types, quality, and downsampling values. Select "Optimize images only if there is a reduction in size" to prevent bloating the file size.

- **Fonts.** The fonts in the document are listed in the dialog, and fully embedded fonts are subset by default. You can unembed those you don't need, such as system fonts or common fonts. If a document is intended for departmental circulation, for example, and you know everyone viewing it uses the same set of fonts, you can delete those from the list.

- **Transparency.** Choose transparency flattening and settings such as resolutions for text, line art, and gradients.

- **Discard Objects.** Decide what objects to remove, such as form fields, alternate images, and search indexes. Some options in this panel are the same as those available in the Examine Document dialog, described in #32.

- **Discard User Data.** Decide what added items can be removed from the document, such as layers, form content, cross-references, attachments, and comments. Some of the options from the Examine Document dialog described in #32 are included in this panel.

- **Clean Up.** Choose other cleanup details, such as removal of invalid links or bookmarks, encoding options, and a method of compressing the document's structure.

Click Save to name and save the settings if you plan to reuse them at a later time. If optimizing is a onetime thing, click OK to close the dialog. Click Save in the Save Optimized dialog to overwrite the original file. To be on the safe side, however, save the document with another name instead, and after you are satisfied with the results, delete the original.

Save It Again

One of the simplest ways to reduce file size is to save a file as itself. If you have been working with a document— for example, adding and removing pages—an iteration of the file is saved each time you save it. These iterations can really add up to a huge file size. Choose File > Save As. In the Save As dialog, leave the name as is and click Save. A prompt asks if you want to overwrite the file; click Yes. The file is resaved, and content is consolidated. You may be surprised how much smaller the file becomes!

#**34** Exporting PDF Documents in Other Formats

Pick a Format— Any Format

How do you know what format to use for exporting from PDF? Here are some tips:

- Acrobat lets you save a PDF file in two formats to use in Word or other document-processing programs. If the document contains a lot of structural elements, such as columns, use the DOC format. For simpler content that is intended for other word or text processing, use RTF.

- If you want to use a PDF document as a Web page, use one of two HTML formats.

- If you want to use the data, use XPDF or XML formats. Converting your document's data to XML or XPDF reduces the complexity and creates data that can be read by many types of applications. Use XML format when you want to export a document for data exchange, such as for use in spreadsheets or databases. Use XPDF when you want to use the data for data exchange in a variety of PDF formats, such as forms and documents.

(continued on next page)

You can use a PDF document for a variety of purposes and pass it through various programs. For example, you can create a document in Microsoft Word, convert it to a PDF using PDFMaker, and then export it from Acrobat as an HTML Web page that includes PNG images, or as a PDF file compliant with a standard.

To save a PDF document in another file format (in this case, Word):

1. Choose File > Save As. Select a format in the "Save as type" pop-up menu (**Figure 34a**). Alternatively, choose File > Export, and select the format to open the Save As dialog. The file format extension is appended to the filename and the Settings button becomes active.

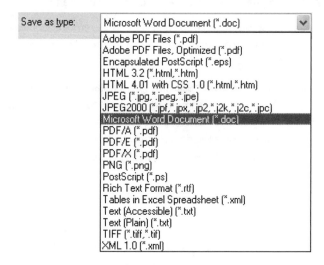

Figure 34a Choose from a variety of export options, ranging from optimized and standards-based PDF formats to image and Web formats.

2. Click Settings. The available options in the Settings dialog are specific to the file format you chose and appear as part of the dialog's name. Check out an overview of the Word export settings in the sidebar "What's the Good Word?"

3. Adjust the settings in the dialog, and click OK to return to the Save As dialog.

4. Click Save. Acrobat exports your file in your chosen format.

Creating Output: Saving, Exporting, and Printing

Note

You can choose among a number of similar formats for exporting from Acrobat. Many are composed of document, text, and code formats for use in Word, document processing, Web, and data exchange applications and programs—read about them in the sidebar "Pick a Format—Any Format."

- Choose the accessible or plain text option for output when you don't want any applied styles or formatting.

Acrobat 9 Pro includes options to save an ordinary PDF file according to a specific standard. That's right—you don't have to run Preflight on the file first! Here's how it works:

1. Choose File > Save As and choose a standards format (PDF/A, PDF/E, or PDF/X) from the "Save as type" pull-down list. Click Settings to open the Preflight: Convert to PDF/[*standard*] dialog. The dialog name varies according to the standard selected (**Figure 34b**).

Figure 34b Export settings vary according to the type of file you are producing; the example is for exporting a Word DOC file.

2. If there are multiple standard choices, choose a standard from the options. For example, PDF/A may be either PDF/A-1a or PDF/A-1b, while PDF/E has no optional conditions; PDF/X has four choices.

3. To ensure that your document is up to standards, select "Create PDF/[*standard*] according to the following PDF/[*standard*] conversion profile." In the case of PDF/X conversions, you can also choose from multiple conversion profiles.

4. Choose a viewing or printing condition from the drop-down list, or leave the default.

(continued on next page)

5. Click Overview (?) to open a small dialog (also shown in Figure 34b) listing the fix-ups and corrections Acrobat includes in the conversion profile; click OK to close the dialog and return to the main Preflight: Convert to PDF/[*standard*] dialog (read about fixups in Chapter 6, "Complying with PDF and Accessibility Standards").

6. Click OK to close the settings dialog and return to the Save As dialog, and then click Save to convert the file. Acrobat starts to process, fix, and evaluate the file according to the standard. If there are errors that can't be corrected, you'll see a notice that the file needs to be evaluated using Preflight. You can read about Preflight and standards in Chapter 6.

What's the Good Word?

Here are some pointers for exporting a PDF file as a Word document:

- To specify a layout option that may help keep a complex document (with images, text wrap, columns, and so on), choose either Retain Flowing Text or Retain Page Layout.

- Include Comments is selected by default; deselect it if you don't need comments in the exported document.

- Don't export the images if you don't need them. They add to file size and processing time.

- If you want to export images and your PDF file contains both color and grayscale images, choose Determine Automatically from the Use Colorspace pop-up menu.

- If you don't need the images to be in color, select the Grayscale option, since the files are processed faster and are smaller in size.

- To save file size, you can click Change Resolution and choose an option to downsample the images.

#35 Saving Image PDF Files

Suppose you don't want to save a file in some variation of a text format, but instead would like to save it as a set of image pages, or export the images to use elsewhere.

To save a PDF as an image, do the following:

1. Choose File > Save As and select an image export option from the Format pop-up menu.

2. Click Settings to open the Settings dialog. Modify the options in the Save As [type] Settings dialog according to your requirements, which vary depending on the file format you selected.

3. Click OK and return to the Save As dialog. Click Save to convert the file. Acrobat converts each page of your document to an image: The image will be the same size as the document page.

You can also export the images alone, and specify the extraction size and other details. Follow these steps:

1. Choose Advanced > Document Processing > Export All Images. Browse for the folder you want to use to store the images in the Export All Images As dialog.

2. Choose an image format from the list at the bottom of the dialog. Your choices include JPG, TIF, PNG, and JPEG2000.

(continued on next page)

Show Your Viewers

An image of a document makes a very nice link from another document. When you are building a large project incorporating several types of material, you typically link the documents together. Instead of using text to link, use a thumbnail-sized image of the first page of linked documents, such as image samples or slide shows. Be sure the outcome is worth the effort—don't use an image of an all-text page, for example.

3. Click Settings. In **Figure 35**, the resultant dialog shows Export All Images As TIFF Settings. The dialog is similar to that used for configuring export settings for any format that allows for image export.

Figure 35 Specify how to export a sequence of images in a document.

4. Click Save to export the images to the folder and save them using the file's name and an incremental number.

#36 Choosing Settings for Basic and Production Printing

Acrobat 9 Pro includes a suite of Print Production tools you can use to evaluate and prepare documents for high-end printing. Choose Advanced > Print Production or View > Toolbars and select Show Print Production Toolbar to display the set of tools. To access the toolbar from the shortcut menu, right-click (Control-click) the toolbar area at the top of the program window and choose Print Production from the toolbar listing.

Although the tools are intended for high-resolution printing, several tools can be useful in many business-based production situations as well:

- Click Output Preview 🔲 to open the Output Preview dialog. From the Simulation Profile menu, choose options to show you how your document would look using different types of paper, different monitors, different color profiles, and so on (**Figure 36a**). Read more in the sidebar "Soft Proofing."

Figure 36a The Output Preview gives you a good idea of how a document looks printed on different types of paper.

- To open the Crop Pages dialog, click the Crop tool 🔲. Use the settings to crop off unwanted areas of the page or to increase the size of the page. Read more about the Crop tool in #51, "Cropping and Rotating Pages."

- Click the PDF Optimizer tool 🔲 to open the PDF Optimizer dialog, which lets you choose settings to compress or remove content and decrease the size of files. The PDF Optimizer is discussed in #33, "Optimizing a PDF Document."

(continued on next page)

Soft Proofing

Use the Output Preview dialog features to simulate different document conditions. In Acrobat, you don't have to print a hard copy to preview the colors. Instead, soft proofing shows you how a document will look in print. Select the Simulate Black Ink check box to preview how the document would look printed in black ink. Select Simulate Paper Color to preview the color of your document printed on white paper. Select Set Page Background Color and choose a color from the color palette to see how your document looks against a colored paper background.

Handling Proofs

Traditionally proofs are printed and then the proof and the original are compared side by side. Instead of printing paper proofs, use the Commenting summary feature to produce a single document that shows the comment in the summary with a connector line to the correction or comment added to the document. Choose either to split the view with document and comment pages separated, or to place the comments and document page on the same page. Read more about comment summaries in #77, "Setting Comment Status and Creating Summaries."

Avoiding White Patches

Click the Transparency Flattening tool to open the Flattener Preview dialog. Where you have layered images in your documents, unless the layers are flattened before printing, transparent areas print as white—not what you usually want to see in your masterpiece. Choose the desired settings and click Apply.

- Click the Fix Hairlines tool to open a dialog that allows you to define a page range, the size of line to target, and the replacement width. Increasing the width of very thin lines makes it easier to see them onscreen.

Printing from Acrobat can be much more complex than clicking the Print button: You can control what you print as well as where and how a document is printed. In addition, Acrobat lets you print to a printer or to a file, define a portion of your document for printing, or create a PostScript file.

Choose File > Print. In the Print dialog (**Figure 36b**), you can choose specific print characteristics, such as the print range and number of copies.

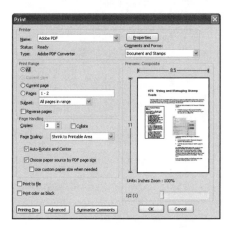

Figure 36b The Print dialog offers many ways to configure and prepare a document or its components for printing.

Let's take a look at the Print dialog options:

- Choose a printer from the Name pop-up menu in the Printer area of the dialog; in Mac OS, choose an option from the Presets pop-up menu. Your operating system's printer and printer driver installations, as well as your network configuration, determine the Presets and Printer lists.

- In Windows, select the "Print to file" check box to create a PostScript file.

- Specify Print Range and Page Handling options. Select a Page Scaling option such as None (the default), shrinking or tiling pages, printing multiple pages per sheet, or using booklet printing. For some selections, additional options display, such as using Labels or CutMarks with tiled pages.

- Choose Document (the default setting), Document and Markups, Document and Stamps, or Form Fields Only from the Comments and Forms pop-up menu.

- Click Summarize Comments to open the Summarize Options layout, and choose settings for printing the comments in the document. See #77, "Setting Comment Status and Creating Summaries," for more on printing comments.

- Click Advanced Print to open the Advanced Print Setup. In this dialog, choose settings for precise printing features, including Output, Marks and Bleeds, Color Management, and PostScript Options.

Before printing, preview the page in the Preview area of the dialog. If you like, drag the slider below the Preview area to show the other pages in the document. Click OK to start the print job.

Print What You See

Suppose you want to print a portion of an image that shows your new company logo or your dog's face. Resize the program window to show only the content you want to print; use the scroll bars and magnification tools to get the placement correct. Then choose File > Print and click Current view in the Print Range settings of the Print dialog. The area displayed in the program window displays in the Preview area. Choose other print settings, and click OK to print.

More Printing Options

Look for these other settings in the Print dialog:

- If you are working in Windows and using a drawing that contains colored lines, such as an engineering drawing, click Print Color As Black to force all nonwhite color to print as black. This allows the lines to be readily visible on a black-and-white printed page.

- You can quickly change the size of a printed document. Choose Shrink to Printable Area or Fit to Printable Area from the Page Scaling pop-up menu. Your document is reset at the page size selected in the printer properties.

- Choose Booklet Printing to print a document ready for collating, folding, and stapling. When the paper is folded, the pages are in correct order: First and last page are paired, second and second-to-last page are paired, and so on. Your printer must be able to do automatic or manual duplex printing, which is printing on both sides of the paper.

#37 Choosing and Using Fonts

Before converting a document to PDF, make sure your fonts can be used and viewed by others. Access the settings from a PDFMaker, Distiller, or the Adobe PDF Printer driver. Here's an example using Word:

1. In Word, choose Adobe PDF > Change Conversion Settings. Click the Advanced Settings button to open the Adobe PDF Settings dialog; then click the Fonts folder in the left column to display the Fonts settings (**Figure 37a**).

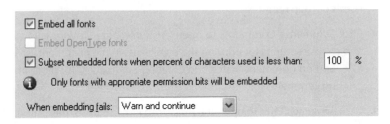

Figure 37a Select embedding and subsetting options for your file conversion.

   - Depending on the conversion settings option you are using, you may find the "Embed all fonts," "Embed Open Type fonts," or the "Subset embedded fonts" check boxes at the top of the pane already selected.

2. In the lower portion of the window, select the font you want to embed from the list at the left and click Add. The font is added to the Always Embed list at the right if it can be embedded. A locked font, which shows a lock icon to the left of its name, can't be embedded (see the sidebar "You Can't Break the Lock").

3. Click OK and name the joboptions file in the prompt dialog that opens. Back in the source program, convert the document to PDF.

A common error is to preview a document only on your computer using your installed fonts, which isn't how other computers display your file unless the font is embedded. **Figure 37b** shows the text using fonts installed on my computer in the upper heading example. To preview the file without local fonts, choose Edit > Preferences (Acrobat > Preferences) and choose Page Display from the left column. Clear the "Use local fonts"

You Can't Break the Lock

A lock symbol 🔒 to the left of a font's name in the Fonts settings dialog indicates that the font is locked. If you select that font, Acrobat displays a message below the Font Source menu stating that the font's license does not permit embedding. In this case, you have two options: Either you must purchase the font for everyone who uses the document, or you should change to a font that can be embedded.

check box and click OK. The same document, without benefit of local fonts, is shown in the lower heading example of Figure 37b.

Figure 37b Unless you have permission, a locked font (upper heading) is replaced by a default font (lower heading)—the Viking is purely decorative!

The difference is clear. The font used—Everyday Formula—is a locked font and can't be embedded. If I sent someone this document, my spiffy headings would be replaced by something far tamer.

You can check the Document Properties for confirmation. Choose File > Document Properties and select the Fonts tab to show the font information (**Figure 37c**). The information for the Everyday Formula font is as you would expect: The dialog states that the actual font used is Adobe Sans MM.

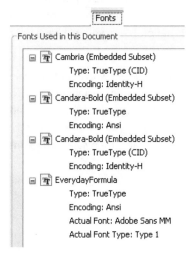

Figure 37c The Document Properties dialog lists information for the embedded, subset, and substituted fonts.

Embedding and Subsetting

Embedding means that information about all the characters in the fonts is automatically attached for use after the document is converted to a PDF. *Subsetting* refers to a percentage of the font's information based on the number of characters used in the document.

When you embed a font, the text in the document using that font displays correctly. Preserve the content precisely using subsetting. It's a good idea to subset at 100%—the difference in file size is hardly noticeable. If you use half of the possible characters in a font and subsetting is set to 100%, all your information is used. If you use half the possible characters in a font and have subsetting set at 25%, other characters may be substituted.

Subsetting is important for documents sent to a print service or press. When the document is printed, it uses the information in your document, not that of the printer's version of the font, ensuring precise results.

#38 Print Troubleshooting 101

Here are some basic tips and hints that you may find handy in times of stress (usually one minute before a deadline!). If you're having trouble printing a PDF, try the following:

- Rewrite the file. Choose File > Save As, and resave the file as itself (don't change the name). Click OK when prompted to overwrite the existing file and prevent storing multiple copies of the same file. When you choose Save As and resave it as a PDF, Acrobat overwrites all the stored versions created each time you save the file, sometimes clearing a stored problem.

- Try using the Examine Document process to remove elements from the file. The problem may be solved by removing content such as metadata and data from other applications. (See #32, "Using the Examine PDF Process," for information on using the Examine Document process.)

- Re-create the PDF file using a different method; for example, if you originally converted the file using PDFMaker, try again using Acrobat Distiller.

- If you are using a Web file, download the PDF again and try printing once more.

- Try exporting the file as an image file, and print the exported image pages (refer to #35, "Saving Image PDF Files," for information on image exports). Although you won't solve the problem, you will have your printed output.

- Print the file as an image. Sometimes a document won't print because of errors in interpreting the text or font information—neither of which is required when printing an image of the page. Click the Advanced button at the bottom left of the Print dialog (shown in Figure 36b) to open the Advanced Print Setup dialog, and then select the Print

Don't Print Everything

In a pinch, you can try printing the file in sections. You may find the printing problem comes from one object on one page, and that single error could prevent the document from printing. Once you isolate the problem, you might have to re-create a page, but that is much simpler than starting over.

Picking Pages

You can use Acrobat's Pages pane to select portions of a document to print—great for trying to troubleshoot a print issue:

- To select a group of pages, click the first page to select it, hold down the Shift key, and click the last page to select it. Acrobat selects all pages in between as well.

- To select noncontiguous pages, click the first page to select it, hold down Ctrl (Command), and click the other pages you want to print.

Creating Output: Saving, Exporting, and Printing

As Image check box (**Figure 38**). The Settings option switches from Acrobat Default to Custom as a result. Click OK to close the dialog, and then click OK to try printing again.

Figure 38 Print the document as an image file using the Advanced Print Setup dialog.

- In a layered document, merge or flatten the layers in the PDF file to determine if a layer is causing the printing issue. To preserve your original, save the document with another name after flattening layers.

- If you are using a PostScript printer, set the printer to display printing errors. Check that the PostScript Printer Description (PPD) file is up to date, and that you are using the PPD file recommended by the printer manufacturer.

- If the document you are trying to print has color separations, print a composite of the document to see if a color plate is causing the problem.

Help!

If you run into printing problems, click Printing Tips at the bottom left of the Print dialog to open Adobe's print troubleshooting site—an excellent and comprehensive knowledge base that is sure to offer some insight into your issue.

CHAPTER SIX

Complying with PDF and Accessibility Standards

Traditionally, the preflight process tests files for compliance with certain printers or standards. The concept of preflight has changed from that of a testing tool to one of the most powerful features in Acrobat. Along with evaluation, you can also employ fixups, which modify your document for everything from flattening form fields to moving comments off the printing area.

Acrobat 9 Pro takes the evaluation and fixup process further than ever before, letting you specify a particular area or view to evaluate or repair, or even create layers to separate your document's objects. Just as you might certify a document with a digital signature to indicate you are the author or approve the content, Acrobat 9 includes a preflight audit trail, adding a digital signature automatically to certify your document's standards compliance.

If you find opening dialogs and running preflight profiles repetitious, make yourself a program to run features automatically from the desktop.

Output standards also apply to accessibility features. Acrobat 9 offers a range of features that allow users who are visually or motion impaired to work with PDF documents. You'll find testing options to establish whether a document complies with different accessibility standards, and evaluation reports that help you correct accessibility issues.

Tags are a key element in making accessible documents. Acrobat contains a number of ways in which you can apply tags to a document, evaluate the status of the document, and use the tags for manipulating the document and its contents.

#**39** Testing and Fixing a Document with Preflight

Preflight Profile Categories

There are several basic categories of preflight profiles:

- Create PDF layers, used for dividing content in a file according to object type

- Digital printing and online publishing, used for basic printing and online use (optimized for either quality or size)

- PDF analysis, which evaluates files for components, such as hairlines, color, or object types

- PDF fixups, used for making specific changes, such as converting color space, decreasing image resolution, or managing transparency

- PDF/A compliance, used to evaluate a document for compliance with the Archival standard and to make repairs

- PDF/E compliance, used to evaluate a document for compliance with the Engineering standard and to correct compliance errors

- PDF/X compliance, used to evaluate a document for compliance with Print standards and to make repairs

Preparing a print job, whether intended for prepress or your company's annual report, can be a laborious and time-consuming process. Acrobat 9 Pro includes a suite of preflight tools you can use to evaluate your files for problems, compliance with standards, and analysis of objects like hidden text and transparency. The Preflight dialog includes preflight profiles (groups of settings), as well as individual checks and fixups.

To test a document for compliance with a profile, follow these steps:

1. Choose Advanced > Preflight or click the Preflight button ▨ on the Print Production toolbar to open the Preflight dialog and load the profiles.

2. Click Select Profiles ▨ on the Preflight toolbar to load the existing profiles. Click Show All and choose an option from the pop-up menu—view a list of the Preflight categories in the sidebar "Preflight Profile Categories."

3. Click the arrow next to a category label to view the profile list and select the profile to apply (**Figure 39a**). You'll see information about the profile display in the dialog.

Figure 39a Select the profile you want to run from the list in the dialog.

4. Click Analyze if you've chosen a profile that verifies or evaluates some aspect of the file; click Analyze and Fix if you choose a profile that tests and makes changes. Acrobat evaluates and applies changes as required.

5. The Results tab displays the results. As you see in **Figure 39b**, there are some errors, and the source file, although an RGB file, isn't successfully converted to a PDF/E-compliant document.

Figure 39b Evaluate the results of your profile.

6. Click the plus sign (+) to the left of any error message to display detailed information.

#40 Ensuring Standards Compliance

Every version of Acrobat introduces more standards, as well as methods for evaluating a document according to those standards. Acrobat 9 is no exception, as you can see in the sidebar "Variations on a Theme."

To test a document for compliance with a profile, follow the steps outlined in #39, "Testing and Fixing a Document with Preflight." For the PDF standards, you'll usually find profiles that let you convert to the standard, verify that the file complies with the standard, or remove the standard's information (**Figure 40a**).

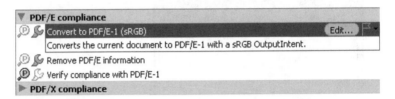

Figure 40a Choose a standards-compliant profile from one of the categories, such as the PDF/E-1 profile used in the example.

Once the file is saved, your recipient can guarantee its conformance with the standard by viewing the information in the Standards pane, new in Acrobat 9. Once you open a PDF file that conforms to a standard, the Standards pane opens automatically (**Figure 40b**).

Figure 40b Information about the document and its applied standard appear in the Standards pane.

In the Standards pane, you can do the following:

- Click Verify Conformance to evaluate the file. If the Status is listed as "verification succeeded," you know the file complies with the standard and the listed OutputIntent.

- Click Check Profile Fingerprint to be sure the audit trail matches the listed profile.

- Click Remove Preflight Audit Trail to delete the content, which you may want to do if you are the final recipient of a file.

Variations on a Theme

You can choose from a number of PDF print standards. The one you select depends on the final processing of the document:

- All PDF/X standards are designed for graphics exchange. The files must contain specific page content and resources.

- All compliance options contain an OutputIntent and a printing profile.

- A document destined for digital press uses a PDF/X-1a standard; this standard has versions for 2001 and 2003.

- Choose PDF/X-3 standards that are 2002- or 2003-compliant; the PDF/X-3 standard includes color usage options—CMYK and spot colors only or calibrated color.

- PDF/X-4 prepress digital data standards based on PDF 1.6 as either complete exchange of printing data (PDF/X-4) or partial exchange with an external profile reference (PDF/X-4p).

- PDF/X-5, also based on PDF 1.6, offers three levels based on graphical content and ICC profiles.

- Specific named standards such as Sheetfed Offset (CMYK) are based on best practice guidelines recommended by industry associations.

Use the PDF/A standard for documents intended for long-term storage in PDF format. The file can't include external players, external links, or protection in order to ensure viewing and printing over the long term. PDF/A standard has two variations—1a and 1b.

The PDF/E standard is designed for engineering PDF document exchange. PDF/E files can contain 3D models and annotations. However, the content and resources must be embedded in the file to guarantee reliable viewing and printing.

Apples and Oranges *Are* Different

Don't expect to be able to convert any file to a standards-compliant file simply because you can choose a profile that will convert the file. Sometimes there simply aren't enough pieces of document information or metadata to allow for the conversion. For example, if you have a file converted from a Word document that used online settings, you won't be able to convert that smoothly into a PDF/X file compliant with print standards.

The solution? If possible, return to the source program and reproduce the PDF file using the standard you need. If you don't have the source file, you may get the result you want using a couple of profiles.

#41 Fixing Print and File Issues Automatically

Along with testing a file for compliance with different standards or analyzing the content of a file, you can fix problems that prevent a file from meeting your PDF file goals. Click either "Select single checks" 🔍 or "Select single fixups" 🔧 on the Preflight dialog's toolbar, and follow the steps listed in #39, "Testing and Fixing a Document with Preflight."

You don't have to use one of the presupplied profiles for making repairs. Instead, create one from scratch like this example fixup, following these steps:

1. Click one of the Profile buttons in the Preflight dialog, then click the Options menu. The choices in the menu depend on whether you've clicked Select profiles, "Select single checks," or "Select single fixups." Read about which option to use in the sidebar "Which to Choose?"

2. Choose Create New Preflight Profile to open the Preflight: Edit Profile dialog (**Figure 41**).

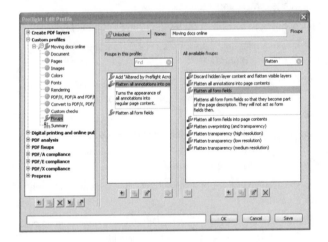

Figure 41

Tip
If the profile is locked, select Unlock from the Locked pop-up menu at the upper left of the dialog to allow you to make changes.

3. Type a name for your new profile; the default is *New Profile 1*. The example is named *Moving docs online*.

Complying with PDF and Accessibility Standards

4. Click the icon to the left of the profile category name in the left column of the dialog to open the nested list of components.

5. Select Fixups from the items under the profile to display the "Fixups in this profile" and "All available fixups" lists at the right of the dialog. Select a fixup from the "All available fixups" column and click the left-facing arrow just below the "All available fixups" column to move the fixup to the column on the left, as shown in Figure 41. You can read information about the selected fixup in either list.

Tip
Rather than scrolling through dozens of fixups, type a term in the search field to filter the options.

6. Continue adding fixups as required.

7. Click Save to store your new profile and continue working in the dialog; click OK to save your new profile and close the dialog.

8. Click OK. Your new profile is added to the list alphabetically.

Which to Choose?

How do you know whether you want to edit a process, duplicate it, or start a new one? And do you want a new profile? Or a new check or fixup?

- Start with a duplicate of an existing profile if you want to make some changes to specific components (such as image resolutions) but need the overall profile.

- Start with a new profile if you want to combine some specialty items that aren't likely to be in an existing profile, such as flattening comments and form fields, and cropping the pages (the example used here).

- Start from an existing check or fixup if you want to change parameters, and the check or fixup allows modification.

- To change parameters for a locked check or fixup, start from a duplicate. The item is named *(Copy 1)* by default, so you won't overwrite the original.

#42 Making Preflight Work for You

Not only is preflight one of the most powerful features in Acrobat 9, but it's also one of the more misunderstood and underutilized features.

To help make preflight work for you, here are some ideas to keep in mind:

- Filter the list of profiles to decrease confusion. There are literally hundreds of profiles, checks, and fixes. To start, click the Select profiles, "Select single checks," or "Select single fixups" button on the Preflight toolbar to choose the area you want to work in. Then, click the Show All button and select a category.

Tip

In the Preflight dialog, the Select profiles, "Select single checks," and "Select single fixups" buttons are all referred to as Preflight profiles, even those that deal with a single issue.

- If you need to reuse a profile that you applied last week, click Show All, and choose "Most recently used"; for a profile that you use regularly, choose "Most frequently used."

- Designate profiles as favorites. Locate the profile you want to use as a favorite, and click its listing. You'll see a description of the profile's action and a flag icon at the right of the listing. Click the flag to designate it as a favorite (**Figure 42a**). The next time you are searching for profiles, simply choose Favorites from the Show All menu.

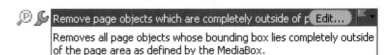

Figure 42a Designate a profile as a favorite to make it simpler to find.

- Specify a subset of a document for Preflight. In the Preflight dialog, click Further Options and choose "Run Preflight checks for visible layers only" in a layered file, or select a page range in a multipage document.

- For some items, such as images, you can select the object in the Results list, and click Show in Snap to view a close-up of the error. The Snap view is useful if you have a lot of graphics in close proximity to one another.

- Acrobat 9 Pro offers a new method for tracking the integrity of a document. Click Embed Audit Trail at the bottom of the Results tab to embed information about the Preflight profile and the results, and then add an invisible digital signature that confirms the status of the document at the time you ran the Preflight profile. Click OK in the information dialog, and save the signed file.

- Click Create Report to open a Save As dialog where the file is renamed as *[filename]_report.pdf*. Choose PDF report options, such as how to highlight error details, and click Save.

- If you create the report after embedding an audit trail, the resulting report defines the audit trail's signature as invalid. In the Signatures pane, you'll see the extra page added for the report, as well as all the comments identifying errors in the file (**Figure 42b**). By the way, notice that the document was signed by Adobe Acrobat 9 Preflight, not using a personal signature.

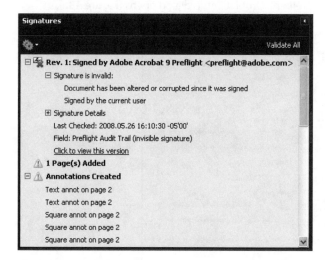

Figure 42b An audit trail's signature is invalidated if you create a Preflight Report after embedding the signature.

Spread the Word

To share information about a document's status with your workgroup, click Options > Insert Preflight Results as Comments to transfer the error information from the Results tab in the Preflight dialog to the document itself. Acrobat draws a comment box on the appropriate area of the document and adds a comment note to the Comments list.

You can also generate a report on the status of the document. Click Report in the Preflight dialog; a Save As dialog opens. The file uses the document's name and appends *_report* to the name. Click Save to save the document.

#**43** Creating and Using a Printing Droplet

It's Raining Droplets

If your specialty is print production, you will often find you have a series of preflight tests you have to run, depending on your client. Take a few minutes to build droplets and storage folders for each of your regular jobs. You can store the droplets on the desktop or in any folder on your hard drive. Why not a folder on the desktop for easy access? Need to check a file for Client A? Open your folder and drag the file to the appropriate droplet. Acrobat opens and runs the Preflight process, storing the document and reports according to the droplet's settings.

In Windows, you can add the droplet right to the system's Start menu if it is on your desktop. Right-click the droplet to open the shortcut menu and choose "Pin to Start menu." Then drag your document for testing to the Start button and hold it for a second or two until the Start menu opens. Then, simply drop the file on the droplet item.

A Preflight droplet is a special application you build to modify or evaluate documents. With a droplet on your desktop, you don't even have to open Acrobat dialogs to process a file! In addition to using droplets to evaluate files, you can use them to separate your files by their results and create reports automatically. Build the droplet in Acrobat through the Preflight dialog.

Note
If you intend to create folders to store both files that have been processed successfully and those that generate errors, add and name the folders before building the droplet to save time.

Follow these steps to construct the droplet:

1. In Acrobat, choose Advanced > Preflight. When the profiles are loaded, select the profile you want to convert to a droplet.

2. Click Options in the Preflight dialog and choose Create Preflight Droplet. The Preflight: Droplet Setup dialog opens (**Figure 43a**).

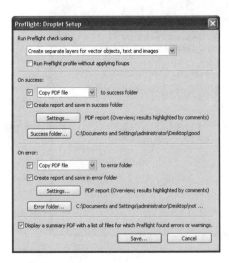

Figure 43a Specify features and storage locations for the Preflight droplet.

3. Choose options for a successful test. You can move, copy, or create an alias of the document in a specified folder. Click the Success folder button to choose a folder in which to hold the successfully processed files.

Complying with PDF and Accessibility Standards

4. Select the "Create report and save in success folder" check box and then click Settings to open the Preflight: Report Settings dialog:

- Specify the type of report—PDF, XML, or Text.

- Include an overview or details.

- For a detailed report, select a method for highlighting problems using a mask, a comment, or layers.

5. Click OK and return to the Droplet Setup dialog. The report settings now appear in the dialog.

6. Choose options for a test that generates errors. Your choices are duplicates of the ones offered for a successful test.

7. Click Save; the "Save droplet as" dialog opens. Choose a location to store the droplet and click Save to create it.

When you want to test a file, locate and select the file on your computer. Then drag it to the Droplet icon. Acrobat starts and tests the file. Depending on the outcome and your settings, the file is processed and saved, and reports are generated (**Figure 43b**).

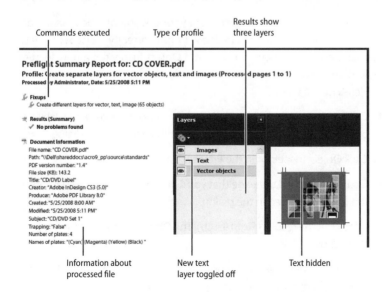

Commands executed   Type of profile   Results show three layers

Preflight Summary Report for: CD COVER.pdf
Profile: Create separate layers for vector objects, text and images (Processed pages 1 to 1)
Processed by Administrator, Date: 5/25/2008 5:11 PM

Fixups
Create different layers for vector, text, image (65 objects)

Results (Summary)
✓ No problems found

Document Information
File name: "CD COVER.pdf"
Path: "\\Dell\shareddocs\acro9_pp\source\standards"
PDF version number: "1.4"
File size (KB): 143.2
Title: "CD/DVD Label"
Creator: "Adobe InDesign CS3 (5.0)"
Producer: "Adobe PDF Library 8.0"
Created: "5/25/2008 8:00 AM"
Modified: "5/25/2008 5:11 PM"
Subject: "CD/DVD Set 1"
Trapping: "False"
Number of plates: 4
Names of plates: "(Cyan) (Magenta) (Yellow) (Black) "

Layers
Images
Text
Vector objects

Information about   New text   Text hidden
processed file   layer toggled off

Figure 43b The Preflight droplet evaluated the file and added the fixup—in this case, adding separate layers for different types of objects.

Modifying Droplets

Sometimes your requirements change, and you need to make a change to a droplet. It's easy—in the Preflight dialog, click Options to open its menu, and choose Edit Preflight Droplet. Locate and select the EXE file you want to change to open the Edit Droplet dialog, where you'll find the same settings as those shown in Figure 43a with one addition. If you'd like to save the droplet into your Preflight profiles, click Capture, select the Group from the pop-up menu, and click OK. When you've finished editing the droplet, click Save to update it.

Share and Share Alike

If you are involved in a group project, using the same criteria for processing files can certainly save time and decrease error. A Preflight droplet is an independent executable file that performs a Preflight task that you can e-mail or distribute as you like.

Examining a
Document's Output

Black and White Simulations

Use the Output Preview dialog features to simulate different document conditions. In Acrobat, you don't have to print a hard copy to preview the colors. Instead, soft proofing shows you how a document will look in print. Select the Simulate Ink Black check box to preview how the document would look printed in black ink. Select Simulate Paper Color to preview the color of your document printed on white paper. Keep in mind that not all profiles in Acrobat will support these two soft proofing options.

One of the Acrobat Preflight tools you may not have used before—but should be taking advantage of—is the Output Preview tool.

Click Output Preview to open the Output Preview dialog. From the Simulation Profile menu, choose options to show you how your document would look using different types of paper, different monitors, different color profiles, and so on (**Figure 44a**).

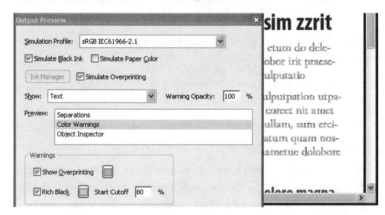

Figure 44a Select an object type or color profile to view different document conditions.

If you aren't sure of some aspect of your document—be it an image, the font used, or why an image doesn't print correctly—discover what's happening in your document with the Object Inspector, a new feature in Acrobat 9 Pro.

Here's how it works:

1. Choose Advanced > Print Production > Output Preview, or click Output Preview on the Print Production toolbar to open the dialog.

2. Click Object Inspector in the Preview list.

3. Click an object on the page that you'd like to examine. The contents of the object are listed in the dialog.

4. Check out the results (**Figure 44b**). The Object Inspector describes the following:

   - The stacking order of the objects below the cursor; the objects are listed from background to top layer.

   - Fill and stroke information for objects, as well as details like color space, overprinting, and so on.

Complying with PDF and Accessibility Standards

- Image information, including resolution, format, and size.

- Text object information includes the color space and color value, font name, font size, and so on.

- Transparency settings, types of blending modes, and other image manipulation settings applied.

5. Close the dialog when you've finished examining your file.

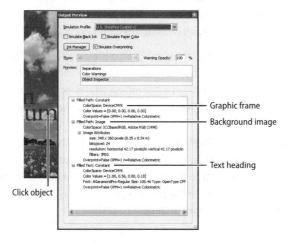

Click object

Graphic frame

Background image

Text heading

Figure 44b The Object Inspector shows details about the page contents at the cursor location.

The Dish on Overprinting

One term you may have heard, and not understood, is *overprinting*. Simply put, overprinting blends the color of an object (like some text) with the color of an underlying object. For example, if a background is 100% cyan (blue) and the text is 100% magenta, the areas that overlap look violet.

In Acrobat 9, overprint simulation is on by default. For an individual document, you can deselect the Simulate Overprinting check box in the Output Preview dialog.

By the way, the opposite of overprint is *knockout*, where the overlying object's color is opaque.

#45 Navigating a Document

Using a mouse isn't the only way to move around a page. Acrobat can also magnify and reflow documents, automatically scroll, read the page aloud, or enable the use of keystrokes.

Magnification and reflow. For some, it's important to zoom in to a very high magnification in order to read the screen. Acrobat offers reflow, which wraps text automatically regardless of the magnification. Reflow is great if you are reading a single column on a page. For complex layouts, you need to define articles, which create a reading path through a document. Read about reflow in the sidebar "Wrapping with Reflow"; read about articles in the sidebar "Organize Reading with Articles."

Automatic Scroll. Use scrolling when you're looking for a particular element such as an image. Choose View > Automatic Scroll, or press Ctrl+Shift+H (Command+Shift+H). The scrolling starts at the current location in the document, and stops when you reach the end of the document.

Automatic scrolling uses Continuous page layout. To change speed, press the up arrow key to increase or the down arrow key to decrease, or you can type a number from 0 to 9—the higher the number, the faster the speed. Want to reverse? Press the minus key (–) on the keyboard or number pad; press Esc to stop the scrolling.

Tip
Since Acrobat pauses the scrolling and applies the selected tool if you use the mouse, be sure the Hand tool is selected. That way, you aren't adding extra steps to deselect a tool.

Read Aloud. Acrobat can use system resources to read a document aloud—terrific when your goal is to make your documents more accessible as Acrobat simulates some features of a full-blown screen-reader program:

- Choose View > Read Out Loud > Activate Read Out Loud to get started; choose View > Read Out Loud > Deactivate Read Out Loud to stop.

- Locate the page you want to read and then choose View > Read Out Loud > Read This Page Only, or choose View > Read Out Loud > Read To End Of Document.

Tip
You can also have the voice read a selected object. Click a paragraph on the page with the Hand tool and it is read aloud.

Read It Your Way

To customize Read Aloud preferences, choose Edit > Preferences (Acrobat > Preferences), and choose the Reading heading in the Categories list. Look for these options:

- Choose an option for Reading Order, the method in which Acrobat automatically moves through a document. The default, and recommended option, is "Infer reading order from document."

- Define whether you want the screen reader to read only the currently visible pages, the entire document, or the currently visible pages in a large document. The default size for defining a document as "large" is 50 pages; type a different number to change the definition of a large document.

- In the Read Out Loud Options section, set a volume, and choose a voice, pitch, and speed. Both Windows and Mac offer several voices—on Mac some of them aren't even human!

(continued on next page)

Complying with PDF and Accessibility Standards

You can customize a few reading features in the Preferences dialog (**Figure 45**). Read about the customizations in the sidebar "Read It Your Way."

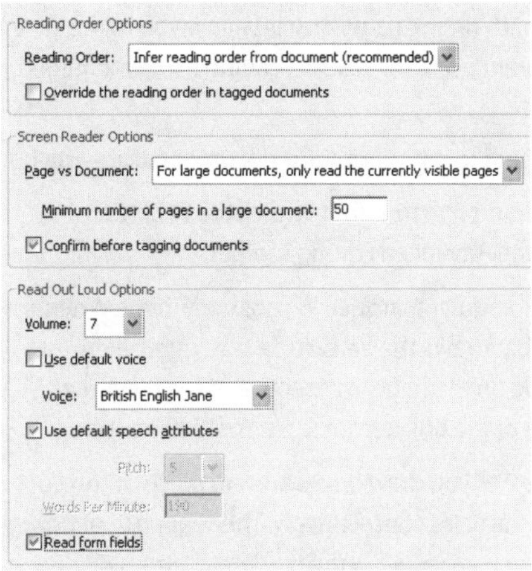

Figure 45 Customize the way Acrobat reads to you in the Preferences dialog.

Keystrokes. Acrobat offers full keystroke access to navigation and program items. Unlike other Adobe programs, like Photoshop and InDesign, Acrobat doesn't have you define keystrokes yourself. Choose Help > Adobe Acrobat 9 Pro Extended Help to open the Adobe Help Viewer. Scroll down to the Keyboard shortcuts listing in the left frame of the window—you'll find lists of shortcuts for work areas, getting around the program, and using tools. (For a short list of keystrokes used to activate features like Read Aloud, check out Table 49.1 in #49, "Enhancing PDF Accessibility").

• Select the "Read form fields" check box to have text fields, check boxes, and radio buttons in fillable forms read aloud.

Wrapping with Reflow

Readers using assistive devices or very small screens like those on personal digital assistants (PDAs) often experience a problem called *reflow*. When you zoom in closely to a page, what happens? You see a few words and maybe an image. Not only do you have to scroll back and forth to see the entire line, but also it's difficult or impossible to understand where you are in the document at any given time.

Choose View > Zoom > Reflow to automatically wrap content on the page, regardless of the level of magnification. Keep in mind that reflow is not a permanent format: Whenever you reset the magnification, reflow is turned off.

Organize Reading with Articles

There are two options for making a page flow properly regardless of the magnification: Either you can revise the layout to have a single column, or you can use articles to define a reading path on the page. Articles allow you to design a document both for visual appearance and for ease of reading using magnified views.

Follow these steps to control a reading path through a document using articles:

1. Choose Tools > Advanced Editing > Article Tool or click the Article tool to select it if you have opened the Advanced Editing toolbar.

2. Click and drag to create a rectangular marquee in your document. When you release the mouse, Acrobat draws the first article box, numbered 1-1. The Article tool draws a shape on the page irrespective of the contents. Anything within the margins of the box becomes part of the article.

3. Continue adding article boxes; as you draw boxes around pieces of text or images, Acrobat numbers the articles consecutively. The sequence of boxes using the same article number is called an *article thread*.

4. Press Esc (or Return) or select another tool to stop the article drawing and open the Article Properties dialog. At a minimum, you need to name the article.

5. Click OK to close the dialog.

For editing articles, such as deleting or adding boxes or combining articles, select the thread you want to work with, and choose the commands from the shortcut menu.

#46 Specifying Accessibility Requirements

Both Acrobat 9 and Adobe Reader 9 offer a wizard for configuring the programs to optimize display and interaction for assistive devices.

To run the wizard, choose Advanced > Accessibility > Setup Assistant to open the five-screen wizard. Click Next to move to each screen; click Done when you have made selections on all screens.

Note

The wizard is the same in both Acrobat and Adobe Reader, aside from references to the programs' names. In Adobe Reader, choose Document > Accessibility Setup Assistant.

Look for these features on each screen:

- **Screen 1.** Choose the device you are working with: a screen reader, a screen magnifier, or all options. You can also click the "Use recommended settings and skip setup" button to close the wizard and apply the preprogrammed settings.

- **Screen 2.** On this screen choose a high-contrast color scheme and colors for fields, producing a page like the example shown in **Figure 46**. Choose the option to disable text smoothing (producing sharper-looking text). Since some assistive devices can have problems with Acrobat's use of different cursors for different tools, you can select "Always display the keyboard selection cursor."

Figure 46 Be careful when designing documents that may be viewed using a high-contrast color scheme. In this example, although it's easy to read the left sample, using a high-contrast color scheme makes some of the text barely legible, as in the right sample.

(continued on next page)

Set It Here, Set It There

The Accessibility Setup Assistant brings together settings from a number of panels in the Preferences dialog:

- The options for reading order and screen reading are available in the Reading Order Options section of Preferences.

- The "Confirm before tagging documents" option is also in the Reading preferences in the Screen Reader Options section of Preferences.

- The document colors options are in the Accessibility preferences.

- The form field color preferences are in the Forms preferences.

- Find other color settings in the Full Screen, Measuring, Spelling, and Units & Guides preferences.

Colors to Avoid

If you know that vision-impaired users will be viewing your documents, be careful with the colors you choose. One of the biggest problems is light-colored backgrounds. Although a pale background behind a title looks attractive on a white background, if you use a high-contrast color scheme, for example, the text becomes virtually illegible. The light background and the light text used for high-contrast schemes are too similar in color, making the text hard to read—like the example in Figure 46.

- **Screen 3.** Choose tagging options. You can choose to let Acrobat infer the reading order or specify a preference. Also in this panel, choose to override reading order in a tagged document, or confirm tagging in an untagged document.

- **Screen 4.** Select an option for viewing large documents. You can choose to deliver the visible pages or the entire document, or you can let Acrobat decide. If you prefer, you can have all the pages delivered for a small document. Click the Maximum number of pages in a small document field and type a number. The default is 50 pages. Choose an option to have Acrobat override a page layout style and use the single page default, which is best for many screen readers. Finally, specify a default document zoom value.

- **Screen 5.** The fifth and final screen gives you an option to disable document auto-save, which, when enabled, can cause the document to reload and begin reading from the start of the document. You can choose to reopen the document from the last viewed page—which is terrific when you're working with long documents. Finally, you can also choose to open a PDF document in Acrobat or a browser; opening a document in Acrobat is less confusing for some assistive devices.

Planning Documents for PDF Accessibility

The key to successful tagging of a document as well as making it comfortable for a user working with a screen reader is to use your source programs' features efficiently. Plan ahead:

- Configure the document pages correctly. For example, don't add blank lines to make a space.

- Check the styles attached to inserted material such as images and charts.

- Group tables and charts or convert them to an image to prevent creating individual tags for each line and word segment.

#47 Basic Document Tagging

Some program features that are used to enhance accessibility don't work properly or predictably unless a document is tagged, which means it has a logically defined structure. Tags are a part of the document's information that defines relationships among elements in the document, including tables, lists, images, and text.

Tagging can be done in the source document (if you're using a PDF-Maker) or in Acrobat. To tag a document using a PDFMaker, choose Adobe PDF > Change Conversion Settings. In the Settings tab, select "Enable accessibility and reflow with Tagged PDF" and then click OK. The tags are created when the PDF file is generated.

Open the document in Acrobat and choose View > Navigation Panels > Tags. Click the Tags icon to display the document's tags in a hierarchy (**Figure 47**). The figure shows a section of the Tags pane for an Excel spreadsheet. The parent tag <Workbook> holds a <Worksheet> that contains a <Table>, which contains tags for the table rows <TR>, which in turn contain tags for table cells <TD>, which contain the cell's <Content>, which are text objects.

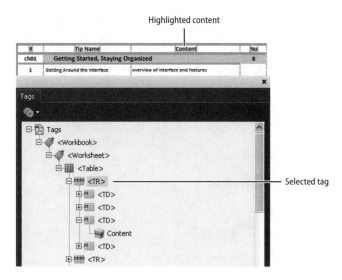

Figure 47 The tags in a document are listed in a hierarchy.

In the figure, notice that the top row of text is highlighted—a useful behavior for locating content on the page quickly. Choose Highlight Content from the Options menu. Selecting a parent tag, such as the <TR> tag, automatically selects the child <TD> tags.

Checking for Tags

Check for preexisting tags by choosing Advanced > Accessibility > Quick Check. The Accessibility Quick Check looks for a document structure (tags). An untagged document displays a message stating that the lack of structure may cause a problem with reading order.

A Structure and Tags Aren't Equal

Some programs create a structured document that often is fine for reading in Acrobat. For example, creating a Word document using styles in a heading hierarchy is an example of a structure. A structure doesn't provide some of the qualities in an accessible document such as word spacing; you must tag a document to make it compliant with accessibility standards.

Touching Up Properties

When correcting the accessibility status of a document, you can modify the properties of individual tags. Select the tag in the Tags panel, and choose Properties from either the Options menu or the shortcut menu. The TouchUp Properties dialog opens; make changes to the properties, such as the type or the alternate text, and then click Close.

Many document-creation programs don't offer tagging options. You can easily add tags from within Acrobat:

1. Choose Advanced > Accessibility > Add Tags to Document. Acrobat processes the document and adds tags. An Accessibility Report displays in the How To area at the right of the Document pane in the program window. Refer to #48, "Reporting On and Repairing a Document," for information on working with tags and reports.

2. Check the document again by selecting Advanced > Accessibility > Quick Check. The new message will state that there are no accessibility problems with the document, meaning it is tagged.

3. Choose File > Save to save the document with its tagged structure.

#**48** Reporting On and Repairing a Document

In addition to tagging your document, Acrobat can evaluate the accessibility level and generate a report with repair hints. Use these advanced evaluation methods if you are preparing documents that must comply with government or other regulatory accessibility standards. Before you start, ensure that the document is tagged (refer to #47, "Basic Document Tagging," for instructions).

1. Choose Advanced > Accessibility > Full Check to open the Accessibility Full Check dialog (**Figure 48a**).

Figure 48a Choose a standard and specify features in this dialog.

2. Select from the options according to your requirements:

- **Report and Comment Options.** In this area, you can select whether or not to create the report and define a storage location for the report (which is automatically named using the PDF document's name). The option "Include repair hints in Accessibility Report" is selected by default—leave the option selected to save time repairing your document. If you are the type of person who likes to see what's what close up, select the "Create comments in document" check box to show the found errors and irregularities in comments.

- **Page Range.** Here you can choose the visible page, a specified range, or the entire document.

- **Checking Options.** In the Name pop-up menu, you can choose a testing option according to a set of standards (see the sidebar "Evaluating Against Standards" for more details).

(continued on next page)

Evaluating Against Standards

Prior to Acrobat 8 Professional, forms were tested according to Adobe PDF accessibility only. Now, test a document against these standards, selected in the Accessibility Full Check dialog:

- **Adobe PDF standards.** These are the default standards, and they consider such features as alternative descriptions, character encoding, tab order, and list and table structure.

- **Section 508 Web-based intranet and Internet information and applications (1194.22).** These are U.S. government standards subsequent to the Rehabilitation Act. As you see in Figure 48b, the standards are numbered. Click "Browse Section508. gov" for information on the standards.

- **W3C® Web Content Accessibility Guidelines 1.0.** These standards include options defined in three categories of priority,

(continued on next page)

with Priority 1 standards required for accessible use, and Priority 3 standards useful for accessible use. Click "Browse WCAG Guidelines" for more information.

- **W3C® Web Content Accessibility Guidelines 2.0 (Working Draft 27 April 2006).** This is the successor to the original guidelines, arranged in three levels. Click "Browse WCAG Guidelines" for more information.

Touching Up Properties

When correcting the accessibility status of a document, you can modify the properties of individual tags. Select the tag in the Tags panel, and choose Properties from either the Options menu or the shortcut menu. The TouchUp Properties dialog opens; make changes to the properties, such as the type or the alternate text, and then click Close.

- You can further specify options according to the format you select. The default option is to check all options for compliance. You can check for options such as alternative descriptions, text languages, object structures, and so on. Deselect the items that aren't in your document for faster processing. For example, if your document doesn't contain JavaScript, deselect (I) Scripts from the Section 508 guidelines, or if you don't have a form, deselect "All form fields have descriptions" in the Adobe PDF guidelines.

3. Click the Start Checking button to start the evaluation. When the check is complete, a results summary displays; click OK to close the summary and open the report.

4. The Accessibility Report opens in the Navigation pane at the left of the program window (**Figure 48b**). The report is an HTML document, and contains links within it to help you identify and correct errors. If the option to include repair hints was active when the report is generated, you see information on how to repair your document. Click Collapse to close the Accessibility Report when you have finished.

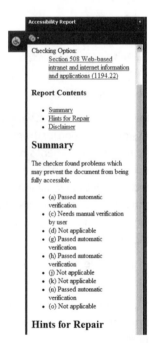

Figure 48b The report shows errors and offers links to repair hints.

#49 Enhancing PDF Accessibility

There are several conditions to consider when making a PDF document accessible. Forms, for example, offer specific challenges in their design, such as their *tabbing order,* the way a user moves through the form using the keyboard. For any document, examine the *reading order,* which defines how a document is read.

Forms. Forms are handled differently from regular documents with regard to accessibility. The form fields have to be configured correctly so that a screen reader or other device can recognize them (**Figure 49a**). When designing a form, be sure to do the following:

- Label each field on the form.

- Draw text fields and lines using graphic tools; typing characters, such as a string of underscores, confuses the structure of the field and its content.

- Include instructions or descriptions as necessary.

- Include alternate text for form fields.

- Add tags to the fields either in the source program or in Acrobat.

Tab order. Be sure a user can move through a form logically using the keyboard. You can test the tab order in Acrobat Pro 9 following these steps:

1. Click the Pages icon in the Navigation pane to display the Pages pane, and select the form's thumbnail.

2. Choose Options > Page Properties to open the Page Properties dialog.

3. Choose a tabbing option that is logical for your form:

   - Use Row Order to move left to right across the page.

   - Use Column Order to move through the columns from left to right and top to bottom.

   - Use Document Structure to move the tab in the order specified in the document.

(continued on next page)

Order Up Reading Order

Here are some ideas to help you organize and work quicker with the TouchUp Reading Order tool, and ordering in general:

- Decide how to handle images and captions. A screen reader defines a caption within a figure tag as a part of the image and it isn't read. On the other hand, using the figure/caption tag separates the caption from the body text.

- If you need bookmarks, tag selections as headings, and then convert the heading tags to bookmarks (see Chapter 15, "Controlling Action and Interaction," to learn how to work with bookmarks in Acrobat).

- Extra spaces and tabs are identified in the reading order. Either delete the object, or define it as a background element, or *artifact.*

(continued on next page)

- If there is too much correction to do, it may be quicker to start over. Click Clear Structure and then rebuild the page's structure.
- Use the listings in the Order pane to change reading order. Drag the icon to the left of the object you want to reorder until the horizonal indicator bar is in the correct location. Then release the mouse to change the order.

Tabbing Through

Test the form's tab order and form field function:

- Press the Tab key to move the focus to the next field.
- Press Shift+Tab to move focus to the previous field.
- Press the Spacebar to move through a field's options.
- Press the arrow keys to select list, check box, and radio button form items.

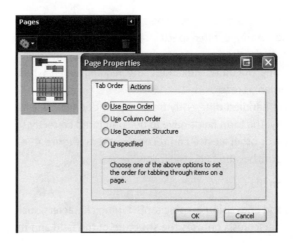

Figure 49a Choose a path for the user to tab through the document.

4. Click OK to close the dialog and test the tab order. Check out the sidebar "Tabbing Through" for a list of keystrokes to use for testing.

Reading Order. The path taken through a document is called its *reading order*. Acrobat offers the TouchUp Reading Order tool to define and order individual content elements on a page.

Select the TouchUp Reading Order tool on the Advanced Editing toolbar. Alternatively, you can choose Tools > Advanced Editing > TouchUp Reading Order Tool or Advanced > Accessibility > TouchUp Reading Order.

Click the PDF page with the tool. The TouchUp Reading Order dialog opens, and the content of the page is shown in separate gray numbered blocks. The numbers identify the document's reading sequence (**Figure 49b**). Read some tips for using the tool and touchup process in the sidebar "Order Up Reading Order."

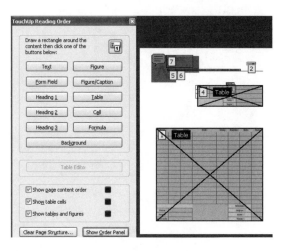

Figure 49b Display and modify the reading order in a document.

As with other features and processes in Acrobat, you can use keystrokes to activate accessibility tools and commands (**Table 49.1**).

Table 49.1 Accessibility Keystrokes

Action	Windows Action	Mac OS Action
Change reading settings for the current document	Shift+Ctrl+5	Shift+Command+5
Quick Check tool	Shift+Ctrl+6	Shift+Command+6
Reflow a tagged PDF and return to unreflowed view	Ctrl+4	Command+4
Activate and deactivate Read Out Loud	Shift+Ctrl+Y	Shift+Command+Y
Pause reading out loud	Shift+Ctrl+C	Shift+Command+C
Read only the current page out loud	Shift+Ctrl+V	Shift+Command+V
Read out loud from the current page to the end of the document	Shift+Ctrl+B	Shift+Command+B
Stop reading out loud	Shift+Ctrl+E	Shift+Command+E

CHAPTER SEVEN

Transforming Document Pages

Acrobat offers a number of tools you can use to manipulate the content of a document. The techniques described in Chapters 2 and 3 show how to combine elements from various documents and using different sources, such as scans and Web pages.

Combined or merged documents can include all or select pages from a document, but what if you aren't sure what you need to use in a project? Or if you change your mind as you are working? In this chapter, you'll discover methods to combine and manipulate the contents of documents by substituting pages from one document for those in another.

Once a document is complete, you can further enhance it by adding structure. In this chapter, you'll also learn how to balance page sizes through cropping, and add page numbers to the document using standard page or Bates numbering. You'll see how to add features that add a cohesive touch, including headers and footers, and watermarks and backgrounds. Finally, you'll learn how to save time by using automation features you set up as batch sequences.

This chapter shows you how to build the content manually—check out the new Flash-enabled Acrobat 9 Portfolio feature in Chapter 4 to see how to use content from various sources and present it automatically.

#50 Changing Pages and Their Contents

Here's a time-saving process that's terrific for visual people. Rather than extracting, combining, and deleting content through dialogs, you can do it visually using the Pages pane.

Here's how to do it with two documents, but you could use as many documents as you can manage:

1. Start with two documents, one to which you want to add pages (the recipient) and the other from which you're taking pages (the donor).

2. Click the Pages icon in each document to show the thumbnails.

3. Select the page thumbnails from the donor document's Pages pane and drag them to the recipient document's Pages pane.

4. A vertical black line indicates the location where the content will be dropped—release the mouse when you are in the right spot and the job is done.

Acrobat 9 offers a few ways to handle document contents. In this technique, check out examples of when to use each type of action, selecting commands from the Pages pane's Options menu. By the way, most actions can be performed from the Pages pane, or via commands in the Document menu.

Delete and insert pages. Sometimes when you combine files, you have extra pages you don't need. To delete pages, open the document, and click the Pages icon ▦ at the left of the program window to open the Pages pane (**Figure 50a**). Click the thumbnail(s) for the content you want to delete, and drag them to the trashcan 🗑. Click OK in the confirmation dialog, and Acrobat removes the pages.

Figure 50a Select thumbnails for pages you want to remove in the Pages pane.

Suppose you want to add pages containing tables from one PDF file to the end of another PDF file. Open the PDF document and the Pages pane, and then click the thumbnail before the location where you want to insert additional pages. Next, choose Options > Insert Pages to display the Select File To Insert dialog. Locate the file you want to use, and click Select to close that dialog and open the Insert Pages dialog. Since you preselected the location in your open file, you'll see it listed in the dialog. Click OK to close the dialog and add the new content.

Extract Pages: Let's say you have a multipage document and you want to send part of it to a number of colleagues. You can extract the pages (either a single page or group of pages) from the Pages pane. Select the

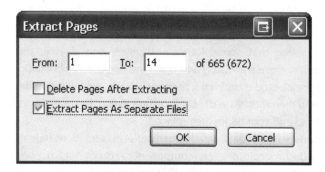

Figure 50b Choose an option for pages extracted from your document.

thumbnail(s) and choose Options > Extract Pages to display the Extract Pages dialog (**Figure 50b**). Make your choice:

- Click Delete Pages After Extracting to separate the content from the original. Click OK to close the dialog; the content is processed and opens in Acrobat as a separate document using the prefix "Pages from" in the filename.

- Click Extract Pages As Separate Files if you want to create individual PDF documents from each page you select in the dialog. Click OK to close the dialog; select a storage location for the extracted content in the subsequent Browse for Folder dialog, and click OK. The pages are extracted and saved with the page number—for example, MyBigFile 22—appended to the filename.

- Deselect both check boxes if you want to keep the original intact, and extract the pages into a single document.

Replace Pages: Suppose you have a PDF document that needs some editing that is much simpler to do in the source program. However, you've added several links and some comments that will be lost if you simply delete the pages—so what do you do? Easy: Simply replace the pages instead. The new content slides into place in your document, leaving all the work you've done in Acrobat intact.

In your source program, open the file and make the changes. When you re-convert the file to PDF, you can convert just the pages to replace (find out how in the sidebar "Pick What You Want" in #10, "Using PDFMaker in Microsoft Word").

Do the Splits

Here's a cool tip to use if you have several documents that you'd like to split more evenly, such as by file size or number of pages. You don't have to open a document in Acrobat to split it, nor do you have to split one document.

Begin by choosing Document > Split Document to open the Split Documents dialog. Click Apply to Multiple to open a secondary Split Documents dialog, where you'll list the files to split. Choose either Add Files or Add Folders from the Add Files pop-up menu. Select the files or folders you want to work with to include them in the dialog's list. Click OK to close the dialog. The regular Split Document dialog opens—continue with the steps listed in the technique.

Adding Document Pages

If you choose a PDF document, the pages are added immediately. If you choose another type of file, the document is converted to PDF before the page is inserted into your document. This is a great time-saver, since you don't have to reopen the document's source program and the file, convert to PDF, and then return to Acrobat.

Power Deleting

Instead of using commands to delete multiple pages, use the thumbnails and keyboard keys. Click the thumbnail of the page you want to delete, hold down the Shift key, and click additional pages to select them, and then press Delete on the keyboard. The confirmation dialog opens asking if you really want to delete the pages. Click OK and the pages are gone.

Back in Acrobat, open the document where you want to replace pages, select the thumbnails in the Pages pane, and choose Options > Replace Pages. In the dialog that opens, locate and select your replacement file. Click Select to close the dialog and open the Replace Pages dialog. Because you preselected thumbnails, they are already shown in the dialog. Click OK and then click Yes in the confirmation dialog that opens next. The dialog closes and your pages are replaced.

Split Document: In the past, we'd have to perform extractions repeatedly to break a document into several component parts, but not anymore. Acrobat 9 now offers a feature to split PDF files into multiples based on different criteria.

Note
Any attachments in your document aren't copied to the split component files.

Open your document in Acrobat and follow these steps:

1. From the main menu, choose Document > Split Document to display the Split Document dialog.

   • Choose an option for splitting—"Number of pages" (and specify the Max pages), "File size" (and specify the Max MB), or "Top-level bookmarks."

2. Click Output Options to open a dialog where you can select a folder for storing the split files, as well as a method for naming the files (**Figure 50c**).

Figure 50c Specify how to store and name the components of your split document.

3. Click OK to close the dialog and process your document.

Delete and Insert or Replace?

What's the difference? It depends on what else is on the page.

For example, you may have a page with a large number of comments, links, or form fields on it. If you merely inserted an edited version of the page and deleted the one you want to remove, you'd lose all your comments and links. When you use the Replace command, Acrobat replaces the underlying page, keeping the overlying content (such as comments, links, or form fields) untouched.

Insert Pages in Front

Sometimes you need to insert a new page before an existing page in your document. For example, you may need to add a cover page to a catalog or marketing brochure. In the Insert Pages dialog, simply click the Location pop-up menu and choose Before. Click OK and Acrobat adds the page to your document precisely where you want it.

#51 Cropping and Rotating Pages

If you combine several documents from different sources, you may find discrepancies in the page sizes or orientations. Use the crop and rotate features in Acrobat to get the pages looking cohesive. Read about rotating in the sidebar "Spin It Around."

If you are cropping a single page, display it in the Document pane; if you are working with more than one image, select the thumbnails in the Pages pane.

Follow these steps to crop a page:

1. If you have the Advanced Editing toolbar open, click the Crop Tool to select it. Then click and drag on the page to draw a marquee the size of the area you want to crop.

2. Double-click within the cropped area to open the Crop Pages dialog. The area you drew on the document page is shown in the preview, like the box surrounding the bird in **Figure 51a**. The settings for the margins are already entered as well, based on the preselection.

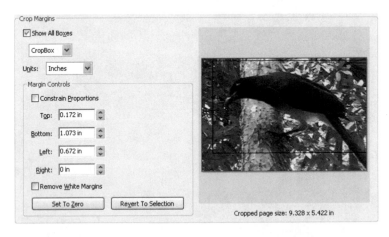

Figure 51a An area selected with the Crop Tool appears automatically in the preview area of the dialog.

Tip
You can also select the thumbnail in the Pages pane and choose Options > Crop Pages from the pane's menu, or choose Document > Crop Pages. There aren't any markings on the preview when you open the dialog.

3. The page appears as a thumbnail at the top right of the Crop Pages dialog, and the Show All Boxes check box is selected by default in the Crop Margins area of the dialog. Change the measurement used in the cropping in the Units pop-up menu.

4. Adjust the crop settings using the four margin fields in the Margin Controls area, described in the sidebar "Specifying Margins."

5. Change the page size to a larger size. Use a fixed size by selecting an option from the Page Sizes pop-up menu, or click Custom and type custom values.

   - By default, the existing content is centered on the expanded page. If you resize the page, you can also specify a location for the content by entering XOffset and YOffset values (**Figure 51b**). Click Center to recenter the content.

Figure 51b Type locations for the X and Y coordinates—either positive or negative values—to place the content on a page.

6. Finally, specify the page range you wish to crop. If you preselected pages from the Pages pane, they are identified in the fields. You can also specify whether to crop all pages, only even pages, or only odd pages by choosing an option from the Apply to pop-up menu.

7. Click OK to close the dialog, and Acrobat resizes the page. You can see the effects of the cropping in the Document pane, as well as in the Pages pane's thumbnails.

Note
You can't undo a crop by choosing Edit > Undo or using the shortcut Ctrl+Z (Command+Z). If you change your mind after cropping, choose File > Revert to return to the uncropped version of the document.

Cropping Multiple Pages

You can crop several pages at once. Select the pages' thumbnails in the Pages pane (the files can be contiguous or spread throughout the document). Once in the Crop Pages dialog, you can see the selected pages listed at the bottom in the Page Range section. If you do this, make sure the content of the pages is laid out the same.

Specifying Margins

As you change the values, the cropping outline in the preview image changes to reflect the new values.

- Type values in the fields or use the arrows to adjust the settings.

- Select Constrain Proportions to crop the page equally on all four sides.

- Move the marquee in the Document pane to adjust the Margin Controls settings automatically.

- Click Remove White Margins to have Acrobat automatically set margins tight to the page content.

#52 Applying Page and Bates Numbering

Numbering Nuggets

Keep these things in mind when numbering your masterwork:

- Whenever possible, remove visible page numbers from source material before converting it to a PDF. Using Acrobat-based page numbering is easier when the pages contain no numbers to conflict with the numbers displayed on the status bar or in the Pages pane.

- Consider the document's use. Many documents need simple page numbering. However, if you are assembling a technical manual, you will likely use prefixes identifying content based on chapters, systems, and so on.

- If you are building a book structure, consider how the book will look when printed. Books use front matter such as a table of contents and other introductory material that is numbered differently from chapter content.

(continued on next page)

Acrobat and Adobe Reader show page numbers on the Page Navigation toolbar numbered in logical order—that is, the first page is page 1, the second is page 2, and so on. Acrobat offers several ways to number pages. You can number them manually, use a numbering system called Bates numbering, or insert page numbers as part of a page footer, described in the next technique.

In a sample document, I have two sections to number separately; each section will start with text (such as Contents); the second includes a number with the text, followed by page numbers. Sounds complicated, doesn't it? Acrobat can handle it.

Here's what you do:

1. In the Pages pane, select the pages for the first section (I am using pages 1–5 in my example). Choose Options > Number Pages to open the Page Numbering dialog. The Selected option is already active because I selected the pages in the Pages pane (**Figure 52a**).

Figure 52a You can use custom numbering for different sections in a document.

2. Leave the "Begin new section" option selected in the Numbering section of the dialog. Then choose a page format from the Style pop-up menu. As shown in Figure 52a, our example uses numbers for the page renumbering.

3. Enter a value in the Prefix field, as well as punctuation if desired, such as *Contents_* in the example. The numbering starts at "1" by default, as shown in the Start field. Click OK to close the dialog.

Acrobat modifies the page numbers; as **Figure 52b** shows, we now have pages Contents_1 through Contents_5. The remaining pages in the document are renumbered as well. The second section is done the same way, but this time the Prefix is *Chapter01:*. In the Page Navigation toolbar, the page numbers reflect both the page count as well as the numbering you added.

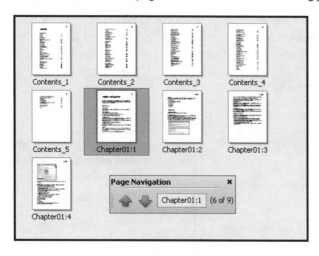

Figure 52b Custom numbers used to differentiate sections in a document are shown in the Page Navigation toolbar.

Bates numbering. The legal community uses a specialized type of page numbering to identify pages of content with unique numbers. Acrobat 9 lets you number pages across a set of files. See the sidebar "Who Is Mr. Bates?" for a description of the Bates numbering system.

Add Bates numbers by following these steps:

1. Choose Advanced > Document Processing > Bates Numbering > Add to open the Bates Numbering dialog.

2. Click the Add Files button, and choose either Add Files or Add Folders to open a Browse dialog. Locate and select the files you want to include, and click Add Files to close the dialog and list the files in the Bates Numbering dialog.

(continued on next page)

Tip
Click Output Options at the lower left of the dialog to open the Output Options dialog. Here you can specify how to name the files—keep the original filename, add a prefix or suffix, replace filenames with Bates numbers only, or overwrite existing files. If you want to track the process, select "Create log file" and specify a storage location. Click OK to return to the Bates Numbering dialog.

- If you have to add more material to a section of your project, select the page thumbnails, choose Options > Number Pages to open the Page Numbering dialog, and check that the settings are correct for the section you are numbering. Then click "Extend numbering used in preceding section to selected pages."

Who Is Mr. Bates?

Bates numbering is used in the legal system for identifying documents. The system is named after the Bates automatic numbering machine, where an arbitrary unique numeric or alphanumeric identifier is generated for each page of each document used in a legal case. The number is unique to the documents disclosed or produced in a case, but there isn't a standardized algorithm for determining the number.

3. Order the files in the list as you wish—select a file and click Move Up or Move Down. When your list is in order, click OK to close this dialog. The Add Header and Footer dialog opens.

4. Click Insert Bates Number to open the Bates Numbering Options dialog (**Figure 52c**) and choose options according to your requirements. Read about the different choices in the sidebar "Numbering Strategies."

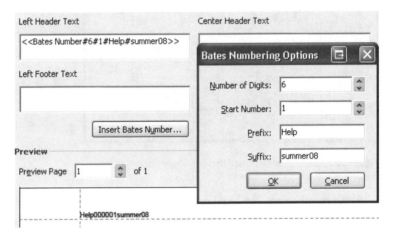

Figure 52c Bates number settings are shown as a formula in the Header area, and in the Preview.

5. Click OK to close the dialog and generate the numbers. In the Add Header and Footer dialog, the number is shown in its default position in the left of the header. In the Left Header Text field, the automatic numbering formula is written as <<Bates Number#6#1#Help#summer08>>.

6. Check the Preview area; the header is written as Help000001summer08.

7. Click OK to process the files; the Add Headers and Footers dialog closes automatically. Click OK to close the confirmation dialog when the numbering is complete.

#53 Inserting Headers and Footers

Instead of adding pagination to your document for navigational purposes, you can add precise headers and footers to the pages. Here's how to add a footer, including custom text, to a sample document:

1. From the main program menu, choose Document > Header & Footer > Add to open the Add Header and Footer dialog.

2. Choose the font name and size from the pop-up menus at the top of the dialog.

Tip
Read how to tweak the page layout in the sidebar "Appearance Tidbits."

3. Make entries in the fields as desired (**Figure 53**). There are three text entry fields each for Header and Footer content—left-justified, centered, or right-justified on the document page. The example uses a date (shown as <<mm/dd/yy>>), custom text, and page numbering. Before adding either an automatic entry or custom text, click the text entry box where you want to add the content in the dialog:

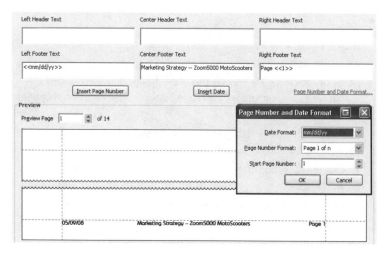

Figure 53 Specify the content for the header or footer text in the dialog, and check the preview before adding to the document.

- To insert the date or page numbers automatically, click the Insert Page Number or Insert Date button.

(continued on next page)

Appearance Tidbits

Select the Appearance Options check box at the upper left of the dialog to open a small Appearance Options dialog. There are two neat options:

- Click "Shrink document to avoid overwriting the document's text and graphics" to decrease the size of the content on the page and allow the header/footer content to be seen clearly.

- Click "Keep position and size of header/footer text constant when printing on different page sizes" to show a uniform location throughout a document.

Saving Settings

Save your custom headers or footers in Acrobat 9 and reuse them at a later time. Configure your perfect layout in the Add Header & Footer dialog and then click Save Settings at the top of the dialog. Type a name in the name dialog that opens, and click Save to store the file with the other program settings. When you want to reuse them, select your custom settings in the Saved Settings pop-up menu.

Modifying Headers and Footers

To modify headers or footers after you've applied them to the document, choose Document > Header & Footer > Update. A dialog asks if you want to edit the header and footer content; click Yes to open the Update Header and Footer dialog (identical to the Add Header and Footer dialog). If you want to remove them, choose Document > Header & Footer > Remove.

- To customize the date or page number appearance, click the Page Number and Date Format link and then choose a format in the resulting dialog (also shown in Figure 53). Click OK; the choices are used as the default until you choose again.

- To add custom text, type in the text entry box where you want to add the text (left, center, or right).

- To remove text, select it in the text box and press the Delete key.

4. Adjust the margins in the Margin fields at the top right of the dialog (not shown in Figure 53).

5. In the Preview area of the dialog, click the up and down arrows to see previews of the upper and lower edges of the pages. Make adjustments to the margins and appearance as necessary.

6. Click OK and apply the header and footer. The content and numbering are applied to the page in the area specified.

Pick a Page, Any Page

You don't have to apply your headers and footers on every page. Click the Page Range Options link in the Preview area of the dialog (hidden under the Page Number and Date Format dialog in Figure 53) to open the Page Range Options dialog.

Select the pages to which the headers and footers are applied. The default is All Pages, or choose another option:

- Click the Pages from button and type the page numbers in the Pages from and to fields.

- Choose "Odd pages only, Even pages only" from the Subset pop-up menu, or leave the default as "All pages in range."

Click OK to return to the main Add Header and Footer dialog.

#54 Adding Watermarks and Backgrounds

A good way to create a cohesive-appearing document you have constructed from multiple source documents is to use a watermark or background. Watermarks overlay the page content; backgrounds are behind the content. In this technique, you'll see how to apply and configure graphic backgrounds. Watermarks and backgrounds have separate commands and open separate dialogs. The content in both dialogs is identical, with the exception of the text insertion options, available only for watermarks. Read how to use text at the end of this technique.

Note
As with headers and footers, you can save and reuse custom settings for watermarks and backgrounds. Refer to the sidebar "Saving Settings" in #53, "Inserting Headers and Footers," for further details.

Our sample document has four pages, each containing one large image.

1. Choose Document > Background > Add/Replace to open the dialog shown in **Figure 54**.

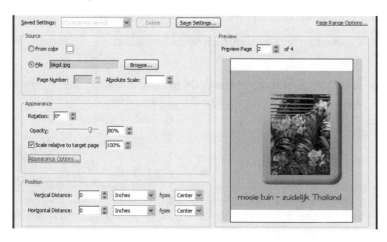

Figure 54 Configure the settings for the background in the dialog.

2. Click File in the Source area of the dialog, and click Browse (Choose) to select a source document to use for the background. If the source document has more than one page, select the page you want to use as an example.

(continued on next page)

Picking Watermark and Background Features

To specify how the watermarks and backgrounds are shown on the page, click the Appearance Options link at the bottom of the Appearance section.

In the resulting dialog, choose from these options:

- "Show when printing"— Use this option when you want to circulate a document that has a specific status, such as Draft to prevent readers from assuming it's the final version, or Confidential to maintain the integrity of the document.

- "Show when displaying on screen"—If you intend to circulate a document for review or collaboration online only, make sure the recipients can see a watermark when reviewing the file. It's important for participants to understand a special status, view dates and other document data, or see a background that you've inserted.

(continued on next page)

- "Keep the watermark's appearance constant regardless of the page size"—Placing the watermark in a consistent location saves time when processing a document for printing if your pages are of different sizes; this option doesn't apply to backgrounds.

Image Protection

Do you need to distribute a lot of images? And do you spend a great deal of time adding a watermark to the images? Save yourself a whopping load of time by combining the content into one PDF document and adding a watermark through Acrobat. Add text or use your watermarking image and adjust the transparency.

3. Modify the position, appearance, and size of the background content as desired. Then set the horizontal and vertical alignments and rotation. Adjust the opacity by using the slider.

4. To apply the background to a subset of the document, click the Page Range Options link at the top right of the dialog and choose the specific pages you want to receive the background.

5. Check your adjustments in the Preview area; click the arrows to move through the previews of different pages. When you are satisfied with the results, click OK to close the dialog and apply the background.

Rather than using a graphic image background, add text as a watermark by following these steps:

1. Choose Document > Watermark > Add to open the Add Watermark dialog.

2. Click the Text radio button in the Source area of the dialog.

3. Type the text to use for the watermark in the text field.

4. Choose font and color characteristics, and adjust the text location as required.

5. When the text is just right, click OK to close the dialog and apply the watermark.

Preplanning a Project

It's important to plan ahead. Before you start, create the background or watermark content and save it as a PDF file if you intend to use an image; if you are using text, you can create it right in the dialog. Knowing you can add distinguishing content in Acrobat saves time finding and organizing the source material, applying a background or watermark, and then creating the PDF version.

#**55** Batching Tasks to Save Time

Suppose your usual workflow entails repeating the same tasks, document after document. Wouldn't it be nice to click a couple of buttons and have Acrobat do the work for you? Well, you can take out the ho-hum using the batch sequence feature in Acrobat 9 Pro. Acrobat includes eight default batch processes, and you can easily write your own custom sequence.

Working with batch sequences or scripts isn't something that many Acrobat users do every day. To make batch sequencing simpler, Acrobat 9 brings the idea of completing tasks in batches to the foreground. In some program areas where you are likely to do the same task over and over, such as exporting files, adding backgrounds or watermarks, or recognizing text using OCR, you'll see a new command that includes the words *multiple files*. Click to open a dialog to select files for processing, and your mini-batch is applied.

For those times when you want the program to do a number of tasks in a sequence, build a custom batch sequence. In this example, you'll see how to build a batch process that deletes comments, adds a watermark, and then saves the file with another name.

Follow these steps:

1. Choose Advanced > Document Processing > Batch Processing. Click New Sequence in the Batch Sequences dialog.

2. A small dialog opens, allowing you to name the sequence. Type a name and click OK—be sure to use a meaningful name for the sequence. The Edit Batch Sequence [*name*] dialog opens.

3. Click Select Commands. In the Edit Sequence dialog (**Figure 55a**), select a category of action, such as Document or Page, in the column at the left. Select an action and then click Add to move the action to the list at the right.

4. Add other actions for your sequence. You can reorder them by clicking the Move Up and Move Down buttons; click Remove to delete an action if you change your mind.

(continued on next page)

Do It Your Way

Actions that show a box icon ☐ in their Edit Sequence dialog listing offer configurable settings. If you want to apply a configurable action, such as using the Watermark with the same appearance all the time, double-click the command's name—the dialog to open the appropriate dialog—in this case, the Add Watermark dialog. Configure the settings and click OK to close the dialog. When the sequence is run, Acrobat won't stop when it reaches the Add Watermark command but instead applies what you've configured.

If you want to make changes each time the sequence is run, click the box icon to the left of the command to toggle Interactive Mode ☐. When the batch script is run, Acrobat stops when it reaches the interactive command and opens the appropriate dialog so that you can choose settings. When you're done, click OK and the batch sequence continues.

Plan Ahead

To get you into the batch sequence mindset, here are a few things to consider:

- Plan ahead. As you start working on a project, consider what repetitious tasks could be handled by a batch sequence.

- Put the files you plan to batch into a separate folder. It's easier to keep track of where you are in your workflow. You can include files other than PDF documents in your batch sequence.

- Configure and tweak a sample file. When you are satisfied with the appearance, you are ready to build and use a batch sequence for the rest.

- Write and test your batch sequence at any time. You don't need to be working with a project's files to write the sequence.

- Consider writing a group of batch sequences.

- Pay attention to how you like to work. As you construct a batch, you can allow for prompts that let you check documents.

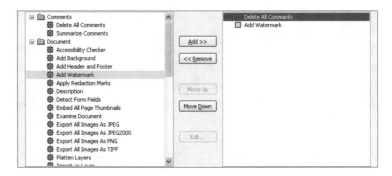

Figure 55a Choose from a long list of actions to include in the batch sequence.

5. Configure the settings or assign an Interactive Mode to actions you want to control manually. In the example shown in Figure 55a, the action for deleting comments has no icon to the left of the command's name—comments are deleted or they aren't. The Add Watermark action has an icon to its left meaning it can be made interactive, but isn't an interactive command in the example. Read more in the sidebar "Do It Your Way."

6. When you have finished adding commands, click OK to return to the Edit Batch Sequence [*name*] dialog. The commands are listed in the dialog (**Figure 55b**).

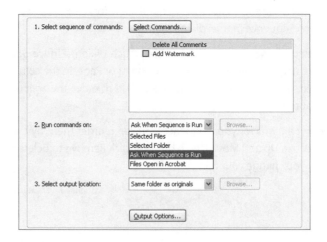

Figure 55b Specify the settings for running your custom batch sequence in the dialog.

7. Choose an option from the "Run commands on" pop-up menu based on the requirements of your project (see the sidebar "Everything in Its Place").

8. Choose an option from the "Select output location" pop-up menu according to your project's needs. If you think you might use the sequence repeatedly, choose Ask When Sequence is Run. If the files are intended for the same output folder, choose Specific Folder and select the folder.

9. Click Output Options so you can configure the processed files further in the Output Options dialog (**Figure 55c**).

Figure 55c Specify filename and file format options for the batch sequence.

10. Select custom options for your project. For example, you can do the following:

   • Append characters to the original filenames and specify whether or not to overwrite the original files.

   • Choose an output format from the menu, such as Web pages, Word documents, text, and so on.

   • Select Fast Web View to minimize file size.

   • Run PDF Optimizer options (read about the PDF Optimizer in #33, "Optimizing a PDF Document").

   • Export the processed files in one of the Acrobat export formats (learn more about exporting in #34, "Exporting PDF Documents in Other Formats").

(continued on next page)

Everything in Its Place

If you are building a sequence for a specific project and have stored the files in one folder location, choose that option. If you have files in several folders, choose Selected Files. The option you choose determines the other selections that are available. For example, if you choose Files Open in Acrobat, the rest of the dialog is dimmed.

But What About …?

In the Edit Sequence dialog, if you choose a specific folder on which to run the commands, a Source File Options button appears. Click the button to open a list of file formats—any type of file you can convert to PDF can be included.

1-2-3 of Batch Sequences

What to use, why bother, and where to put the stuff? To simplify, and make these questions easier to answer, simply decide these four factors and you are on your way to batch sequence success:

1. Decide which commands you want to run.

2. Decide on the characteristics of the files you intend to process—are the files usually in a particular folder, or scattered all over your computer?

3. Do you want to store the finished files in a regular location, or are you more likely to need them saved all over your hard drive?

4. What file format do you need for the finished documents?

11. Click OK to close the Output Options dialog, and then click OK again to close the Edit Batch Sequence [*name*] dialog, returning you to the original Batch Sequences dialog. Your new sequence is included in the dialog's list.

12. If you are ready to use the process (either a custom sequence or one of the defaults), click Run Sequence. You can also rename it, edit it, and delete it by clicking the appropriate buttons.

As the process is applied, you may see dialogs, depending on the commands you added to your sequence and whether or not you specified Interactive Mode.

CHAPTER EIGHT

Touching Up and Modifying a PDF Document

It's ten to five. Your client wants the draft of a proposal by end of business today. You have ten minutes, and the boss decides that an image should be replaced here and a title changed there. If your security settings allow changes, use that crucial last ten minutes to make those modifications and save the day. Why? Because you work in Acrobat.

Acrobat offers a number of touch-up tools you can use for making simple corrections. You can adjust text, images, and objects right in Acrobat. If you have a document scanned as an image, Acrobat can convert it to editable text. Use the Redaction tools to block out sensitive content, including metadata.

#56 Selecting and Editing Text in a PDF

Suppose you want to combine a couple of pages from one document, a table from another, and a block of text from another. You could go to the source documents and programs and rebuild the content, import different formats from document to document, and export a PDF file. Or you could try combining the content in Acrobat, which is often the more efficient approach.

Use the Select tool, located on the Select & Zoom toolbar, to select text, images, and tables, and to perform object-specific actions available from the tool's pop-up menu of options. Select is an intelligent tool that behaves differently depending on what you're selecting on a document.

Note
Don't confuse the Select tool on the Select & Zoom toolbar with the Select Object tool located on the Advanced Editing toolbar. The Select Object tool selects items like links and form fields.

Here are your options:

- Click the Select tool on the Select & Zoom toolbar and then click and drag over some of the text you want to select; the text is highlighted in the document (**Figure 56**).

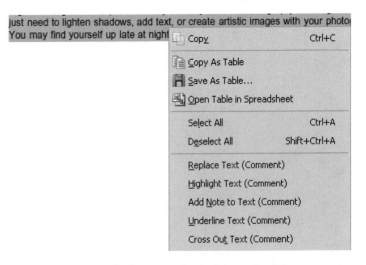

Figure 56 Select text in the document using the Select tool and choose content-specific commands.

- Hold the pointer over the selected text for a couple of seconds until the Select Text icon displays ▶📄. Right-click (Control-click) to display the menu listing options you can choose depending on the content selected, also shown in Figure 56.

- As with other select tools, if you hover the pointer over the table, the Select Text icon displays. Right-click (Control-click) to open the short-cut menu. The table-specific options, shown in Figure 56, include the following:

  - **Copy As Table.** As its name indicates, this option allows you to copy the table to the clipboard. Open the document you want to paste the table into, and choose Edit > Paste.

  - **Save As Table.** Name the table in the Save As dialog that appears when this option is selected, and choose a format.

  - **Open Table in Spreadsheet.** When selected, your spreadsheet application, such as Excel, opens and displays the imported table in a new worksheet.

In both Word and Excel, the tables taken from the PDF document are editable and ready to use.

Tag It

If your document is tagged and you merely want to copy and paste a table, don't spend time selecting tools, selecting text, and selecting commands. Instead, open the Tags panel and click the table's tag. Choose Options > Copy Contents to Clipboard. Then open the document in which you want to use the table and paste it in. The table is pasted and includes its data as well as formatting such as borders, fonts, and so on. How cool.

Adding More and More

The more you click, the more you select:

- Double-click a word to select it.

- Triple-click to select a line of text.

- Quadruple-click to select all the text on a page.

- Press Shift and the Left or Right Arrow key to add text one letter at a time.

- Press Shift+Ctrl (Shift+Command) and the Right Arrow key to add text one word at a time.

#57 Editing Text and Modifying Attributes

To touch up a word or line of text, simply use the TouchUp Text tool in Acrobat. Here's how:

1. Right-click (Control-click) the toolbar well and choose Advanced Editing to open the Advanced Editing toolbar.

2. Select the TouchUp Text tool  from the Advanced Editing toolbar and click the tool within the text you want to edit. The paragraph is surrounded by a bounding box.

3. Drag the I-beam pointer I to select all or part of the paragraph, or position the I-beam within the text you want to edit (**Figure 57a**).

Figure 57a Use the TouchUp Text tool to make simple changes to the content of a page or to add new text.

4. Type the replacement text or add new text at the position of the I-beam pointer. Click outside the highlighted area to deselect the text.

You can modify properties of new text as well as text already in the document, including the following:

- Font and font size

- Fill and stroke options

- Font embedding and subsetting

- Spacing between words and characters

- Baseline adjustments

Tips for Tranquil Text Tweaking

Keep these ideas in mind when touching up text:

- If you need to select an entire paragraph, use the shortcut keys Ctrl+A (Command+A).

- To add new text, with the TouchUp Text tool active, Ctrl-click (Option-click) within the document where you want to add the text. The New Text Font dialog opens with the default options: Arial text and horizontal writing mode. Select the font and writing mode (horizontal or vertical), and click OK. The default text "New Text" displays on the page. Select it, and then type the new text. Click outside the new line of text to finish the process.

- Only fonts with a vertical writing mode will write vertically. An error message means you've selected a horizontal-only font.

(continued on next page)

Touching Up and Modifying a PDF Document

1. With the TouchUp Text tool, first click the row of text or select the words or characters you want to edit.

2. Right-click (Control-click) the text to open the shortcut menu and choose Properties. The TouchUp Properties dialog opens (**Figure 57b**).

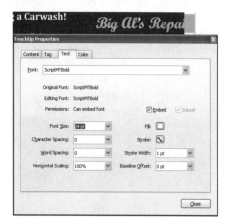

Figure 57b Adjust the characteristics of text in a document by modifying its properties.

3. Choose a font from the Font pop-up menu. Adjust other text attributes as desired and as the font's attributes allow, shown in the figure. As you make adjustments, the changes are automatically previewed in the selected text. Click Close to apply the settings.

- If the text isn't behaving as text, maybe it isn't. Scanned text that hasn't been captured behaves like an image: see #61, "Extracting Active Text from an Image."

- If you add text and it won't wrap to the next line, choose Edit > Preferences > TouchUp (Acrobat > Preferences > TouchUp) and select the Enable Text Word Wrapping check box.

Gimme a Break!

In addition to adding text, you can add line breaks. Click the location on the text block where you want it to break, and then right-click (Control-click) to open the shortcut menu. Click Insert > Line Break. Then press Enter (Return) to wrap the text to the next line. You can use the same method to insert other items, including soft hyphens, nonbreaking spaces, and em dashes.

Copy That

The better you understand some of the intricacies of text selection, the faster you can get your work done. Here are some suggestions:

- Choose Edit > Preferences > General (Acrobat > Preferences > General) and click "Make Hand tool select text and images." This way, when you hold the pointer over text in a document, it automatically works as the Select tool.

- If you are copying and pasting text and intend to send it on to others, be aware that unless a recipient's computer has the same font, it can't be preserved. Acrobat replaces that font with the closest match.

- When a document is tagged, you can use the Copy With Formatting option. This option is especially useful if your document contains columns.

- If you can't copy text, check to see if the document has security settings. The author may have specified that copying be restricted.

Beware of Fakes!

Sometimes the touch-up results aren't what you expect—often related to fonts used in the source program. For example, many Word documents seem to use bold or italic text. In reality, this is probably just a bold or italic text appearance. Unless you are using a named font, such as Arial Bold or Arial Italic, when you try to touch up text in Acrobat you won't have an exact match for the replacement font, since Acrobat doesn't simulate a bold or italic appearance.

#58 Object TouchUps

The TouchUp Object tool ![icon], located on the Advanced Editing toolbar, is useful for organizing content on a page imported as part of the document, such as text, images, and multimedia objects. For example, if you have added extra text to a page and need to shuffle the location of a colored background, use the TouchUp Object tool to select the background object and drag it to a new location (**Figure 58**).

Figure 58 Use the TouchUp Object tool to move content on a page.

Here are some tips:

- You can cut, copy, and paste objects.

- Although you can't select an object on one page and drag it to another page, you can cut an object from one page and paste it to another page.

- You can select more than one type of object at the same time.

- If you click and drag the tool over objects on the page, it will select all the objects within the marquee. Ctrl-click (Option-click) an object to add it to the selection.

- If you click to select an object, you can then right-click (Control-click) to display the shortcut menu. From here, choose Select All, and all the objects on the page are selected.

What Else Does It Do?

In addition to cut, copy, paste, and move options, you can use the TouchUp Object tool to do other types of editing in your document. Select an object or objects, and from the shortcut menu, pick from one of the following:

- Click Delete Clip to remove any objects that are clipping the selected object.

- Click Create Artifact to remove the object from the reading order so it isn't identified by the Read Out Loud feature or a screen reader program (read about screen readers and other accessibility issues in Chapter 6, "Complying with PDF and Accessibility Standards").

- Click Edit Image (to edit a bitmap) or Edit Object (to edit a vector object). The commands change based on the object type; specify the program to use for the editing in the Preferences dialog.

- Right-click (Control-click) an object with the Touch-Up Object tool and choose Properties. In the TouchUp Properties dialog, you can edit the object's content, tag, color, and text information.

Out of the Way, Please

If you are trying to select an image on a document that has overlying text, you could be in for some serious frustration unless you change one of the preferences. Choose Edit > Preferences > General (Acrobat > Preferences > General) and select the "Make Select tool select images before text" check box from the Basic Tools menu.
By default, the General Preferences include a setting to select text before images.

Reuse and Recycle

Once you have an image or image segment copied, you can reuse it. You can also save the image as a file. Select the image in the document, and then right-click (Control-click) to open the shortcut menu. Choose Save Image As, name the image, and specify the save location.

Take a Shortcut

For those who prefer to work with mouse and shortcut keys, click the first object with the TouchUp Object tool, and then press Ctrl+A (Command+A) to select the page's or document's objects.

#59 Reusing Images

You can handle images in a document in three ways—by reusing them, "snapping" portions of them, or inserting other images.

Unless a document is secured against image use, you can reuse individual images in the document.

1. Click the Select tool on the Select & Zoom toolbar. The Select tool automatically changes to an arrow when the pointer is clicked over an image; the selected image is indicated by a highlight.

   - If you want only a portion of the image copied, drag a marquee over the image with the Select tool.

2. Wait a second or two, and the Select Image icon displays on top of the selected image (**Figure 59a**).

Figure 59a A selected image shows a different icon when the pointer hovers over the object.

3. Right-click (Control-click) to open the shortcut menu. You can choose one of two image commands—copy the image to reuse it in another application or document, or choose Save Image As to save a copy of the image as a discrete file.

   ### Note
   If you like, you can use the selected image as a navigation element by bookmarking the image or using it as an image for a link. (Read about both bookmarks and links in Chapter 15, "Controlling Action and Interaction.")

4. Click outside the selected image or click another tool to deselect the image.

Information Overload

Many commands show you information dialogs—something you don't really need to see more than once. Fortunately, the dialogs include a check box that you can click to hide the message. Go ahead. Click it.

Drag-and-Drop Shot

You don't have to mess around with copying and pasting when you're moving images. Open the recipient document next to the document with the image and arrange the documents on the screen. Then, select the image in the PDF document and drag it to the other document.

If you want to reuse some page content that contains both text and graphics, don't bother to copy and paste each element. Instead, use the snazzy Snapshot tool.

1. Add the tool to the Select & Zoom toolbar by right-clicking (Control-clicking) the toolbar well, choosing More Tools, and then selecting the Snapshot tool from the More Tools dialog. Or, if you are snapping a shot as a onetime activity, choose Tools > Select & Zoom > Snapshot Tool .

2. Select the content from the page:

   - Click anywhere on the document to capture the visible content in the Document pane.

   - Drag a marquee around a portion of the page, or around a portion of an image on the page (**Figure 59b**).

Figure 59b Specify a portion of a page's content (left) to capture as a clipboard image (right).

3. You see a flash as the image's colors are inverted within the marquee and the content is captured. The selected area is highlighted until you deselect the tool or select another tool. An information dialog appears telling you that the content has been copied to the clipboard. Click OK.

4. Paste the clipboard content wherever you need it, or use it to create a new PDF document; refer to #22, "Creating a PDF from a Scan in Acrobat," to see how that's done.

#60 Round-trip Editing an Image

Fine-tune images at the last minute and still make that deadline. Round-trip editing lets you work from Acrobat, make changes to content in another program, and then integrate those changes automatically in the PDF document. You use the TouchUp Object tool and a designated editing program, such as Photoshop or Fireworks, to make changes that are then returned to the PDF document: round-trip editing at its finest. You can even select several images and change them all at once.

Follow these steps to change image content:

1. Select the TouchUp Object tool on the Advanced Editing toolbar, and right-click (Control-click) the image or images you want to edit to open the shortcut menu.

2. Choose Edit Image. Your specified image editor opens, and displays the image or images.

3. Make your changes. If you have added any layers, choose Layer > Flatten Image to flatten the layers.

4. Choose File > Save. The image is saved, closed, and replaced in Acrobat (**Figure 60**).

Figure 60 Make changes to images, like the "before" image at the top, within Acrobat. The "after" image at the bottom has had the background faded and a radial blur applied.

Image Editing Oops

Watch out for some things that can make your editing experience less than miraculous:

- A resized image's location will often need tweaking in Acrobat. Use the TouchUp Object tool to reorganize the content if required.

- Transparency is preserved only for masks specified as index values in an image using indexed color.

- When you change image modes, such as from RGB to grayscale, your image may not be saved automatically; instead, Photoshop opens a Save dialog and will save the image as a Photoshop PDF separate from your original PDF document.

- Not every image can be read. If you see a checkerboard instead of your image, you can't edit using the round-trip method. Check your Photoshop configuration.

- If the image looks a little odd when it opens in Photoshop, check the pixel aspect ratio. Acrobat instructs Photoshop to use pixel aspect ratio correction for previewing.

Choosing an Editing Program

Specify the programs you wish to use for editing images and text in the Preferences dialog. Choose Edit > Preferences (Acrobat > Preferences) and choose TouchUp from the Categories menu.

Click either Choose Image Editor or Choose Page/Object Editor to open a browse dialog. Locate the program you want to use and select it. Click Open to close the dialog and assign the program to the function. Then, click OK to close the dialog and set the preferences.

Keep the Connection

The image connection exists only as long as the object is selected in Acrobat. If you are working with an image in Photoshop and then deselect the object in Acrobat, you have to start over.

#61 Extracting Active Text from an Image

A page scanned in older versions of Acrobat, or one created from a photo or drawing, is only an image of a page, and you can't manipulate its content by extracting images or modifying the text. However, Acrobat can convert the image of the document into actual text or add a text layer to the document using optical character recognition (OCR). Be sure to evaluate the captured document when the OCR process is complete to make sure Acrobat interpreted the content correctly. It's easy to confuse a bitmap that may be the letter *l* with the number *1*, for example.

To capture the content of an image document, do the following:

1. Choose Document > OCR Text Recognition > Recognize Text Using OCR. The Recognize Text dialog opens. Specify whether you want to capture the current page, an entire document, or specified pages in a multipage document.

2. Click the Edit button to open the Recognize Text - Settings dialog. Choose one of three options in the PDF Output Style pop-up menu:

   • Searchable Image compresses the foreground and places the searchable text behind the image. Compressing affects the image quality.

   • Searchable Image (Exact) keeps the foreground of the page intact and places the searchable text behind the image.

   • ClearScan rebuilds the page, converting the content into text, fonts, and graphics.

   • If you select either Searchable Image or ClearScan OCR choices, you can choose one of four options from the Downsample Images pop-up menu—anywhere from 600 down to 72 dpi. Downsampling reduces file size, but can also result in unusable images.

   Click OK to return to the Recognize Text dialog.

(continued on next page)

Rounding Up the Suspects

Converting a bitmap of letters and numbers into actual letters and numbers may result in items that can't be definitively identified, known as *suspects*. Here's how to fix it.

Select Document > Recognize Text Using OCR > Find First OCR Suspect to open the dialog where Acrobat identifies suspect characters for you to confirm.

Work through the suspects using several options:

• Select the text in the Suspect field and type the correct letters.

• Click Not Text when the suspect isn't a word at all.

• Click Find Next to go to the next suspect.

• Click Accept and Find to confirm the interpretation, and go to the next suspect.

• Click Close to end the process.

Depending on the characteristics of the document's text, you may have to modify some conversion results, such as the font or character spacing, using the TouchUp text tool.

3. Click OK to start the capture process. Be patient. Depending on the size and complexity of the document, the process can take a minute or two. When it is complete, the dialog closes and the results of the conversion are shown in the document (**Figure 61a**).

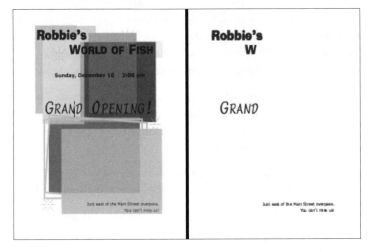

Figure 61a A poster image converts with all content visible using Exact Image OCR (left); using ClearScan converts only content that doesn't overlay the denser parts of the poster image (right).

The point of OCR is to produce searchable text in your document. OCR isn't foolproof, and you're going to have some errors, even though Acrobat doesn't recognize them as such. (See the sidebar "Rounding Up the Suspects" to learn how to manage suspect content.) The example shown in **Figure 61b** is a case in point. At the top of the figure, the title of #60 was reset using a complex font. Then, the first paragraph from #60 was captured as a screenshot image, and the text recognized using OCR in Acrobat. At the bottom of the figure, notice how many errors there are in the captured text.

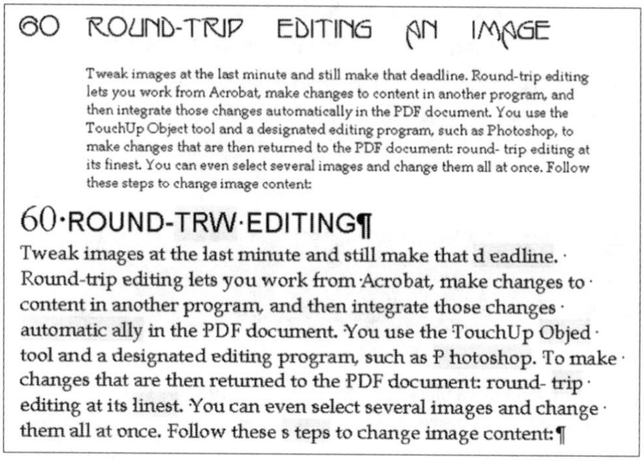

60 ROUND-TRIP EDITING AN IMAGE

Tweak images at the last minute and still make that deadline. Round-trip editing lets you work from Acrobat, make changes to content in another program, and then integrate those changes automatically in the PDF document. You use the TouchUp Object tool and a designated editing program, such as Photoshop, to make changes that are then returned to the PDF document: round- trip editing at its finest. You can even select several images and change them all at once. Follow these steps to change image content:

60·ROUND-TRW·EDITING¶

Tweak images at the last minute and still make that d eadline. ·
Round-trip editing lets you work from Acrobat, make changes to ·
content in another program, and then integrate those changes ·
automatic ally in the PDF document. You use the TouchUp Objed ·
tool and a designated editing program, such as P hotoshop. To make ·
changes that are then returned to the PDF document: round- trip ·
editing at its linest. You can even select several images and change ·
them all at once. Follow these s teps to change image content:¶

Figure 61b Acrobat tries to interpret as much as possible of the page's content as text, but won't recognize text on a dark-colored background.

Note

If you're wondering where the captured text came from, it's simple: All I did was select and copy the paragraph in the PDF file, and then I pasted it into a Word document. The highlights were added in Word for illustration.

Scan and Convert

If you are scanning a document in Acrobat 9, creating searchable text is a default part of the scanning process. See #21, "Creating a PDF from Web Pages in Acrobat," for more details.

#62 Redacting Content

Commenting & Markup tools such as the Rectangle or Highlighting tool can appear to cover up images or text. In a printed PDF page the underlying content is hidden, which isn't the case in a digital file—the underlying content is merely covered up (**Figure 62a**).

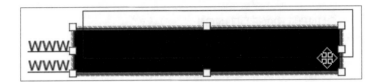

Figure 62a Covering text with a black rectangle is fine for printing. In a document, all you have to do is move the box out of the way.

Permanently removing content and replacing it with a placeholder of some type, such as a colored box, default text or code, or blank space, is called *redaction*. Acrobat 8 introduced a set of redaction tools, which are enhanced in Acrobat 9 Pro.

To use redaction, your PDF file must do the following:

- Contain searchable text, described in technique #61.

- Not be encrypted. Read about encryption in Chapter 16, "Making Your Documents Secure."

Follow these steps to remove content permanently:

1. Right-click (Control-click) the toolbar well and choose Redaction from the shortcut menu to open the toolbar.

2. Click the Mark for Redaction tool 🖉. An information dialog opens explaining that you can use the tool to specify content for removal and then use the Apply Redaction tool to complete the task. Click OK to close the dialog.

3. Move the pointer over the page and drag to select content for redaction. You can select single or multiple words, entire paragraphs, or images. Each item selected displays a bounding box (**Figure 62b**).

Have It Your Way

Personalize the appearance of the redaction marks using colors, text, or code. Click Redaction Properties 🖉 on the Redaction toolbar. The default settings in the Redaction Tool Properties dialog specify a solid black fill for the redaction marks.

Select options for the text including a Redacted Area Fill Color if you'd like the areas filled with a color other than black. Select Use Overlay Text to activate the text options. Choose the font and size (or use auto-sizing), and choose the font color, text positioning, custom text, or redaction code.

If regulations or legislation governing your work requires it, you can specify a code identifying the reason for redaction rather than using text over a solid block of color. In the Redaction Tool Properties dialog, click Redaction Code to activate the code choices. Select a Code Set and a Code Entry.

To add, modify, export, and import code, click Edit Codes. Click OK and return to the Redaction Tool Properties, and then click OK to return to the document. The next time you use the Apply Redaction tool, the custom code is inserted on the page.

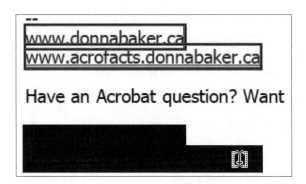

Figure 62b Select and preview content for redaction on the page.

Preserve Your Files to Preserve Your Sanity

In many workflows, it's important to have both redacted and full versions of a document. Once the redacted file is saved, the original content can't be restored. If you apply redaction and change your mind, choose File > Revert to return to the file's status prior to the redaction.

4. Move the pointer over a selected object on the page to see how it will look after redaction, like the lower paragraph in Figure 62b.

5. When you have finished your selections, click Apply Redactions 🔁. A confirmation dialog opens; click OK to apply the redactions to the file.

Note

A second information dialog opens asking if you would also like to examine the document for other content that can be removed. Click Yes to proceed with the document examination as described in #31, "Finding Information about Your Document." If you need to check the redacted files for other content regularly, select "Always perform the selected action" to save a mouse click in the future.

Suppose you have to locate many similar items in a very long document—how tedious! Acrobat 9 offers a new Search tool that lets you track down single words, phrases, or patterns. Read about searching for content using phrases in the sidebar "The Correct Phrase Is …"

Click the Search and Redact tool 🔍 on the Redaction toolbar to open the Search window, and follow these steps to search for a pattern:

1. Specify the locations for searching from the "Where would you like to search?" options.

2. Click Patterns to activate a field, and choose an option from the pop-up menu, such as Dates.

(continued on next page)

Another way to search for
redaction content is using
phrases. Click the Search
and Redact tool ⌨ on the
Redaction toolbar to open
the Search window. Choose
the location for searching,
and select "Multiple words
or phrases" to activate the
Select Words button, which
you click next to display
the Words and Phrases to
Search and Redact dia-
log. Type a word or phrase
and click Add, and repeat.
When you've finished add-
ing terms, click OK to close
the dialog and process the
file. Once the matches are
made, you'll see the contents
identified in your document.
Click Apply Redactions to
complete the process.

But here's the coolest part—
you can import and export
lists of words and phrases
to reuse as necessary. You
won't forget what you have
to locate and redact, nor
will you have to transcribe
a list of terms every time
you need to redact another
document.

- You can search for phone numbers, e-mail addresses, Web addresses,
  social security numbers, employee numbers, credit card numbers,
  and dates. You'll see examples of each pattern in the Search window when you make the selection (**Figure 62c**).

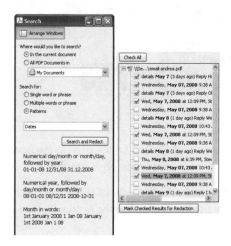

Figure 62c Search a document for patterns,
like dates. In the Search Returns (shown at
the right), select the results you want to redact.

3. Click Search and Redact to get started. The document is processed, and
   the search results are displayed, as shown at the right of Figure 62c.

4. Click the search results you want to redact; click Check All to select the
   entire set of returns.

5. Click Mark Checked Results for Redaction to complete the process.

CHAPTER NINE

Building Content with Adobe Presenter

Acrobat 9 includes a snazzy new tool integrated into PowerPoint called Adobe Presenter. You don't have to be a Flash wizard to use Presenter to produce multimedia presentations, learning materials, and even surveys and standards-compliant quizzes. Once you're done, the same project can be used as a PDF file, on a Web page, or as a stand-alone in SWF format, or it can be published to your Acrobat Connect Pro server.

Presenter offers its own program icon and menu item in your program listings, but it isn't a stand-alone program. Instead, it is installed as a menu in PowerPoint, just like the PDFMaker installed in Office (Windows) programs.

A Presenter workflow requires several components, including these:

- Constructing the base PowerPoint presentation used for the Presenter project

- Specifying how the presentation functions, through options such as playback and quiz interactions

- Defining the viewer interface for the presentation through its theme and text

- Adding Presenter features, such as audio narration and video, to the slides

- Testing and publishing the project as PDF, as SWF, or for use in Acrobat Connect Pro

Presenter isn't installed or activated with other Acrobat 9 Pro Extended components, such as LiveCycle Designer or Acrobat Distiller. Instead, it has its own installation option on the Acrobat 9 Pro Extended installation screen. Click Install Adobe Presenter and follow the prompts. The first time you open it, you have to register the product. If you don't register it, Presenter runs in trial mode for 30 days.

#63 Creating a Presenter Publication

You can build the Presenter publication over your underlying PowerPoint publication at any stage of development—whether you start a new publication from scratch or open an existing slide show.

Tip
To save time when configuring Presenter settings, it's quickest to have the set of slides created and the basic titling finished. That way, when you select some of the configuration options, you won't have to guess at settings.

To get under way, open your presentation in PowerPoint and then choose Adobe Presenter > Presentation Settings to open the four-tab dialog (**Figure 63**).

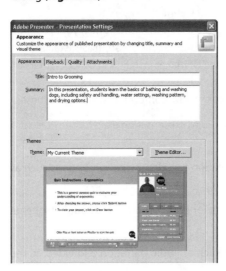

Figure 63 Specify choices for Adobe Presenter in this dialog.

Use the settings in the dialog to configure the presentation features:

1. In the Appearance tab, change the publication appearance:

- Type an alternate title for your presentation if you don't want to use the default title, which is the PowerPoint file's name.

- Type a summary for the presentation to describe its purpose and contents. If you use your presentation on Adobe Connect Pro, the summary is shown with other presentation data; in a PDF or local presentation, the summary isn't used.

- To configure the appearance and function of the SWF interface, select and edit a theme. Read about using themes in #64, "Specifying a Theme."

2. In the Playback tab, choose settings for playing the presentation:

- Select "Auto play on start" to have the presentation begin immediately after loading. Otherwise the user has to click the Play button on the presentation's interface to start the presentation.

- Presenter runs the presentation once and then stops by default; if you want it to loop—like presentations used in a kiosk or public display—select Loop presentation.

- Select "Include slide numbers in outline" if you want to include slide numbers in the Outline pane of the presentation (a handy option for different presenters with varying levels of familiarity with the content).

- If you want the presentation to stop after a slide's animation is complete, choose "Pause after each animation." That way, a viewer has time to make notes or check out the finished slide before continuing.

- Slides display according to the length of their audio or video; for slides without media, specify a display time in seconds. The default is 5 seconds.

3. In the Quality tab, choose image and audio qualities based on how you intend to use the presentation.

- Click the Publish For drop-down arrow and choose from My Computer, Adobe Connect Pro, or Adobe PDF to automatically optimize the levels, or select the options manually.

- Select the Control Preloading check box, and choose either "Download slides completely before playback" or "Disable preloading of embedded Flash content," based on your presentation's characteristics. Read about the differences in the sidebar "To Preload or Not to Preload: That Is the Question."

- Save some time configuring future projects by selecting the "Use these settings for new presentations" check box.

(continued on next page)

Exceptions to the Rules

For the most part, Presenter default choices for image quality are fine—with a few exceptions. To prevent blurry content, be sure to set image quality to high in your presentation if it includes charts, Smart Art, Word Art, Quick Styles, or shapes using 3D effects, like shadows.

You can view presentations on mobile devices such as cell phones and PDAs that use Flash Lite 3. If you intend your output for mobile devices, use the low-quality setting for images and audio to reduce the size of the finished file.

What about Playing Flash?

You don't have to worry about installing Flash Player, or whether you have the right version. The latest version of the Flash Player (Flash Player 9) is installed when you install Presenter.

Taking It Mobile

Presenter output can be used on mobile devices that run Flash Lite 3. Many features are supported, including slide animations and backgrounds, audio, and embedded SWF and FLV files.

Some Presenter content isn't supported in Flash Lite 3, including the side panel, quizzes, themes, and the playbar.

4. In the Attachments tab, select and add files to attach to the presentation. Click Add to open the Add Attachment dialog, where you can locate content such as spreadsheets or charts that you want to provide with the presentation. An attachment can be either a file or a link—to discover how to use links and attachments, check out #66, "Including Attachments."

5. Once you've finished modifying the settings, click OK to close the dialog.

Create slide titles to give users easy access to any slide. Check that titles appear in the PowerPoint outline for all slides, including graphic-only slides, before publishing your presentation.

#64 Specifying a Theme

Presenter publications show a presentation running inside a customizable interface called a *theme*. You can customize features such as color, tab display, graphics, fonts, and interface functionality. Once you have chosen, customized, or created a theme, save it for reuse.

Adobe Presenter uses a default green-colored presentation theme named Sage, but you can alter it. Open your presentation in PowerPoint and then follow these steps:

1. Choose Adobe Presenter > Presentation Settings. Click Theme Editor to open the dialog shown in **Figure 64a**.

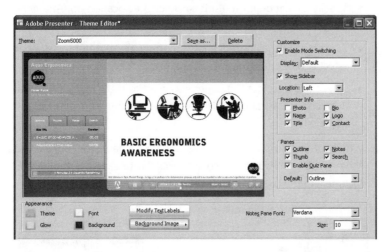

Figure 64a Select details to customize the appearance of the theme according to your company, brand, or club colors.

2. Choose a theme to start customizing from the Theme pop-up menu. The new theme appears in the preview window.

3. Change Appearance options as desired:

- Click the color swatch for different interface elements to open color pickers and choose custom or branding colors.

- Click Modify Text Labels to change the text in different areas of the theme, such as the field names in the Search tab or the label assigned to a quiz score. You can't change the column headings "Slide Title" and "Duration" on the Outline pane.

(continued on next page)

Speaking Your Language

So you plan to distribute your presentation to colleagues in Germany? Or Japan? No problem. The text labels in the presentation automatically display in German, French, Japanese, or Korean if the viewer's operating system is set for one of those languages. You can choose from several other languages, including Chinese or Dutch, in the Player Text Labels dialog, which displays when you click the Modify Text Labels button in the Theme Editor window.

If Your Saved Theme Isn't Quite Right …

Fear not. Pay attention to how you customized the features in the Theme Editor. If you make changes to a default theme and saved it, then made some more changes, the unsaved modifications aren't included in the theme. How to tell if you have unsaved settings? Check the label at the top of the Theme Editor. If you see an asterisk following the label, that means there are unsaved settings. Click Save As again,

(continued on next page)

retype the name of your theme, and click Save. You're asked if you want to over-write the existing theme—which you do, of course.

Customize the Loading Text

By default, Presenter displays a loading screen that reads "Adobe Presenter" while your presentation is loading.

Personalize the presentation with your business name or other text on the loading screen instead. Open a presentation in PowerPoint, and save and publish the presentation to your computer to copy the files locally.

To change the text for a presentation, follow these steps:

1. In Windows Explorer, locate this folder: c:\Documents and Settings\ *[user name]* \ My Documents\My Adobe Presentations\ *[PresentationName]* \ data.

(continued on next page)

- Click Background Image > Change to open a dialog where you can locate and select a JPEG image to use as the background behind the slides, playbar, and toolbar.

- Choose a font and size from the Notes Pane Font pop-up menus.

4. To select Customize options, do one of the following:

- Click the Enable Mode Switching check box, and select either Default or Fullscreen from the Display pop-up menu to offer users optional presentation sizes.

- Specify a location for the sidebar. Click the Location pop-up menu and choose Right or Left.

- To customize the content shown at the upper right of the sidebar, select and deselect the Presenter Info check boxes.

- Select and deselect the panes you want to show in the presentation; choose a pane to display as the default from the Default pop-up menu.

5. When you've finished, click Save as, and type a name for your custom theme in the dialog that displays. Click OK to save the theme and include it in the Theme list for future use (**Figure 64b**).

Figure 64b The customized theme is shown as the default theme.

6. Click OK to close the Theme Editor and return to the Presentation Settings dialog. Notice how the theme you've customized is now shown in the Themes area of the dialog, and the label displays as *"My Current Theme."* Click OK to dismiss the dialog and return to your project.

In order to see the changes you've made to the theme live, you have to publish the presentation. See how in #69, "Previewing and Publishing."

Note

If you have too many custom themes, select the names in the Theme Name pop-up menu, click Delete, click Yes to confirm, and click OK to remove it. You can't delete the default themes.

Change It Once—Use It Forever

Rather than leaving the default Adobe Presenter preload text, or customizing the text for each presentation, you can modify an Adobe Presenter program file to change the text for all your presentations. Here's how:

1. Locate the Themes folder on your hard drive:

   - On Windows XP, in Windows Explorer, locate C:\Documents and Settings\ *[user name]* \Local Settings\Application Data\Adobe\Adobe Presenter\ Themes.

   - On Windows Vista, from the desktop click Start > Run and type *%LOCALAPPDATA%\Adobe\Adobe Presenter*. Click OK to close the Run dialog and open the folders; double-click on the Themes folder.

2. Right-click on the language.xml file and open the file using an XML editor or Notepad.

3. Look for the `<language id="en">` section close to the start of the file, and type this code, inserting your custom text as the value:

   ```
   <uitext name="ADOBE_PRESENTER" value="Insert Your Custom Text"/>
   ```

4. Save and close the language.xml file.

5. Back in PowerPoint, save and publish the presentation to your computer, selecting the View output option.

6. Click the logo to test the new content.

2. Open the vconfig.xml file in an XML editor or Notepad.

3. Scroll down about one-half page to the `<language id="en">` section, and type this code on a blank line, inserting your custom text as the value:

   ```
   <uitext name="ADOBE_PRESENTER" value="Insert Your Custom Text"/>
   ```

4. Save and close the vconfig.xml file.

5. Open the index.htm Web page holding the presentation, located at c:\Documents and Settings\ *[user name]* \ My Documents\My Adobe Presentations\ *[PresentationName]*. When the page opens, view your custom text as the presentation loads.

#65 Recording and Using Audio and Video

The Scoop on Using Flash Files

Keep these construction tips for integrating Flash content in mind as you develop your presentations:

- Author your content at 30 frames per second (fps) to match the Presenter frame rate of 30 fps.

- Develop content on a canvas no larger than 720 x 540 pixels to fit within the Presenter parameters.

Keep these programming tips in mind as well:

- You can't use external variables, including _level#, _global, or stage.

- Use relative paths to reference movie clips, not _root paths.

In addition to adding existing audio files, you can record your own audio files to use in Presenter presentations. Recorded files are saved in MP3 format.

To record audio, choose Adobe Presenter > Record Audio and read the test message. When the Input Level shows OK, click OK to open the Record Audio dialog (**Figure 65a**). Using the controls on the dialog, add and review audio to use for your presentation.

Play button

Record button

Figure 65a Record and review audio to add to your presentation.

Consider these tips to ensure that you are recording the best audio possible:

- Specify the audio recording quality. Choose Adobe Presenter > Preferences > Quality. Select from CD Quality (highest) to Low Bandwidth (lowest). Balance the required quality against the file size; the higher the quality, the greater the file size.

- Preview the audio as you record it in the Audio Editor. You can also preview later from the PowerPoint window. Choose Adobe Presenter > Edit Audio > View > Slide Show to display the Edit Audio window overlaying the presentation slides.

Use video you import from other locations, or record and customize it directly through Adobe Presenter—perfect for adding those talking head features to your presentation:

- Choose Adobe Presenter > Capture Video to open the Capture Video dialog. Choose the slide to link to, select your device and quality, and click Record. Click Stop to stop, and review by clicking Play. When finished, click Save to open a dialog where you name the file and choose a storage location.

- Select the slide where you want to add the video, and choose Adobe Presenter > Import Video to open a dialog. Select the video to import, click Open, and wait while the file is processed. You'll see a white box overlaying the slide on which the video is placed.

Regardless of the method you use for bringing video into a presentation, you can edit it via Adobe Presenter. Here's how:

1. Select Adobe Presenter > Edit Video to open the dialog (**Figure 65b**).

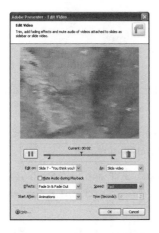

Figure 65b Edit features of the video you import or record.

2. To preview the clip, click Play ▶; click Stop/Pause ❚❚ to stop the preview.

3. Adjust the length of the clip by dragging the start and end markers in from the edges of the playbar if desired.

4. Specify other features for the video:

   - Choose how to play video by selecting the slide or sidebar option.

   - Choose a Fade or Speed option from the Effects pull-down menu.

   - Choose when to play the video by selecting an option from the Start After pop-up menu. You can indicate a time delay, or specify that the movie start after the slide's animation or audio.

(continued on next page)

Check Your Assets and Give Users Playback Control

If you want to check your presentation's inventory of Flash files, choose Adobe Presenter > Manage Flash to open a dialog listing the files according to the slide number. The listings include the SWF files' names.

The SWF files in your presentation are controlled by the playback controls in the Presenter playbar, or by using the playbar in the original SWF file. The default uses the Presenter playback option. To change the setting, select the Controlled By Presentation Playbar check box for any files you want to control from their original playbar.

Stamp Your Own Brand

Another location to use a SWF file is in the finished project. Replace the Adobe logo in the lower-left corner on the published interface with your own logo or branding information.

Design or resize a copy of your logo at 47 x 27 pixels and save it as logo.swf in the Presenter templates folder. Republish your presentation to see your custom template. Read about publishing a Presenter project in #69.

5. To edit another slide's video, choose the slide's name from the Edit on pop-up list (**Figure 65c**).

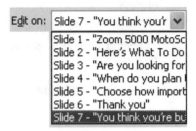

Figure 65c Select a slide from the list to edit its video.

6. Continue until you've finished your edits, and then click OK to close the dialog.

7. Save the file. To view the video, you can either render the project or choose View > Slideshow from the PowerPoint menu.

Last—but certainly not least—add Flash SWF and FLV (Flash video) to your presentation for some extra interest and excitement, following these steps:

1. Select Adobe Presenter > Insert Flash. Locate and select the SWF file.

2. In the Import Options, choose a slide from the Import On pop-up menu, and specify whether to add the content as a slide or sidebar animation.

3. Click Open to dismiss the Insert Flash dialog, and add your SWF to the slide, positioned at the center. Click and drag to reposition the file if you like.

4. Repeat the process to insert other content on other slides.

Tip
If you want to preview the SWF content, choose View > Slideshow from the PowerPoint menu.

#66 Including Attachments

Just as you can attach all sorts of files to a PDF document (check out #24, "Attaching Source Files to a PDF" for details) you can attach PDF files, documents, spreadsheets, other presentations, Flash files, and so on to your presentation.

Follow these steps to add attachments to your presentation:

1. Choose Adobe Presenter > Publish Settings > Attachments and click Add to open the Add Attachment dialog (**Figure 66a**).

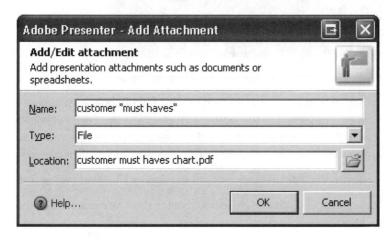

Figure 66a Specify characteristics of attachments or links.

2. Add a description for the attachment.

3. In the Type pop-up menu, select File or Link—click Browse to locate and select a file to attach, or type the URL in the text box to attach a link.

4. Click OK to close the dialog and list the attachment in the dialog.

5. Click Add again, and attach other files as required.

When the presentation is rendered, click Attachments in the Add Attachment dialog to see the list of content attached or linked to the presentation (**Figure 66b**).

Testing, Testing, 1-2-3

Broken links are undoubtedly one of digital life's greatest irritations. Make sure that doesn't happen in your Presenter publications.

Once you've added your links, save the presentation, and then publish it (learn how in #69, "Previewing and Publishing"). When the presentation displays in your Web browser, Acrobat 9, or Adobe Reader 9, start testing links. Fortunately, if there are broken links, it's simple to repair them. If you see a message that starts "Cannot find 'file://c:\Documents and Settings…\resources\ *[filename]*,'" open the path in Internet Explorer and look for your missing file. Copy or move the file into the subfolder. Republish and try again.

174

Linking by Hand

Links from a presentation to files need to be configured by hand due to the way PowerPoint manages links. It takes a few minutes, but it's worth it. Follow these steps:

1. Open the folder where you have stored the PPT or PPTX file, and create and name a subfolder. The name doesn't matter—I usually call it "Links" (for obvious reasons!).

2. Move or copy the files you intend to link into the Links folder.

3. In PowerPoint, create the links to the files from the presentation slides.

4. Publish the presentation on your computer.

5. Locate and open the published project folder; copy your Links subfolder into the Data\ Resources subfolder.

Does that seem like too much work? You can use attachments instead of links. Attached files are included as part of the project's resources when you publish the project.

Figure 66b View the list of attached content from the playbar.

Rather than attaching files, you can add links to online resources or Connect Pro Server storage locations. Adobe Presenter treats hyperlinks attached to text on slides as a type of attachment. For example, you could create a link from text on a slide to a spreadsheet, following these steps:

1. Display the slide where you want to add the link, and select the link text.

2. Right-click and choose Hyperlink from the shortcut menu to open the Insert Hyperlink dialog.

3. Specify the settings for the hyperlink, including the file location, a tooltip, and so on. Click OK to close the dialog and return to the slide.

4. The text now shows a hyperlink, as well as a tooltip, if you specified one in the dialog (**Figure 66c**). Clicking the link opens the hyperlinked document in another window.

Figure 66c Insert a hyperlink to content stored elsewhere on your system or server.

In case of link issues, be sure to read the sidebar "Testing, Testing, 1-2-3."

Don't Let IE Give You the Presentation Runaround

Internet Explorer may not allow attachments to presentations to display properly when you publish them locally—that is, to a zip file or a CD-formatted file, for two reasons:

- Security settings in Internet Explorer prevent an Internet page from accessing and running files on a local system. While this feature is terrific for protecting your system, it adds a touch of aggravation to your development process.

- An Adobe Presenter publication runs locally in your Flash Player, and Internet Explorer deems file downloads via Flash Player as unsafe. Another touch of aggravation.

What to do? Here are some options. The best choice depends on how you need to use the content:

- Create PDF output (the simplest solution—read about it in #69).

- Store the attached files on a Web server or network drive and make hyperlinks in PowerPoint rather than via Adobe Presenter.

- Publish the presentation to an online LMS storage repository, like Connect Pro Server.

#67 Working in the Quiz Manager

Learning Management Systems (LMSs)

A Presenter quiz integrates easily with Connect Pro Server LMS, and creates the manifest files required for other learning management systems. The XML manifest file includes an identifier, title, and data that complies with international standards for Web-based training, issued by the Aviation Industry Computer-Based Training Committee (AICC).

See the Presenter Help files for particulars on building Sharable Content Object Reference Model (SCORM) manifest files for integration with a third-party LMS.

Learn about AICC online at www.aicc.org. Find out about SCORM at www.adlnet.gov/scorm/.

Use the Quiz Manager to—you guessed it—manage quizzes added to a Presenter publication. You can add one or more quizzes, each having numerous questions, all without writing a single line of JavaScript.

The structure of a quiz is complex, and it's based on a hierarchy of relationships and values that make up a learning management system (LMS). Whether you are writing content for a formal e-learning experience or gathering opinions from fellow garden club members, the Quiz Manager takes care of the relationships for you invisibly. All you have to do is select the question types, their content, and their outcomes.

Before you dive into quiz construction, take a few minutes to process some terms and concepts key to using the Quiz Manager effectively:

- **Quiz boundary.** The Quiz Manager encases all the slides in a quiz within an invisible boundary. For example, the quiz shown in **Figure 67** includes five slides in the quiz, although there are only three questions—the quiz boundaries include the instruction slide and the thank-you slide.

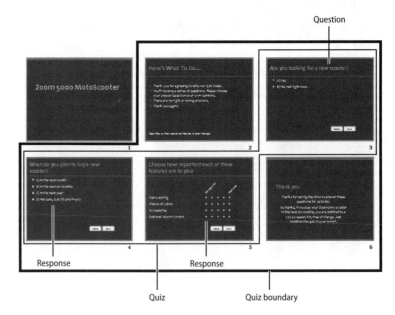

Figure 67 The Quiz Manager controls several aspects of a quiz presentation.

- **Quiz.** One presentation can have one or more quizzes. Each is a named container that holds the individual questions. The Quiz Manager can assign an Objective ID to a quiz to coordinate with an objective in your learning management system.

- **Questions.** The actual interactions your viewers perform. Each question is given an Interaction ID.

- **Responses.** The selection of possible answers for a question. Each may be assigned a value, and the correct responses can vary.

Other features not identified in Figure 67, but important in many types of quizzes, include the following:

- **Question group.** Often, a quiz displays different questions in different orders to different users. In Presenter, all your questions make up a question group; you decide how many questions are used in the quiz presented to your user. For example, you may have a question group containing 30 questions, and specify a subset of 20 questions for the actual quiz.

- **Report and feedback.** Tracking responses, called *reporting*, lets you track the number of attempts, whether or not the responses were correct, and if the results are a pass/fail. You can specify the feedback given to quiz-takers based on their responses. If you are involved in a formal education system, reporting data can be sent to Connect Pro Server or other LMS.

To customize the content further and make your e-learning more specific, branching lets you specify what happens when a user answers a question. For example, if a user answers a question incorrectly, you can have the presentation return to a review slide followed by a review quiz, and return to the main quiz; a right answer moves the user to the next question in the main quiz.

Staying Inside the Boundaries

Presenter uses quiz boundaries to set limits—a concept we all understand—in several ways:

- Specify that Presenter displays a message if the user tries to leave the quiz boundary without answering required questions.

- Use the Quiz Pane, one of the optional panes you select when designing your theme. When the user is within the quiz boundary, the Quiz pane is visible; when the user moves outside the quiz boundary, the Quiz pane disappears.

Come to Order

The Quiz Manager acts as a controller for your quiz-building efforts. Keep your quiz on track and decrease frustration by keeping these ideas in mind:

- Since each quiz slide/question has a unique interaction ID, don't copy and paste a slide to create a new quiz slide. The Quiz Manager can't automatically change the interaction ID, which causes a problem with LMSs.

- If you make changes to a question on the slide (rather than in the Quiz Manager), reopen the Quiz Manager before you publish your presentation. That way, the quiz content is validated and updated.

- If you want to make a change to some aspect of the quiz appearance, such as the font or text color, do it before publishing but after closing the Quiz Manager. Otherwise, if you make changes and then open the Quiz Manager, the questions are rendered again, and your new formatting could be lost.

#68 Writing a Quiz

Adobe Presenter offers six types of questions you can use in your quiz design. Here are their program buttons and short descriptions:

- **Multiple choice:** Users choose one or more correct answers from a list.

- **True/False:** Users choose from two options.

- **Fill-in-the-blanks:** Users complete a statement by typing a response or choosing one from a list.

- **Short answer:** Users write a response to an open-ended question like "What's your favorite aspect of the Zoom5000 hybrid scooter?"

- **Matching:** Users match content among items in two lists.

- **Likert:** Users agree or disagree with statements on a sliding scale, the type of question you often see in consumer surveys.

You don't have to organize the presentation to include slides for the quiz. A new slide is added automatically for each new question you build in the Quiz Manager using the PowerPoint master slide template to configure its appearance. Writing your quiz has two parts: configuring the way the quiz functions, and adding the actual quiz questions.

To get a quiz set up using the default quiz included in Presenter, follow these steps:

1. Open the presentation (or create and save a new one) in PowerPoint.

2. Choose Adobe Presenter > Quiz Manager to open the dialog, which lists a default quiz named "Quiz." Click Edit to open the Quiz Settings dialog (**Figure 68a**).

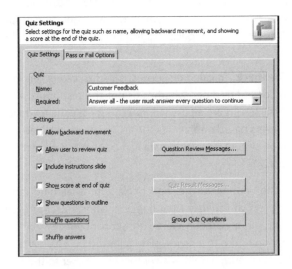

Figure 68a Design the questions for your quiz.

3. Change the name of the quiz if you like, and select an option from the Required pop-up menu to define the level of user interaction (see the sidebar "What's the Rule?" for information on the options).

4. Select the functional characteristics for the quiz, such as whether users can go backward in the quiz, if they can review the quiz, if they can see

their score, and so on. Choose options to shuffle content in the questions and answers, and to display the name of the question slide in the Presenter outline or in a simple Quiz label.

Tip
If the quiz is self-administered, offer users the option to review and show results. Click the corresponding Question Review Messages and Quiz Result Messages buttons to open dialogs where you can add text to display when users check their responses.

5. Click the Pass or Fail Options tab and choose options for two criteria:

- Choose how to show the passing score, such as a percentage or number correct, in the Pass/Fail scoring area.

- Choose actions for the presentation that occur in response to both passing and failing grades. For example, when users pass the quiz, give them the option of moving to the next slide to continue the presentation. Specify criteria for failing a quiz (such as the number of attempts) and how the presentation is to continue. For example, choose an action to go to a slide that allows users to branch out into remedial lessons.

Click OK to close the Quiz dialog, and return to the main Quiz Manager dialog. Now you're ready to add some questions!

In the Quiz Manager, follow these steps to add your quiz questions:

1. Click Add Question to open the Question Types dialog and choose a question type to display the New [question type] dialog. (Read about the different questions in the sidebar "The Question Is …")

2. In the Question pane of the dialog, type a name and the content of the question in the appropriate fields at the top of the dialog.

3. Click Add to activate a response field, and type an answer to include the response in the Answers section of the dialog. Depending on the

(continued on next page)

Tweaking and Reorganizing

When you've finished building your quiz, you can move the quiz slides around in your overall presentation with two cautions—all the quiz questions must be moved as a block, and you can't move a question from one quiz to another.

More Configuration Choices

As you might have guessed, the ability to customize the quiz structure and contents is virtually limitless. The Quiz Manager offers several more tabs on which you can make these sorts of changes:

- **Output Options.** Choose settings for showing questions, scores, tooltips, and other test response features.

- **Reporting.** Specify where and how to report quiz results, such as LMS, Adobe Connect Pro, types of reports, and so on.

(continued on next page)

- **Default Labels.** Specify the text shown on Submit and Clear buttons, as well as how feedback messages are shown.

- **Appearance.** Choose fonts for question elements, where buttons are placed, and whether to save and reuse formatting profiles.

Pick a Spot

There's a method to the location Presenter uses for including a quiz in a presentation:

- In Microsoft Office XP, the quiz starts after the first slide in the presentation.

- In other versions of Microsoft Office, select a slide in the presentation to display before the first quiz slide.

- Regardless of your PowerPoint version, if you add a second quiz, it starts immediately after the first quiz.

question type, continue typing responses and adding them to the Answers list (**Figure 68b**).

Figure 68b Customize the content for the questions and responses.

4. Select the Options tab, and specify whether or not the answers are graded, as well as actions for right or wrong answers (such as moving to another slide, opening a URL, or playing an audio clip).

5. Select the Reporting tab and specify whether to report the answer. In this tab, you'll see the ID numbers assigned to the quiz and the question by Presenter.

6. Continue adding questions to your quiz as required. When you've finished, you'll see them listed in the Quiz Manager (**Figure 68c**).

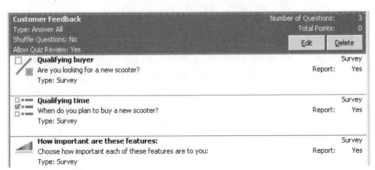

Figure 68c Review the completed questions in the Quiz Manager.

7. Click OK to close the dialog and return to the presentation. The quiz questions are configured and added automatically. Save the presentation to store your quiz.

What's the Rule?

When setting up the quiz, specify how users are required to interact with your quiz, based on your overall goals for the presentation. For example:

- Choose Optional if the quiz is for self-interest, or based on rudimentary information. Users can decide whether it's worth their time based on their level of interest and expertise in the material.

- Choose Required if the user must attempt the quiz. An attempt means answering one question and clicking Submit—the presentation won't move beyond the quiz questions, although the user can navigate among quiz questions.

- Choose Pass Required if the user is participating in an active learning situation where a specified level of understanding (based on the score) must be demonstrated. If you choose this option, the presentation includes a scoring slide explaining the issues.

- Choose Answer All if you need a response for each quiz question, such as feedback on a course module or a survey. The user can't skip questions or move among the quiz slides without responding.

#69 Previewing and Publishing

You've assembled, configured, colored, quizzed, organized, recorded, animated, and, yes, spell checked. Before you publish your masterpiece, take a few minutes and check out the flow of your presentation. Choose Adobe Presenter > Slide Manager to open the Slide Manager dialog (**Figure 69a**).

Figure 69a Make a quick review of the slides and their contents in the Slide Manager.

In the Slide Manager, review features you've set in individual slides in PowerPoint, as well as settings chosen in the Presenter Settings dialog (described in the sidebar "Check Your Info"). You can make individual modifications, or select multiple slides to quickly change properties on a group of slides. When you've finished checking, click OK to close the Slide Manager.

Tip

Rather than opening the Slide Manager from the Adobe Presenter menu, you can click the Slide Manager button in the Publish Presentation dialog, shown in Figure 69b.

Decide how you want to distribute your work. Presenter offers several publishing options, including the following:

- My Computer, to render the project and store it in a location you specify on your hard drive. Choose from either a zip package or a CD package:

  - Use the zip package to compress all the presentation files into a zip file that you can send to a colleague for review. You have

Building Content with Adobe Presenter

to manually locate the files on your hard drive to preview the presentation.

- Use the CD package to produce files you can burn to a CD. The files include an autorun feature, which starts the presentation automatically.

- Adobe Connect Pro, to render the project and store it in a specified server location. You can also select whether to upload the source presentation and its components, such as audio, video, and attachments.

- Adobe PDF, to render the project as a SWF file embedded in a PDF document.

Here's how to publish your presentation as a PDF document:

1. Open your presentation in PowerPoint, and choose Adobe Presenter > Publish to display the Publish Presentation dialog (**Figure 69b**).

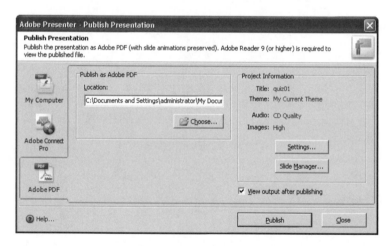

Figure 69b Choose output settings and publish the finished presentation.

2. Click Adobe PDF at the left of the dialog to display the settings.

3. Click Choose to open a browse dialog to select the location where you want to store the publication. Type a name for the file, and click Save to close the dialog and return to the Publish Presentation dialog.

(continued on next page)

Make a Quick Preview

You don't have to wait until you've finished your presentation to check out how it looks. Click View Show 🖥 in the View buttons at the bottom of the PowerPoint program window to run your slide show. To evaluate your presentation within its SWF interface, choose one of the My Computer or Adobe PDF options in the Publish Presentation dialog. Click View output after publishing to automatically open the project in a Web browser (if you choose the My Computer CD package choice) or in Acrobat 9 or Adobe Reader 9 (if you choose the Adobe PDF choice).

4. Select "View output after publishing" to open the PDF file after it is processed.

5. Click Publish. The content is processed, rendered as a SWF, and embedded in a PDF file.

6. View and interact with the finished presentation. The PDF publication requires Adobe Reader 9 or Acrobat 9 to view.

CHAPTER TEN

Commenting in a PDF Document

Acrobat 9 lets you add a wide variety of comments to PDF documents and then share the comments with your workgroup. Unlike manual paper-based commenting, Acrobat's tools include many types of text comment and edit tools; you can attach other documents and sound files to a document, add a comment to a specific frame of an animation or movie, and even integrate your comments directly into their source documents in some programs.

The goal of the techniques in this chapter is to help simplify your workload—with so many tools at your disposal, it's important to understand the reasons why you choose one type of tool over another, and how you can maximize your efficient use of the tools. You also see how to manage comments; review workflows and routing featuring the all-new acrobat.com site is the theme of Chapter 11, "Live Reviewing and Collaboration."

You can access all the commenting types and Comment tools by choosing Comments > Comment & Markup Tools and selecting a tool from the main program menu. Or, take a shortcut—right-click/Control-click the vertical bars at the left of the toolbar to open a shortcut menu. You can choose individual tools, or click Show All Tools to display the full set of tools. Throughout these techniques, I have referred to working from the Comment & Markup toolbar.

You can read about specific types of comments in other chapters. Learn about using a clipboard image as a stamp in #23, "Creating a PDF from a Clipboard Image," or attaching files as comments in #24, "Attaching Source Files to a PDF." Discover how to insert comments into multimedia content (Flash or 3D) in #102, "Inserting Multimedia Comments," and how to use commenting in geospatial maps in #109, "Commenting and Measuring on a PDF Map."

#70 Adding Sticky Notes and Highlighting Comments

Of all the comment tools, you'll probably use the Sticky Note comment most frequently. First select the Sticky Note tool on the Comment & Markup toolbar. Then click the document where you want to place the note, or drag a marquee. A window opens showing an active pointer. Type the text for your note; if you enter more text than fits the size of the pop-up box, the text scrolls. When you have the Properties bar open, you can select text in the note and customize its color, font, and so on directly from the toolbar (**Figure 70a**).

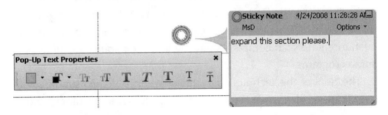

Figure 70a Add sticky notes to the document to point out or describe problems on the page.

To tidy up the page, click the upper-right corner of the pop-up window. You can still read the content of your note; just move the pointer over the note's icon on the page and Acrobat displays its contents in a tooltip. Double-click a note's icon to open the text box. If you want to remove a note, select it on the page and press Delete on your keyboard.

To change a comment's appearance and characteristics, click Options in the note box to open the Note Properties dialog, or right-click (Control-click) to open the shortcut menu and choose Properties. Make changes to the comment, such as the following:

- In the Appearance tab, choose an icon for the note, as well as color and opacity.

- In the General tab, specify a name for the commenting author and a subject.

- In the Review History tab, view information about the comment, such as whether it is a native comment or has been migrated from another file.

The Subject at Hand

It isn't necessary to add a subject for comments, but it's a good practice to develop. For example, you might have two or three people reviewing a document. If they all use the same subject, such as "Mar-Comm," it's easy to figure out what workgroup or department the comments are coming from. The author of a comment and its type make up the Comments list; if you add a subject, it appears below the author's name.

Using the Properties Bar to Modify Comments

To access the Properties bar, right-click (Control-click) in the toolbar well at the top of the program window. The list of toolbars appears; choose Properties Bar.

If you're working with a number of comments using various icons, colors, text, and so on, you may find it easier to use the Properties bar than the comment's Properties dialog to modify comments' properties. Click the note's icon to display the Note Properties dialog; click within the text to display the text options.

Use the three Highlighting tools to underline, highlight, or strike through content. Click the Highlight Text tool 🔏 on the Comment & Markup toolbar. Choose the other two tools from the shortcut menu accessible from the toolbar itself, or choose Comments > Comment & Markup Tools menu, and select the tool.

Drag across the text you want to identify with the tool. As with the Note tool, you can modify the appearance of the Highlighting tools either on the Properties bar or by selecting Properties from the shortcut menu. In addition to identifying content on the page with the tool, right-click (Control-click) on the highlight and choose Open Popup Note to display a note box. Type in your comments. You'll see a small icon at the top left of the highlight area, indicating there's a text note attached to the highlight (**Figure 70b**).

Lock Your Notes

Sometimes you need your comment to stay in place, and don't want to take the risk that another reviewer will go in and change it. Click the Locked option at the lower left of the Note Properties dialog to prevent the comment from being modified or deleted.

discomfort associated with
I have got positive attitude

Highlight	4/24/2008 11:54:20 AM
MsD	Options ▾

Please rewrite: this sounds too clinical. thanks.

Figure 70b Use one of three tools to highlight text in a document for emphasis, and add an explanatory note if you like.

The Same— But Different

The Highlighting tools are used to draw attention to content in your document. There are also three text edit tools that appear to do the same thing. However, the Highlighting tools are used within Acrobat only, unlike their text edit counterparts, which can be exported from the document into a source Microsoft Word or AutoCAD document (Windows). Read about exporting to Word in #78, "Collaborating Live on Acrobat.com."

#71 Setting Commenting Preferences

Once you've been working with comments in Acrobat for a while, you should evaluate how you use them and how you modify them. Ask yourself:

- Do I change the name on the comment box, or the font or text size?
- Am I dragging comments out of the way of other page content and aligning them along the margins?
- Do I find it difficult to keep track of which comment box belongs to which comment?

If you find you make the same modifications repeatedly, it's a good idea to modify the preferences. Begin by choosing Edit > Preferences > Commenting (Acrobat > Preferences > Commenting) to display the Commenting Preferences dialog (**Figure 71**).

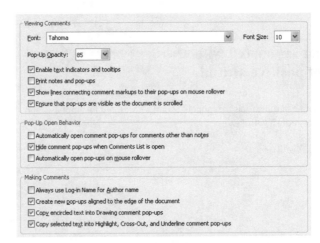

Figure 71 Set commenting preferences according to how you use the tools.

The preferences are set in three categories:

- **Viewing Comments.** Choose options in this section to specify how comments appear in the document. Choose another font in the Font pop-up menu, type a different point size, and choose the opacity percentage for the comment pop-up box. Also in this section of the dialog, you can choose to show connecting lines from the comment box to the comment location, to show text indicators and tooltips, and whether or not to print notes and pop-ups.

- **Pop-Up Open Behavior.** Choose options to define how the comments display in response to actions like mouse rollovers. The default setting for the Pop-up Open Behavior is to hide the pop-up boxes when the Comments List is open. Leave the setting selected if you are working on documents from the Document pane. If you prefer to see the entire pop-up box rather than the tooltip, choose the option "Automatically open pop-ups on mouse rollover." When you usually work with varying types of comments, choose "Automatically open comment pop-ups for comments other than notes."

- **Making Comments.** Choose options to apply to your comment process consistently, such as their alignment on the page or the name displayed at the top of the pop-up box. The first option ("Always use Log-in Name for Author name") is selected by default. If the only name you work with is the login name for your computer, then leave the option selected. If you use another name, or use different names depending on the work or workgroup you are involved with, deselect it. Leave the default option "Create new pop-ups aligned to the edge of the document" if neatness is your passion. Click the final options to copy the content of selected text into comment pop-ups when you circle text using a Drawing tool and for Highlight, Cross-Out, and Underline text comments.

Page After Page

If you select the "Ensure that pop-ups are visible as the document is scrolled" option in the Viewing Comments section of the dialog, the comments are pulled along with you as you move through the document. Some may find it annoying, while others find it extremely useful. Fortunately, Acrobat can accommodate both types of people.

#72 Working with Text Edit Comments

You use the Text Edits tools to edit a PDF document the same way you would with a printed page and a red pencil, but more efficiently. You'll find the tools on the Comment & Markup toolbar. Click the Text Edits arrow to open the pop-up menu listing the tools (**Figure 72a**). If you have selected text on the page, the tools are all active, as shown in the figure. If you haven't selected any text, click the Text Edits tool and drag to select text on the page. Use this option if you need to insert, delete, or replace text.

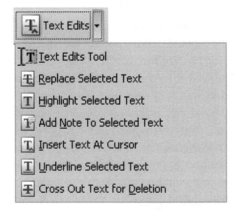

Figure 72a Use the Text Edits tools to mark content for editing just like using a red pencil on a printed page.

Here's how you work with the Text Select tool and keyboard, bypassing the commands in the pop-up menu:

- To insert text, click in the text of the document and type. In the document, you see an insertion caret icon, and the text appears in a pop-up comment box.

- To delete text, select the text to delete using the tool and press Delete or Backspace on your keyboard. The text is crossed out in the document.

- To replace content in the document, select the text and type new text. The replacement text is added to a Replacement Text pop-up comment box, the selected text displays a strikethrough, and an insertion caret is shown at the end of the string of text you selected with the tool (**Figure 72b**).

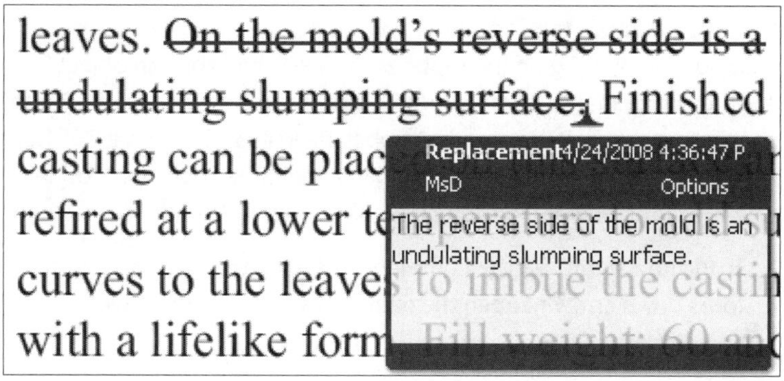

leaves. ~~On the mold's reverse side is a undulating slumping surface.~~ Finished casting can be plac... refired at a lower t... curves to the leave... with a lifelike form...

Replacement 4/24/2008 4:36:47 P
MsD   Options
The reverse side of the mold is an undulating slumping surface.

Figure 72b The insertion caret on the page shows the text edit location. Type the replacement text in the comment box.

If you'd like to use the tools, select text using the Text Edits tool [T] and then choose any of the editing options from the pop-up menu; the tools are described in the sidebar "Care to Make a Comment?"

Which Method Is Best?

You can find some or all of the comment tool options using three or four different methods. For example, if you want to insert text, you can do any of the following:

- Select the Text Edits tool from the Comment & Markup toolbar, click the document with the tool, and then use the keyboard.

- Select the text using the Select tool on the Select & Zoom toolbar, and then choose another tool from the Text Edits pop-up menu.

- Select the text using the Select tool on the Select & Zoom toolbar, and then right-click (Control-click) to open the shortcut menu and choose a tool.

Which is best? It depends on how you like to work. Try them all—you're sure to find a favorite method.

#73 Using and Managing Stamp Tools

Build Up Your Stamp Collection

If you can imagine it, you can use it in a stamp. You can easily add a custom stamp to Acrobat, following these steps:

1. Choose Create Custom Stamp from the Stamp tool pop-up menu. The Select Image for Custom Stamp dialog opens.

2. Click Browse to find the graphic, PDF, or Word file to use for the stamp. The Select dialog opens and displays the chosen file. Click OK and return to the Select Image for Custom Stamp dialog, which shows a preview of the chosen stamp. Click OK; the Create Custom Stamp dialog opens.

3. Click the Category field and type a name for a new stamp category or choose one of the existing categories; then type a name for the stamp. Click OK.

4. To use your new stamp, first open the Stamp tool pop-up menu. The contents of your custom stamp category display thumbnails, just like the program's stamp collections.

The Stamp tools are like the old-fashioned ink stamps you apply to a document (such as Draft, Approved, or Confidential). Unlike ink stamps, some of the Acrobat stamps are dynamic in that they automatically add the time or date when you apply the stamp to the document.

You can even create your own custom stamps. Use the Snapshot tool and the clipboard to capture anything from a PDF page in Acrobat to use as a stamp. Or take advantage of the new feature in Acrobat 9 that lets you use anything on the clipboard as a PDF and copy an object from another program—such as a logo in Illustrator or an image in Photoshop—to create a new stamp in Acrobat. Read #23, "Creating a PDF from a Clipboard Image," and #59, "Reusing Images," to see how that's done.

The Stamp tools are located on the Comment & Markup toolbar.

1. To locate a stamp, on the Comment & Markup toolbar click the Stamp tool's down arrow to open the menu shown in **Figure 73a**.

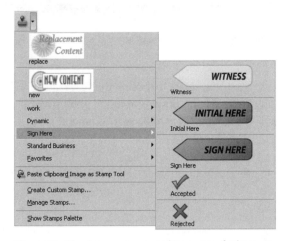

Figure 73a The stamps are arranged in a series of submenus.

2. Click a stamp to select it. The pointer changes to resemble the comment's icon.

3. Click the document where you want to apply the stamp.

An Identity Setup dialog opens when you try to use a stamp for the first time and haven't yet specified an identity as part of a commenting, review, or digital signature setup. Add identity information and click

Complete to close the dialog and apply the stamp. Read about changing information in the sidebar "Who Are You?"

If you move your pointer over the Stamp tool on the Comment & Markup toolbar (not over the down arrow), the last stamp you selected during a session is displayed. Click the Stamp tool and the displayed stamp is active.

The default stamp categories include the following:

- Dynamic stamps display the username, the date, and time the stamp was applied.

- Sign Here stamps are specific formats used for common communications.

- Standard Business stamps are a collection of labels you commonly use to indicate a document's status, such as a confidential or preliminary document, instead of adding note comments or a watermark.

- Favorites can include any stamp from any of the default categories, as well as any custom stamps you like. Keep the favorites together for quick selection.

- Custom is a category holding your own stamps, which you can rename; in **Figure 73b**, the Custom category has been renamed *work*; if you haven't designed any custom stamps, the Custom category isn't listed.

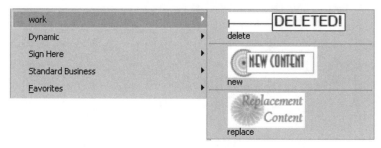

Figure 73b Add categories or change category names as you expand your stamp collection.

5. Click the stamp in the menu to select it, and then click the document page to apply the stamp. Double-click the stamp to add a comment as well.

Who Are You?

The Identity Setup dialog doesn't allow you to change the login name used for stamps or other types of comments. To revise the name, do the following:

1. Choose Edit > Preferences > Commenting (Acrobat > Preferences > Commenting) and deselect the option "Always use Log-in Name for Author name" in the Making Comments section of the dialog. Click OK to close the preferences.

2. Right-click (Control-click) a comment in your document to open the shortcut menu and choose Properties to open the Properties dialog. Select the General tab, type a new name in the Author field, and choose Make Current Properties Default. Click Close to dismiss the dialog.

Get It Together

Use the Stamps palette to keep your stamps straight. Choose Show Stamps Palette in the Stamp tool pop-up menu to display the Stamps dialog.

- Choose a category of stamps to display the collection as thumbnails.

- For the program's stamps, right-click (Control-click) a stamp to open a shortcut menu; make it the current stamp or add it to your favorites.

- For a custom stamp, right-click (Control-click) a stamp to open a shortcut menu and either make it the current stamp or remove it from the favorites list.

Use a Custom Stamp When . . .

Here are some circumstances where it makes sense to take a few minutes to build a custom stamp:

- You write the same comment repeatedly. You may be a department head who needs a date and time stamp as well as a department information stamp. Build a stamp that asks for the information; you can now use a dynamic date/time stamp, and your new custom stamp.

- Your work includes different roles. You may be both a designer and a supervisor. You can build separate stamps defining your role in different situations.

- Your work includes the same role and different moods. Use your imagination and create a suite of expressive stamps. A smiley face can be worth a thousand words—and so can a bolt of lightning.

#74 Drawing and Marking Up Shapes in Acrobat

Say you're one of those people who simply needs to doodle on paper. What happens if someone takes your paper away? Well, just grab a mouse and open a PDF document, because you can draw all sorts of objects, including the aforementioned doodle, using the Drawing tools.

Most of the tools are shown on the Comment & Markup toolbar. The remaining tools, including two Polygon drawing tools and a Pencil Eraser tool, are available from the shortcut menu that opens when you right-click (Control-click) the bars at the left edge of the Comment & Markup toolbar.

Drawing markups are forms of comments. To use a tool, click to select it on the toolbar, and then draw points, click and drag, or scribble with the Pencil or Pencil Eraser tools. For shapes such as a polygon or cloud, click the starting point to close the shape. When you complete the drawing, you can double-click it to open a note and type information about your doodle (**Figure 74a**).

Figure 74a Add information about the doodle in a note.

If you want to show some text in the document in a text box, use the Text Box tool ▤. Find the tool in the toolbox, click it, and then drag a marquee on the page. A yellow text box the size of the marquee is added to the document; click the box and type your message.

Adding Comments to Your Doodles

Need to explain why you deleted a specific paragraph in a document, or just want to leave a note to verify that your changes are correct? Acrobat makes it easy. Once you've added a markup with any of the drawing tools, simply double-click the shape to open a note box, and then type your comment, like the example in Figure 76a.

Circle It

If you are the type of person who uses drawing comments to scribble on a document, there's an option for you. Choose Edit > Preferences > Commenting (Acrobat > Preferences > Commenting) and check the option "Copy encircled text into Drawing comment pop-ups." This way, as you scribble you can add text from the document to the comment's text pop-up without having to select another tool.

A callout is a drawing markup used to pinpoint a specific location on a drawing (**Figure 74b**). Click the document with the Callout tool 📭 and a note box attached to a line with an arrowhead appears. Type your note, and then click anywhere on the page away from the note box. You can drag the box around the page and reposition the arrow's point by dragging as well.

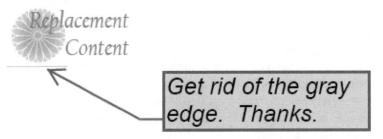

Figure 74b Identify a specific location on the page using a callout.

#75 Working with the Comments List

Each comment added to a document is stored in the Comments List, which is one of the panes displayed in Acrobat 9 by default. Click the Comments icon in the Navigation pane of the program window to open it. Unlike most other panes that open to the left of the Document pane, the Comments List is displayed horizontally below the document (**Figure 75**).

Open comments for page   Choose a filter   Grouped comment

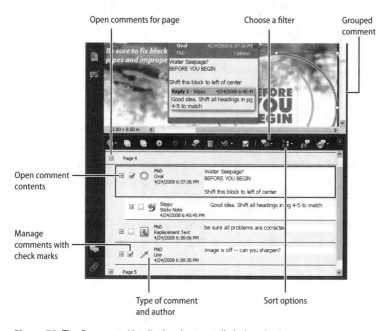

Open comment contents

Manage comments with check marks

Type of comment and author   Sort options

Figure 75 The Comments List displays horizontally below the Document pane.

The plus sign (+) to the left of a page number indicates that the page contains comments. Click a comment in the list. If the comment is located in the portion of the document that is displayed in the Document pane, it is highlighted.

Comments are organized in levels within the Comments List. Here are some tips for viewing comments:

- A multipage document lists comments based on page number. Click a page's plus sign to open the page and display the comments.

(continued on next page)

Get It Together

If you have a large number of comments addressing the same thing, you can collect them together into one grouped comment. When you choose comments to group, only the text for the first comment selected is shown in the Comments List, while the text for the remaining comments is hidden. Select the most important or representative comment first; for example, if Reviewer A adds a comment describing a change that should be made, and then Reviewers B and C agree, select Reviewer A's comment first so that you can see the content of the comment in the Comments List after grouping. To group comments, follow these steps:

1. Click the Hand tool on the Select & Zoom toolbar and click the first comment. Ctrl-click (Control-click) to select the others you want to include in the group. Select the comments from the list or directly on the document page.

2. Right-click (Control-click) the selected comments on the document page,

- The comment type is shown as an icon on the Comments List.

- Click the plus sign to the left of a comment to open its contents. Read details such as the type of comment, author, and date it was applied.

- Clicking plus signs can get tiresome. To quickly open all the pages and all the comments, click Expand All [icon] on the Comments List toolbar. Click Collapse All [icon] on the toolbar to close them again.

- Use the Next arrows on the Comments List toolbar to show the previous or next comments (click the Up and Down arrow buttons respectively).

Working on a long document can involve dozens or even hundreds of comments. That's a lot of information to keep track of. Here are a few suggestions for working with comments:

- Reply to a comment rather than adding one of your own, such as the Skippy and MsD comments in the figure. First, click the comment to select it in the Comments List and then click the Reply button on the toolbar. Type the reply in the text field. Acrobat places the Reply icon before your text.

- Delete comments you don't want to maintain. Click the comment to select it and then click the Delete button on the Comments List toolbar.

- Double-click a comment in the Comments List to open its display in the Document pane, like the Oval comment shown in Figure 75. You see the details of the original comment, as well as any replies that overlay the comment's note box.

The Zen of Comment Organization

You can organize the comments in your document in a number of ways. By default, comments are listed as they appear in the document from start to end. Here are a few tips:

- If you are working on a large document or if you want to check what you have added to a document, sort the comments by selecting them from the Sort By pop-up menu. For example, click Type to reorganize the comments in the Comments List according to the type of comments used in the document. Sorting comments makes it simpler to locate those added by a specific author or a type of comment.

- If you want to see some of the comments, you can filter them. Select a filtering option from the Show pop-up menu, and then specify a type of filter. For example, if you choose Show by Reviewer, a submenu opens listing the reviewers.

- When you apply a filter, the Comments List shows the message "Comments are hidden because a filter is active in the Show menu." The message is a good reminder for you to check whether you have addressed all the comments in the document or whether a certain reviewer has seen and commented on the document.

- In the Comments List, add check marks to identify comments. Check marks are used for any purpose you like, such as making a to-do list, and are not seen by anyone else in the review. Sorting according to the Checkmark Status reduces the list to two categories: Marked and Unmarked. The categories are closed initially; expand a category to reveal its contents.

and choose Group. Don't try to right-click on the Comments List; the shortcut menu doesn't contain the Group command.

3. The comment displays the grouped icon on the Comments List ⌐⊡.

To ungroup the comments, right-click (Control-click) any of the comments in the group and choose Ungroup. Each then becomes a separate item in the Comments List.

Find That Word

Click Search on the Comments List toolbar to open the Search window at the left of the screen. Next, type the search term, specify capitalization and whole words, and click Search Comments. Once Acrobat processes the search, it displays the results in a list in the Search pane. Click a search result to highlight the comment in the Comments List and on the document page.

#76 Exporting Comments to a Word Document (Windows)

Translating Comment Placements

What you see when you integrate comments depends on a few factors. Acrobat uses these concepts to place comments in a revised document:

- Text comments that apply to selected words are displayed within the same words, if they exist in the revised document.

- Stamps, notes, and drawing markups are placed according to the original document's structure (for example, the arrow in the sample document described in this technique).

- If you delete the words or tags where a comment was originally placed, it is placed on either the first or last page of the document.

- If you delete text that originally had text edits, the edits are converted to a note.

- Drawing markups or stamps are placed on the same page as in the original document regardless of position—unless the page is deleted, in which case the comment is placed on the last page of the revised document.

If you're working with a tagged PDF version of a Microsoft Word document generated using the Word PDFMaker, you can have your comments exported directly from the PDF document back into the original document and make the edits automatically.

You can either work from Acrobat and export the comments using the Comment menu's commands, or you can work from Word and import the comments using the commands on the Acrobat Comments menu. Your choice depends on where you are in a particular workflow. If you have finished working with a group of comments, work from within Acrobat; if you have the source document open in Word, work from within Word.

To export comments to a Word document from Acrobat 9:

1. In the Comments List toolbar, click the Options button ⚙ and choose Export Comments to Word. Word opens, and a dialog describes the process.

2. Click OK to close the description dialog and start the import process. The Import Comments from Adobe Acrobat dialog opens. Specify the PDF and Word documents in the dialog, and select the comment import options (read about your choices in the sidebar "Choosing Which Comments to Export").

3. Click Continue. Acrobat processes the comments, adds them to the Word document, and displays the Successful Import dialog (**Figure 76a**). The dialog summarizes the activity and describes how text edits can be integrated. Click Integrate Text Edits to start the process.

4. The Adobe Acrobat Comments dialog opens, displaying the number of comments available for converting. The dialog identifies the first comment in the document and displays the action. Click Apply to make the edit. The text is modified in the Word document (using colored or underlined text if changes are being tracked).

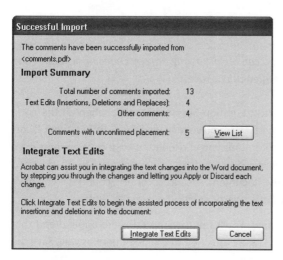

Figure 76a Acrobat tells you when it has finished importing the comments into the document.

5. Click Next in the Adobe Acrobat Comments dialog to continue with the next edit—click "Automatically go to next" to save mouse clicks. Continue until you've viewed and applied all the edits. If you don't want to use the edit, click Discard (**Figure 76b**).

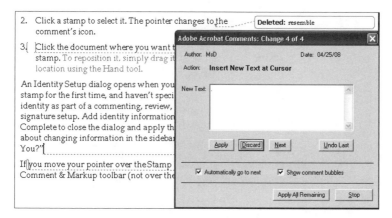

Figure 76b Evaluate each comment and change before applying or rejecting it in the integration process.

(continued on next page)

Choosing Which Comments to Export

You can choose certain groups of comments to export in the Import Comments from Adobe Acrobat dialog. First decide how much you want to edit the Word document, and then choose a type of export accordingly.

- If you have set up a personal commenting system using check marks and want to import only those comments indicated with check marks, you can select the option All Comments with Checkmarks under Select Comment Types to Import.

- If you are editing the document's content using the text edit tools, select the Text Edits only: Insertions, Deletions, and Replaces option. That way, only the comments pertaining to the document's content and structure are transferred.

- Click the Turn Track Changes On Before Importing Comments option if you are involved in an editing or review process.

Note

If you run out of time in the middle of a big job, click Stop. A dialog opens, explaining that you can restart at any time by choosing Acrobat Comments > Continue Integration Process in Word.

6. You'll see the Text Integration Summary dialog when all the comments are processed. After you've reviewed the summary, click Done. Depending on the options you chose in the Import Comments from Adobe Acrobat dialog (described in step 2), you may have instructions for cleaning up the document, such as accepting changes if you have the tracking feature active, or deleting comment bubbles.

7. Check the document. You'll see that the edits are applied and that basic note comments are attached to the document as well. Save the corrected Word document.

Is That Confirmed?

Sometimes the placement of text edit comments can't be confirmed in a source Word document; this occurs when Acrobat can't precisely decipher the structure of the source document's tags. Unconfirmed placements are available in a list in the Successful Import dialog. Click the View List button to see a list of the comments that have unconfirmed placements. In the document you see comments added where Acrobat thinks the comments belong. You can transfer the information from these comments to the document and delete the Word comments.

Birds Migrate, So Why Not Comments?

Suppose you have created a document and then added comments to it. Then suppose you either exported text edits and other comments from Acrobat and integrated them into the source Word document, or revised the source document and then generated a new PDF document. Acrobat 9 lets you add comments to a revised version of a document, as long as the document is tagged (read about tagging a document in Chapter 6, "Complying with PDF and Accessibility Standards").

Open the two documents in Acrobat, and then perform these steps:

1. With the document you want to add comments to active, choose Comments > Migrate Comments to open the Migrate Comments dialog.

2. In the From pop-up menu, choose the file containing the comments. The "Review migrated comments in the Comments List" check box is selected by default; leave this setting.

3. Click OK. The comments are imported into the PDF document and placed in the same locations as those in the document you are exporting from.

The comments may or may not appear in the same location in both documents, depending on the contents of the respective files. For example, a migrated Text Strikethrough comment won't show in a file where the text has been deleted.

Once the comments have been migrated into a document, they are included in the Comments List using the default Migration options.

- Often you develop commenting systems, particularly in large organizations. Acrobat lets you design a custom set of comment-conversion options. Choose Custom Set and then filter the comments you want to export to Word. The filter can be based on the author, status, or check mark.

#**77** Setting Comment Status and Creating Summaries

Once a document has been through a review cycle or two (read about review cycles in Chapter 11), it's time to take care of some last-minute issues. These include defining a status for the comments (both those generated by reviews and migrated comments), creating summaries, and printing comments and comment summaries for reference or archiving.

First select a comment in the Comments List. Then, either right-click (Control-click) a comment in the list or click Set Status on the Comments List toolbar and select Review to display a list of options. You can specify a comment as Accepted, Rejected, Completed, or Cancelled. Unlike the check mark, which is used only on your copy of the document, you can set a status for a comment that can be shared with other reviewers.

When you're collecting feedback from reviewers, or when a project is ending, creating a comment summary is a good idea—that way, all the comments are organized and collated in one handy place for easy reference.

Follow these steps:

1. In the Options pop-up menu on the Comments List toolbar, choose Summarize Comments to open a dialog (**Figure 77a**).

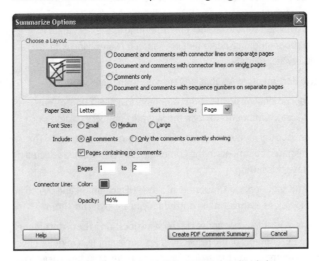

Figure 77a Specify the summary's characteristics in this dialog.

2. Choose layout options (see the sidebar "Choosing a Comment Summary Layout"), paper size, a sort option, which comments to include, and a font size.

3. Click Create PDF Comment Summary to generate the summary.

4. Acrobat opens the summary as a PDF file named Summary of Comments [*filename*] and lists all the comments information sorted according to the option you chose (**Figure 77b**). Save this file for reference.

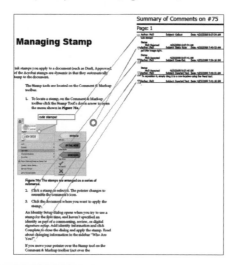

Figure 77b The summary document is created using the settings you selected.

Choosing a Comment Summary Layout

You can generate a summary of comments in one of several ways using the Summarize Options dialog. Choose an option depending on the characteristics of the document and its comments, how you like to work, and what you intend to do with the summary:

- Choosing the "Document and comments with connector lines on separate pages" option is good when you have long comments, although with a printed paper copy you have to follow the lines across pages.

- In a short document or one with short comments, use the "Document and comments with connector lines on single pages" option.

- Use the Comments only option to print just the comments added to a document. If you are the originator of a document and have circulated it to a group for feedback, having a printed list of comments can serve as a to-do list.

- If you have finished a project and want a paper copy for archiving, or want to work on it away from your computer, choose the "Documents and comments with sequence numbers on separate pages" option.

Live Reviewing and Collaboration

Many common workflows rely on communication surrounding a common product, whether that is a product manual, a marketing document, or a chapter in a book such as the one you are reading. One of the strongest features in Acrobat—among a host of strong features—is the ability for a group of users to collaborate and communicate, exchanging ideas and content in a way that can be evaluated and tracked.

The collaboration and review process has developed over the last few versions of Acrobat, from sharing comments and incorporating them into a source document in Acrobat 5, to the revolutionary ability to enable documents for commenting in Acrobat 7 Professional.

Well, it's time for another revolution: Acrobat 9 offers a new way to communicate and manage reviews online. Acrobat.com is a new Adobe service that offers a superb venue for online collaboration in real time—and it's free.

You can work online at Acrobat.com to share a review, and then take the review to a ConnectNow meeting room (for a limited number of participants), or even work on a shared document in Buzzword, Adobe's online word processor. Of course, you'll need tools to start, track, and manage reviews, and Acrobat 9 has enhanced the processes found in earlier versions of the program.

#78 Collaborating Live on Acrobat.com

Manage Acrobat.com Preferences

Modify the program settings to streamline your work with live collaboration. In the Acrobat.com preferences, look for these settings:

- Type your Email Address (Adobe ID) and Password in the fields.

- Click Manage Account to open the Acrobat.com Account Settings area in your browser, and sign in to your account. Here you can change your password, e-mail address, and Meeting URL (for ConnectNow), and set an image. Click OK to accept any changes you've made.

- Click Change Password to modify your login. You first see an information dialog, which explains changing your password at Acrobat.com and informs you that your password in the preferences has now been deleted. Click Yes. In the resulting browser screen, type your login information and follow the prompts to change the password.

(continued on next page)

CHAPTER ELEVEN

The realm of communication and collaboration in Acrobat 9 centers on Acrobat.com, although it is still possible to perform a review the "old way" by e-mail and manual integration of comments.

Acrobat.com is a rich Internet application (RIA) built on Adobe Flash and Adobe AIR. You can access Acrobat.com through your browser, or through program commands using settings you configure in Acrobat 9 and Adobe Reader 9 preferences.

In Acrobat 9 (or Adobe Reader 9), click the Collaborate task button and choose a command (**Figure 78a**).

Figure 78a Choose a collaboration option.

To view the main application interface, go to www.acrobat.com—you'll see a display of the services, accessible through a single login (**Figure 78b**).

Figure 78b Select a service from the Acrobat.com interface.

Live Reviewing and Collaboration

The collaboration and sharing services at Acrobat.com include the following:

Adobe® Buzzword®. Use Buzzword to write and collaborate on documents. The program includes many common word processing features (read more in #83, "Working in Buzzword.")

Adobe® ConnectNow. You can meet with one or two colleagues to use a shared screen for active collaboration (see #82, "Moving to a ConnectNow Meeting Room.")

Create PDF. You can try out the online PDF file converter—read more in the sidebar "Create a PDF File Online."

Share. Use the Share service to store your files, and send your colleagues a link to the file rather than sending or distributing files by e-mail (for more, turn to #79, "Starting a Shared Review.")

My Files. Use the online repository to store and organize up to 5 GB of files (read about using files in #81, "Participating Online.")

To get started through your browser, follow these steps:

1. In your browser, open the site at www.acrobat.com. You'll see a set of five visual links on the page that access the different Acrobat.com features (shown in Figure 78b).

2. Click any of the links to display a dialog identifying the service; click Begin to replace the information dialog with a login screen.

3. Type your e-mail address and password—speed up future logins by selecting the Remember me check box.

- To save time logging in to your Acrobat.com account, select the "Always connect when opening documents enabled for live collaboration" check box.

- If you are working in Acrobat (not Adobe Reader), select the "Copy me when I send an e-mail invitation using Acrobat.com" check box to keep track of your online activities.

Create a PDF File Online

The Acrobat.com service includes five free PDF file conversions. Beyond that number, you can subscribe to the Create Adobe PDF Online service (or convert files yourself in Acrobat).

A file can be up to 200 MB in size. The service can convert multiple file types to PDF, including the following:

- Text as TXT, PS, or RTF

- Image files in BMP, GIF, JPEG, TIFF, and PNG formats

- Microsoft Office files in DOC, XLS, PPT, and PRJ formats

- Open Office files in ODT, ODP, ODS, ODG, and ODF formats

- Star Office files in SWX, SXI, SXC, SXD, and STW formats

- WordPerfect WPD files

If you don't have an Adobe ID, click Sign Up! and follow the prompts.

From Acrobat or Adobe Reader, you can set Acrobat.com access controls in the program preferences. Choose Edit > Preferences (Acrobat/Adobe Reader > Preferences) and choose Acrobat.com from the list to display the settings (**Figure 78c**). Using the preferences, you can manage your Acrobat.com account, as well as specify how to manage invitations and files enabled for live online collaboration. (Read more in the sidebar "Manage Acrobat.com Preferences.")

Figure 78c Specify your settings for Acrobat.com in the program preferences.

#79 Starting a Shared Review

In Acrobat 8, the shared review process was simplified by allowing the initiator to set up a folder on a network without needing IT input. With Acrobat 9 and Acrobat.com, the process is even simpler.

Initiating a shared document review is similar to the process used for distributing a form. However, while Adobe Reader 7 or 8 can be used for a form, only Acrobat or Adobe Reader 9 users can participate in a shared review using Acrobat.com.

Follow these steps to send the review:

1. Click the Comment task button and choose Send for Shared Review to open the Send for Shared Review wizard.

2. Step through the wizard:

   • On the first screen, click Browse to open a dialog to locate and select the file for sharing. Click Next.

   • On the next screen, click the "How do you want to collect comments from your reviewers?" pop-up menu and choose whether to use Acrobat.com or your own server. The default choice is "Automatically download & track comments with Acrobat.com" (**Figure 79a**). Click Next.

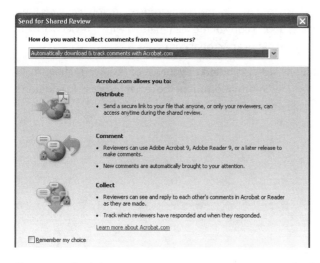

Figure 79a Read about your comment management options in this dialog.

(continued on next page)

Checking for Comments

If you are using one or more shared reviews, specify some preferences to keep track of the process. Choose Edit > Preferences (Acrobat > Preferences), and choose Tracker from the category list at the left of the Preferences dialog. Shared Review and Form Data Collection share settings:

• Check for new comments and form data at a specified time frame, ranging from every hour to never.

• Specify a time to suspend the checks for comments and form data, ranging from 1 month to never.

• Select the notifications you want to see—in the system tray, inside Acrobat, or both. By the way, the notification options are shown on the Tracker window as well.

Choose any of the time intervals by dragging the sliders. Click OK to close the Preferences dialog.

It's a Date!

Don't worry too much if you aren't sure when you need to end a review. The default inserted by Acrobat into your e-mail invitation is for two weeks. You can change the date in the invitation (as described in step 3 of this how-to), or even delete the end date altogether. Once the file is distributed, if you want to change the date, simply click the Review Deadline link on the Tracker to change or delete the date.

Enabling Files

Before you start, enable the file for commenting if your recipients are using Adobe Reader 7 or 8. Open your review file and choose Advanced > Extend Features in Adobe Reader. Click Save Now in the resulting dialog to save and store an enabled copy of the file. Enabling is limited to 500 copies of the document.

When you enable a file by extending features for Reader users, these features are included:

- Saving form data from a fill-in PDF form

(continued on next page)

- On the next screen, type or review the Acrobat.com login information and click Sign In.

3. Once Acrobat.com loads, an e-mail window opens for you to specify the details of the shared review, where you can do the following:

   - Type the e-mail addresses of your reviewers in the To field, and add CC addresses if you like.

   - Review the default Subject and Message text, which you can modify as desired.

   - Click the Access Level pop-up arrow to display your choices. You can allow access to anyone, or restrict access to those you invite to the review.

   - Click the Review Deadline link to open the Change Review Deadline dialog, where you can specify a new deadline date or choose no deadline; click OK to close the dialog and make the change.

   - Select the "Allow page view sharing and chat collaboration in this document" check box to enable users to work with the file online (read about online collaboration in #81, "Participating Online").

4. Click Finish to complete the review process. Acrobat creates the review, as well as adds a copy of the file renamed with "_review" appended to the original name at Acrobat.com.

5. Invitations are distributed to your list of reviewers. The e-mail invitation includes information about the review process, in addition to links to the file online (**Figure 79b**).

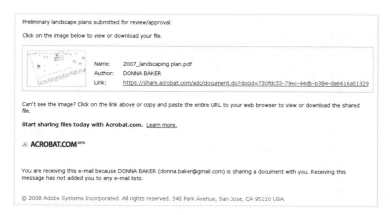

Figure 79b Reviewers are invited by e-mail.

Note

When you use Acrobat.com for shared reviews, you can also allow reviewers to open and share the PDF in a live chat session. Read how that's done in #81.

- Using commenting and drawing markups
- Signing an existing signature field
- Digitally signing anywhere on a document (for Adobe Reader 8 or 9 users only)

Taking Shared Reviews Online

A shared review can be used online in addition to working through Acrobat or Adobe Reader. Comments are synced with the server even when Acrobat is closed, so anyone in a review who logs in can access up-to-date comments.

When you open a shared review, the Welcome Back screen provides updates since the last time you viewed the file, such as the number of new reviewers and comments.

#80 Using an E-mail Review

Sometimes an e-mail review is simpler when you are sending a document for a single person to review, or when it isn't important to share comments among reviewers. An e-mail review cycle has three parts: The review is initiated, the recipient adds comments and returns the comments by e-mail, and finally, the initiator integrates the comments into the master PDF file.

Follow these steps to set up an e-mail review from within Acrobat:

1. Choose Comments > Attach for E-mail Review to open the Send by E-mail for Review wizard. Or choose the command from the Comment task button's menu.

   ### Note
   Alternatively, in any program containing a PDFMaker (Windows) you can choose Adobe PDF > Convert to Adobe PDF and Send for Review, or click the button on the PDFMaker's toolbar.

2. Step through the wizard's screens:

   - On the first screen, choose an open document or click Browse and locate the document you want to send. Click Next.

   - On the next screen, click the Address list and type addresses, or click Address Book to open your Outlook address book and select e-mail addresses (if Outlook is your e-mail program). Click Next.

   - On the third screen, preview the contents of the invitation and then click Send Invitation.

3. An Outgoing Message Notification information dialog opens, explaining what happens next. Depending on your security settings, the e-mail may be sent automatically, or you may need to move through dialogs approving the mail process. Click OK to dismiss the dialog.

   Participants using Acrobat 6 or newer, or Adobe Reader 7 or newer, can review the file. Once the file arrives in the inbox, open the e-mail message and double-click the e-mail attachment to open it in Acrobat or Adobe Reader.

   Make comments as desired, and click Send Comments 🖼 on the Comment & Markup toolbar when you finish. A dialog opens explaining that the comments are being sent back to the initiator, and shows the e-mail address specified by the originator of the review. You can type a different e-mail address or choose one from the Outlook Address Book, just as you can when designing the review. Click Send to close the dialog and send the comments back to the initiator.

Keep Your Sources Safe

It's a good idea to save a copy of the document prior to incorporating reviewers' comments. Edit the document using the copy to preserve the layout and structure. This way, imported comments are in the correct locations on the document. If you want to distribute the document and its comments, choose File > Save As and save with another name. The newly named file is now the tracked PDF file, and the older version, complete with its comments, becomes an archived copy.

Once the comments return to you (the initiator), they are integrated into the PDF. When you double-click the e-mail attachment to open the document in Acrobat, the Merge Comments? dialog displays. You can choose to open the copy of the document, or merge the comments into the tracked PDF file (**Figure 80a**). Click Yes to incorporate the comments and close the dialog.

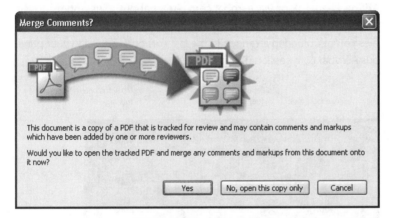

Figure 80a The dialog asks how you want to handle the comments.

You can then review the contents of the Comments List and finish the document's processing (**Figure 80b**). Read about using comment features and tools in Chapter 10, "Commenting in a PDF Document."

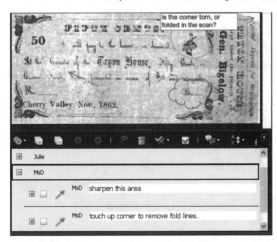

Figure 80b The comments from several e-mail reviewers are incorporated in the master PDF document.

When the Mail Doesn't Work

The Send by E-mail for Review dialog uses a specific filter on the e-mail name you enter. If your e-mail address doesn't use a three-letter suffix—for example, .com, .net, and so on—you may receive an error. Instead, in the Identity pane of the Preferences dialog, type your e-mail address in the e-mail address field, and then click OK.

#81 Participating Online

Going Live Online

Instead of starting a review in Acrobat, share a document directly from MyFiles in Acrobat.com. Although you don't have a wizard on Acrobat.com, the process is similar, with these exceptions:

- To start, click Share on one of the application screens to show the Share fields. By default, the Share fields are added to the MyFiles window, above the file list.

- To identify files for sharing, drag a file from the MyFiles area on the window to the "Choose files to share" list. Click Browse, locate and select a file from your computer, and click Upload to add additional files for sharing. The file is added to the share list and included in the MyFiles listing.

- Click Share With to open a list of e-mail addresses; the list includes only those addresses you've used in Acrobat.com.

Check out #79, "Starting a Shared Review," for more information.

Use the MyFiles feature at Acrobat.com as an online repository to store your files. Depending on workflow, you may want to store files for distributing to others for review or for collaborating in ConnectNow. Or you may want to store files so that you can access them from your laptop during your vacation at the lake.

Open MyFiles online using one of several commands in Acrobat 9, Adobe Reader 9, or via Acrobat.com—read about your options in the sidebar "Finding Your Files." Once the application launches, you see the files you've uploaded arranged in the last sort option used in your previous Acrobat.com session (**Figure 81a**).

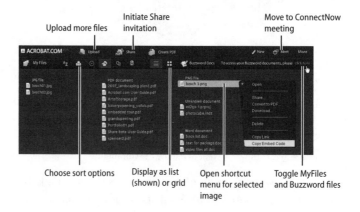

Figure 81a View, organize, and manage your online document collection.

Start a real-time collaboration on a document from your desktop or online (read how to work from Acrobat.com in the sidebar "Going Live Online"). To initiate a session from Acrobat Pro or Acrobat Pro Extended, follow these steps:

1. Choose Send & Collaborate Live from the Collaborate task button's menu—read about working from Acrobat or Adobe Reader in #79, "Starting a Shared Review."

2. Follow the prompts to choose a list of recipients, log in to Acrobat.com, and fill in the e-mail invitation. Your file is enabled for collaboration, saved with _collab appended to the name, and uploaded to Acrobat.com. An invitation is sent to your recipient list.

3. Once your colleagues receive their e-mail and download it, when they open the file in Acrobat or Adobe Reader 9, the document is displayed

along with the Collaborate Live navigation pane on their desktop. The user can sign in as a guest or use the Adobe ID.

4. Back with you, in Acrobat, you'll see the list of Current Viewers and the Document Chat pod shown in the Collaborate Live navigation pane along with the document for discussion (**Figure 81b**).

Figure 81b Collaborate in real time from a document on your desktop.

Tip

The Current Viewers and Document Chat are self-explanatory. Click Start Page Sharing to automatically display the same page and view as you are seeing on your current viewers' computer screens as well; click Stop Page Sharing when you've finished.

Here are the rules for real-time collaboration:

- Users can see a list of participants, and chat with others in the document window.

- Document actions and features, including the mouse pointer, screen view, zoom, layers, and 3D views, can be synchronized.

- Changes are instantly transmitted to the other participants' views.

Finding Your Files

Like all Acrobat.com features, MyFiles can be accessed in several ways. Most of the commands on the Acrobat 9 or Adobe Reader 9 Collaborate task button's menu launch MyFiles as either a full-screen application or one associated with another interface. For example, Send & Collaborate Live shows the MyFiles feature at the bottom of the screen.

Once online, you can toggle between your general Acrobat.com files and Buzzword Docs files (see the toolbar shown in Figure 81a).

Share Files Further

You can use your files stored on Acrobat.com in other online material, such as Web pages. In MyFiles, click a file in the list and then click the arrow to display the pop-up menu:

- Choose Embed Code to copy the code to the clipboard; you can use this to embed the code in a Web page.

- Choose Copy Link to save the file's link to the clipboard. Paste the link into an e-mail, Web page, or chat message to share the file.

- To launch a screen sharing session from within your review document, choose Share My Screen from the Collaborate Live navigation pane's Options menu (read more in #82, "Moving to a ConnectNow Meeting Room").

System Requirements

Your computer has to meet minimal requirements to use Acrobat.com. Depending on your operating system, you need the following:

- Microsoft Windows Vista and XP requires the Internet Explorer 7, Internet Explorer 6.*x*, or Firefox 2.*x* browser, and Flash Player version 9.0.47 or later.

- Mac OS X v10.5 requires the Safari 3.*x* or Firefox 2.*x* browser, and Flash Player version 9.0.47 or later (9.0.115 on Mac OS X v10.5).

- Mac OS X v10.4 requires the Safari 3.*x*, Safari 2.*x*, or Firefox 2.*x* browser, and Flash Player version 9.0.47 or later.

#82 Moving to a ConnectNow Meeting Room

One of the coolest features of Acrobat.com is Adobe ConnectNow, which lets you set up real-time meetings on your desktop using a personal Web conference meeting room. Your personal meeting room has a permanent URL that is easy to remember, so you'll always know where to meet online.

In an online meeting, you communicate with one or two colleagues using live chat, share online whiteboards, and use different audio/video sharing (read your options in the sidebar "Talk Out Loud"). ConnectNow also lets you share your desktop and take remote control access of a participant's desktop.

Follow these steps to start a meeting:

1. Open Adobe ConnectNow by doing the following:

   - Typing your unique meeting room URL into a browser window.

   - Or, in Acrobat, choose Share My Screen from the Collaborate task button's menu. If you are in a real-time collaboration session, choose Share My Screen from the Collaborate Live navigation pane's Options menu.

   Tip
   ConnectNow launches in its own application window—once it is running, you can close the original browser window.

2. When ConnectNow opens, select Invite Others to send e-mail messages and invite participants. If you are collaborating in real time, your collaborators are shown an invitation message and simply have to click View Screen to join the meeting.

3. Attendees join the meeting by logging in to your meeting space from their computers. When a viewer request pop-up appears in the window, click Accept to include the participant in the session.

   The ConnectNow meeting room is made up of several components (**Figure 82a**).

   Note
   If you are the host for the meeting and you are sharing your screen, you can access all the features; however, your participants can't reset the pods layout, for example, or invite another guest.

What to Tell Your Guests

Your guests may not be as computer-savvy or ConnectNow-literate as you are. Give them some information about the service to set their minds at ease:

- A guest doesn't need an account at Acrobat.com but can simply remain a guest.

- Guests don't have to download any software. The ConnectNow application runs via Flash Player, which they will need to have installed in their browser. The only software that might be required is the Connect-Now plug-in if they want to participate in screen sharing.

- Guests don't have to make any changes to their firewalls to participate, as ConnectNow communicates through standard HTTP and Secure Socket Layer (SSL) ports.

Talk Out Loud

ConnectNow offers different audio features: Some are free, while others may include long-distance charges. Here are your choices from the Adobe ConnectNow toolbar:

- Click the Phone icon ☎ and choose Adobe Conference Number to display a text box showing call-in numbers and the meeting ID number. The service is free, but long-distance phone charges apply.

- Click the Microphone icon 🎤 to activate your system's microphone to speak with other meeting attendees using Voice over Internet Protocol (VoIP).

- Click the Webcam icon 📷 to activate your Webcam and use it with sound to add video along with the audio.

Organize and arrange pods as desired   Participants can access and configure tools   Chat in real time

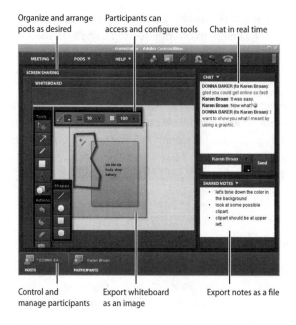

Control and manage participants   Export whiteboard as an image   Export notes as a file

Figure 82a Conduct real-time interactive meetings in your private meeting room.

Look for these features and tools:

- The interaction areas are called *pods*, and are accessible from the Pods pop-up menu. In addition to the ones shown in the figure, you can also open Files and Webcam pods.

- Select administrative commands, such as setting meeting preferences or testing your microphone from the Meeting pop-up menu.

- Find troubleshooting, Adobe Flash, and account settings in the Help pop-up menu—along with Adobe ConnectNow Help, of course.

- Use the tools at the upper right of the window to administer your meeting. For example, click Invite Participants 👤 to add another member to your session; click Share My Computer Screen 🖥 to invoke screen sharing for your group; or click Upload a File 📎 to locate and share a file from your computer.

- Use and manage audio and visual features by selecting the commands on the Adobe ConnectNow toolbar (read more in the sidebar "Talk Out Loud").

- Conduct a live chat with one or both of your participants using the Chat pod.

- Type notes for your meeting that can be saved as a DOC file.

- Use simple drawing tools on the Whiteboard pod. Add shapes, customize their appearance, or add text. You can save the Whiteboard as a PNG file.

Along with the interactive elements listed, ConnectNow lets one participant take control of another participant's desktop. Using remote control to show a specific process or instruction means you don't have to spend time explaining an environment—you are right there.

To assign remote control, click the name of a participant to show the pop-up menu, and choose "Ask this user to share their screen" (**Figure 82b**). Alternatively, you can choose Share My Computer Screen from the Meeting pop-up menu, and the screen is shared by a selected participant.

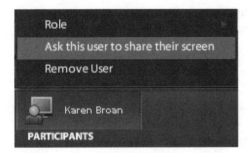

Figure 82b Select a participant for screen sharing.

To return to the regular meeting interface, click the X at the upper right of the Screen Sharing pod.

#**83** Working in Buzzword

Buzzword is the online Acrobat.com document processing application. In addition to writing documents, you can also use commenting tools right in the program, and share the file from the Buzzword interface. Editing, commenting, and revising can be done as a team. Buzzword stores your files and runs from Adobe secure servers, so they are always available on the Web.

Open Buzzword from the Acrobat.com interface or from Acrobat by choosing Create Buzzword Document from the Collaborate task button menu. Once in Buzzword, you can invite others to collaborate on the document using the Share feature at the bottom left of the application window. Invitees can be placed in one of several categories, according to the privileges granted to them—read about the different options in the sidebar "Who's Who?"

Once the application launches, you can do the following:

- Click New ✏️ at the upper right of the browser window to start a new file.

- Click Docs 📄 at the upper right of the browser window to display the Document Organizer, described in #81, "Participating Online," and select a file to work with.

- To import a file from your computer, choose Document > Import from the Buzzword menu, locate and select a file on your computer, and click Open.

Whether you start from scratch or import a document, you work in Buzzword just as you might any desktop application. You may notice that the interface works a bit differently from what you usually see on your desktop. Since Buzzword is written on Flash, most menu items slide in and out of view (read more in the sidebar "Get the Buzz").

You access the panels and menus from the main Buzzword interface (**Figure 83**).

Who's Who?

Buzzword offers four ways for you to interact with documents:

- The Author is the creator and owner of the file, and can delete a file from Buzzword. The Author can write, edit, and add to comments made by other participants. An Author can invite collaborators, change their roles, and remove them from the file.

- A Co-author has the same rights as the Author, except for deleting a document.

- A Reviewer can add comments to a document, but can't add to other comments or share the document.

- A Reader has access to reading the file only, but can't comment or share the file.

You don't have to stay at a particular status. If you save a copy of a file with another name, for example, you become the Author. Although the new copy will include any comments that were added, you have to add collaborators yourself as the list of collaborators from the original isn't transferred to your copy.

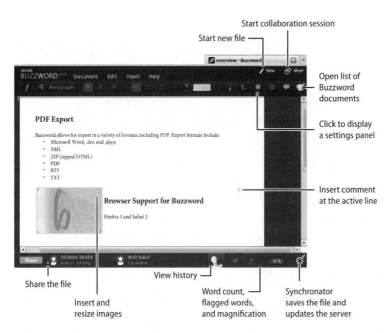

Start collaboration session

Start new file

Open list of Buzzword documents

Click to display a settings panel

Insert comment at the active line

Share the file

Insert and resize images

View history

Word count, flagged words, and magnification

Synchronator saves the file and updates the server

Figure 83 Use the features in the Buzzword application to write, configure, and share a document online.

The application menu contains the sorts of commands you'd expect, such as the following:

- **Document.** Click the Document menu to display commands for managing documents. You'll also find commands for page setup and printing, and for sharing.

- **Edit.** On the Edit menu look for common edit commands, including Check Spelling, which identifies potentially misspelled words with a jagged underline.

- **Insert.** You can insert a range of features into a Buzzword document, such as tables or images, headers and footers, page or line breaks, and even special characters and a limited number of fields.

- **Help.** Use commands in the Help menu to view Help files, and link to Buzzword support sites.

Get the Buzz

Some of the Flash-enabled features added to Buzzword make it simpler for you to work in the interface without having to choose menu items, as you are likely to do when working in an ordinary application. Here are a few:

- Visual guides appear over items on the page when you select different objects. For example, if you drag a column on a table, controls show the amount of the indent; if you add an image, controls for resizing display and show dimensions as you change the image size.

- Activating different items on a page displays arrow buttons. Click an arrow to open a context menu for that item. For example, if you click a column in a table, click the arrow button to show commands to cut/copy/paste the column, or insert more columns.

- A faint comment icon moves along with your pointer on the right side of the page. Click the icon to open a comment box, which is associated with the content on that line of your document.

Tip
Click the Adobe Buzzword logo to open another menu, where you can read about the program and user policies, sign out of Buzzword, or choose Settings & Preferences to open a dialog. Here you'll find the Adobe ID account information, as well as Buzzword preferences that let you specify the unit of measure displayed in the application—inches is the default. You can also choose whether to flag spelling errors, and can construct a word list.

A list of the settings panels and their options are listed in **Table 11.1.**

Table 11.1 Buzzword Options Panels and Settings

Panel Name	Icon	Look for These Settings
Font	*f*	Choose a font name, size, style, and color.
Paragraph	¶	Choose alignment, spacing, and indent.
List	1.	Choose type of list, the icon, the outline level, and commands to skip inserted content between list items.
Image	✳	Select an image to place, then choose a text wrap option and off-set value.
Table	▦	Insert table and configure rows/columns, gridline color, and background color.
Comment	💬	Add a new comment or show existing comments.

#84 Comparing Documents

The Compare feature in Acrobat 9 has come a long way from its earlier versions. In Acrobat 9, differences between two versions of a document are highlighted and commented.

Compare shows differences in text and images based on three different document structures programmed into the feature. To do a comparison, follow these steps:

1. Choose Document > Compare Documents to open the Compare Documents dialog.

2. Click Choose for each of the Compare (older document) and To (newer document) fields, and locate and select the files you want to use. Click the Document pop-up menu to choose any open files for either document option.

3. For both documents, type a page number in the First page and Last page fields to change the comparisons if necessary. The fields list the page numbers for the first and last pages of the documents automatically.

4. Select a Document Description option (read about the options in the sidebar "Matching Descriptions").

5. Click OK to close the dialog and compare the files.

Acrobat processes the files and generates the changes. The contents are displayed in the Compare navigation pane, new in Acrobat 9 (**Figure 84a**).

Matching Descriptions

You choose one of three options when setting up a document comparison process. The choices are based on general types of features found in the named document types. For example:

- **Reports, spreadsheets, magazine layouts.** In these sorts of documents, text usually flows from one page to another, so the feature looks for moves between pages.

- **Presentation decks, drawings, or illustrations.** Each page is treated like a separate document, and Compare looks for changes in order, as you'd often find in a set of PowerPoint slides.

- **Scanned documents.** Acrobat creates temporary images from each document that are then compared as images.

Sure, but Comparing Isn't Reviewing

Isn't it? If you compare two documents, although you aren't inserting comments and markups manually, Acrobat is adding them for you. Once a comparison has been made, use the results page, or a copy of the compared document with comments inserted, and send it for further review with your workgroup.

Figure 84a Manage the views and displays of the compared documents in the Compare pane.

There are several tasks you can take on in the Compare feature:

- Another page is added before the document pages that lists the names of the files, whether differences were found, and a key to the report. You can click links on the Summary page to view either the newer or older document, as well as show the first change in the report.

- Click a page thumbnail to show that page in the Document pane (**Figure 84b**).

- Choose Show Color Legend to display the colors used for different types of comparisons as an overlay in the Document pane.

- To show each of the documents in its own window, choose Show Documents Tiled or Show Documents Side By Side from the Options menu.

- To synchronize the pages while showing both documents in their own windows, choose Synchronize Pages from the Options menu.

- To change the size of the page thumbnails, from the Options menu choose Thumbnail Size > [*option*].

- Drag the splitter bar at the bottom of the Compare pane up to show thumbnails of the old document's pages. Click a thumbnail to open the page in a new window.

Click to toggle settings for color and evaluated items

Click to display in the Document pane

Add your own comments

Identifies types of changes by color

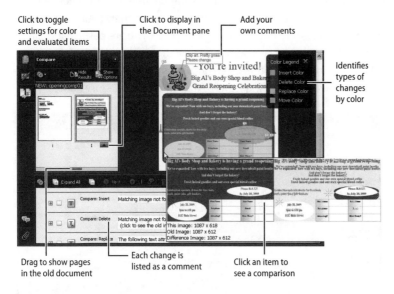

Drag to show pages in the old document

Each change is listed as a comment

Click an item to see a comparison

Figure 84b Evaluate and examine changes in the compared files.

Save the file for future reference.

Apples and Oranges

The new Compare tools in Acrobat 9 offer a lot of customization. If you want to personalize the layout, here are some things to try:

Click Show Options in the Compare pane to toggle the choices. In the options, you can do the following:

- Specify what types of changes to show, such as text, images, formatting, and backgrounds.

- Pick a color scheme to use for displaying the report.

- Drag an Opacity slider to set how transparent/opaque the overlying comments are displayed.

Once you've made your choices, click Hide Options to toggle the options closed. Your choices can be viewed in the Compare pane's Options menu.

#85 Tracking a Review

Initiating and tracking multiple reviews, participating in others, and trying to keep it all straight isn't simple. Fortunately, Acrobat offers the Tracker to help you keep tabs on the process.

In Adobe Reader 9, choose View > Tracker. In Acrobat 9, choose Track Reviews from the Comment task button pop-up menu. All your current reviews—those you have initiated and others you are participating in—along with any servers you are working with—are listed in the left column of the window (**Figure 85**). Open or collapse categories in the Tracker by clicking the corresponding icons to the left of the category name.

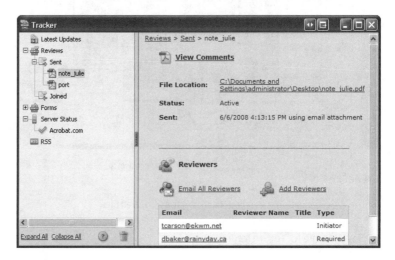

Figure 85 Use the Tracker to keep up with your ongoing reviews.

The range of activities and checks you can perform in the Tracker include the following:

Updates. Click Latest Updates to display information about your reviews. You can also access links for managing and creating more reviews. If the name of a review is shown in bold in the left pane, the review has been updated in some way—new reviewers or comments were added, or the deadline has been updated. If you like, turn on notifications that display icons and pop-ups when an update occurs.

Note
Read about setting update times and preferences in the sidebar "Checking for Comments" in #79, "Starting a Shared Review," earlier in this chapter.

Sort It Out

Suppose you are involved in one large project with one group, and another project with another group. In the course of your usual workday, you participate in a couple of reviews for each project. Each review adds another line to the list in the left pane of the Tracker. To stay organized, follow these steps:

1. Right-click (Control-click) the Sent or Joined labels in the Reviews section of the Tracker and choose Create New Folder. In the dialog that opens, name the folder and click OK.

2. Right-click (Control-click) a review's name to open the shortcut menu, choose Send To Folder, and select the new folder you added. The review is added to the folder.

3. Repeat as necessary until your Tracker structure is simplified and organized.

Viewing a Review's Details. Click the name of a review in the left pane to show the review's details, including a list of participants and the date and time the review was started. From the review's details view, click View Comments to open the tracked file in Acrobat. Click the File Location link in the right pane to open the document in either Acrobat or Adobe Reader 9, depending on which program you are working in. Read how to convert the contents of the Tracker dialog into a PDF in the sidebar "Keeping Track of What You're Tracking."

Communications. Select a review from the list in the left pane, and click Email All Reviewers or Add Reviewers to open the appropriate dialogs.

Note

The Tracker in Adobe Reader can only view incoming reviews; you can't initiate a new review, e-mail the reviewers, add more reviewers, or send a review reminder.

Servers. You can check on the servers you are using for reviewing. Unless you have set up an internal server system, you'll see Acrobat.com listed as the only server. Click the server's name in the left pane to show the details in the right pane, including the names of files served from that location, and the status of the workflow. If you see a green check mark, the server is functioning properly.

Ending a Review. When a review is initiated, you can specify an end date (described in #79, "Starting a Shared Review"). Click the date listed in the review's details in the Tracker and select a different end date, or delete the deadline date. Once a review has ended, the commenting tools are disabled, and your reviewers can't make any more comments on the review document.

Cleanup. You can use folders to sort out the reviews you are involved in, described in the sidebar "Sort It Out." If you are the initiator of a review, select its name in the listing and delete (click 🗑) to remove a review from the Tracker listings. You don't delete the file itself from your hard drive, but you do remove the review files and comments from the Acrobat.com server.

RSS Subscriptions. Add, organize, and view RSS subscriptions. Read more in the sidebar "RSS, Anyone?"

Keeping Track of What You're Tracking

A large review, say one with dozens of participants, can be tiresome to scroll through, even using the slick Tracker interface. To keep a snapshot of a review, right-click (Control-click) the review's name in the left pane of the Tracker, and choose Create PDF From Tracker Details from the shortcut menu. All the content that you review in the right pane of the Tracker is converted to PDF.

RSS, Anyone?

In earlier versions of Acrobat, Web broadcast subscriptions, or RSS (Really Simple Syndication) feeds, were shown in the Tracker. You won't find them in the Acrobat 9 Tracker, but they aren't gone.

Choose Edit > Preferences (Acrobat > Preferences), and choose Tracker from the category list at the left of the Preferences dialog. Select the "Enable RSS feeds in Tracker" check box and click OK to close the Preferences dialog. In the Tracker, you can subscribe/unsubscribe, manage, and read your RSS feeds.

CHAPTER TWELVE

Creating and Handling Forms

Acrobat 9 (both Standard and Pro) offers a new way of working with forms. Acrobat 8 introduced an interface for creating form fields that switched from a design to an active view for constructing and testing a form. In Acrobat 9, the interface is even more streamlined.

As part of a modified approach to form design, Acrobat 9 offers a Form Edit mode that opens in a separate window where you build, preview, and distribute Acroforms. For both Windows and Mac, you can construct forms using the Acroforms forms tools.

You have the same flexibility in designing forms in Acrobat as you do in creating and designing PDF documents of other types. You can design a form in a number of ways and in different programs. And, as with other PDF documents, you can take advantage of both Acrobat.com for file distribution, and PDF Portfolio for collecting form returns.

If you are working with Windows, you have access to the Adobe LiveCycle Designer program, a separate forms design program integrated into Acrobat 9 Pro.

#86 Letting the Form Wizard Guide You

Simplify Your Form Building, Simplify Your Life

Consider these ideas as you build a form:

- Make sure the design of the document can accommodate the size of the fields you intend to use.

- Set options that are common to all fields, such as the font and appearance, when you build the first field.

- Develop a system for adding and naming extra fields.

- When you want to change one property of several fields, such as the alignment, don't change each field individually. Shift-click to select the fields and then open the Properties dialog using the shortcut menu. When you change the alignment, the change is applied to all the selected fields.

- JavaScript is written for each field separately; calculations aren't allowed for a number of selected fields.

Acrobat 9 Standard and Pro offer a form wizard to get your form-building adventure under way. The wizard walks you through several form creation options, such as using existing documents or scanned content. You can start from either the Forms task button or program menu commands.

There are several ways to start the form—in the example, I'm using a fax cover form created from an InDesign file.

Follow these steps to build the form:

1. In Acrobat 9 Standard or Pro, choose Forms > Start Form Wizard to open the Create or Edit Form dialog.

2. Choose one of three options (Windows), including "An existing electronic document" (as in the example), "A paper form to be scanned," or "No existing form," using either a blank page or a template to start from scratch. On the Mac, you have two choices, including "Start with a PDF document" or "A paper form." Click Next.

Note
If you choose the "No existing form" option (available only in Windows), LiveCycle Designer launches and displays the New Form Assistant.

3. Specify the document to use for the form. Choose "Use the current document" if you already have your source file open in Acrobat, or choose "Import a file from file system" and click Browse (Find) to locate and select the file for the form. Click Next.

4. The document is processed, and fields automatically appear on the page using the artificial intelligence feature in Acrobat.

5. An information dialog opens explaining that you are in Form Edit mode and that fields are added to the form (**Figure 86a**). You also see an example of a field and its components. Once you've read the dialog, click "Don't show again" to save a mouse click in the future. Click OK to close the dialog.

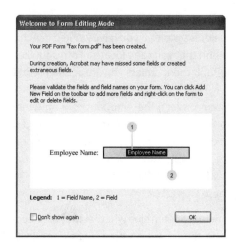

Figure 86a The information dialog explains how the automatic process works, and shows a key to the added fields.

Acroforms vs. LiveCycle Designer Forms

The Acroforms tools and methods are available directly from within Acrobat Standard and Pro versions. LiveCycle Designer forms are available as a separate program accessible via the Forms > Create or Edit Form dialog when you choose the "No existing form" option. A form built in LiveCycle Designer can't be modified in Acrobat, although a form created in Acrobat can be modified in LiveCycle Designer.

The big difference relates to file types. An Acroform uses a PDF file and FDF (File Data Format) data. However, while a LiveCycle Designer form is a PDF file, its data is stored in XML format, which isn't configurable in Acrobat.

Tip

If you are opening an existing form, you won't see the information dialog.

6. The fields are shown on the form and listed in the Fields pane (**Figure 86b**). Complete the structure and layout of the form and save it. (Read how to work with the fields in #87, "Working in Form Edit Mode," and #88, "Drawing and Customizing Form Fields.")

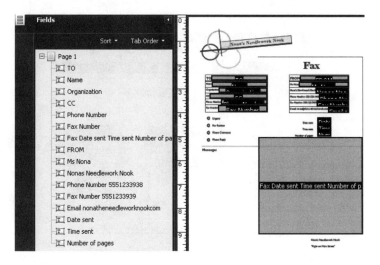

Figure 86b The Form Edit mode shows the fields added to the form automatically.

#87 Working in Form Edit Mode

Why the Changes Happened

Here's a simple explanation for why the Acroforms process is simpler and self-contained—and why you don't find the tools on the toolbars.

Acrobat 9 is the first program version where you don't have an option to open multiple files in the same program window. Instead, based on the architecture of Windows Vista (which influenced the design of Acrobat 9), each file opens in its own program window and offers its own specialized menu. As a result, when you choose one of the Forms commands in Acrobat, the special interface for Acroforms replaces the default view since it's the only document in that program window.

The one file per one window principle is also the reason for the absence of tools and toolbars—unless you're choosing a command that starts a forms process, you don't need the tools.

By the way, the same design/ programming principle is also the reason PDF portfolios function in their own specialized window layout. Read about collecting form data in a PDF portfolio in #94, "Handling Form Returns."

Acrobat 9 offers the same set of Acroform form field tools as previous versions, but the way you view fields is simpler. If you have worked in Acrobat before, you'll be surprised to find that you can't locate a Forms toolbar or choose Forms tools from the Tools menu unless you are actually working with a form.

When you start an Acroform project, the Acrobat program window changes to the Form Edit mode, which offers the form field tools and several other commands for working with the form. In addition, the program menus are displayed, but the available commands are limited to those applicable to building and working with a form. Very handy!

To edit the form, follow these steps:

1. Check through the added fields to determine whether they are needed. Start making corrections in the form (see how that's done in #88, "Drawing and Customizing Form Fields"). You can do the following:

   - Select a field and press Delete to delete it. You can click the field on the form, or select it in the Fields pane (**Figure 87a**).

   - Right-click (Control-click) a field in the pane and choose Properties from the shortcut menu to open its Properties dialog and customize the settings.

   - Add fields as required for your project.

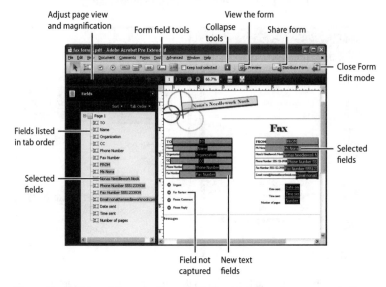

Figure 87a The Form Edit mode shows the fields added to the form automatically.

Tip

You can Shift-click or Ctrl-click (Command-click) to select multiple fields at one time, either on the form or the Fields pane, as in the figure.

2. If you have a lot of work to do with the form using different tools, click Add New Field 🖰 to display the list of form tools and choose Show Tools on Toolbar. You'll see the list of form tools on the toolbar, as in Figure 87a. To collapse the toolbar, click Hide 🔳 . Refer to **Table 12.1** for descriptions of the tools.

3. When you have finished, click Preview 🖳 on the Form Edit mode toolbar to show the form as it appears to a recipient, including instructions and actions on the Document Message Bar (**Figure 87b**).

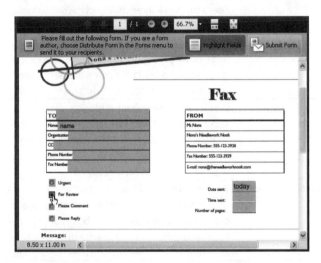

Figure 87b The Preview shows the form as it appears to your user, including active form fields.

4. In the Preview, click and type to test the fields. When you've finished testing, choose Forms > Clear Form to remove the content you've added. To show a background identifying the active form fields, click Highlight Fields.

5. Click Edit Layout 📝 to restore the Form Edit mode if you need to make more changes and adjustments.

6. When you've finished working with the form, be sure to save it. Click Close Form Editing to return to the basic Acrobat program window.

Left or Right

Usually a field is associated with a label to its left side. The conversion process doesn't inherently recognize when a label follows a form field placed to its right.

If you exit the Form Edit mode, you can easily return to make more changes. Choose Forms > Add or Edit Fields to reopen the Form Edit mode. If the file isn't saved, you are prompted to save it prior to returning to Form Edit mode.

Table 12.1 The Tools Found in the Form Editing Toolbar and Their Common Uses

Icon	Tool Name	Common Uses
	Text Field tool	Use this tool to create a field in which your users can type text, such as names, addresses, or favorite colors.
	Check Box tool	Where your user can choose one or more options, use a check box. For instance, if your form includes a list of favorite holiday destinations, your user might like to specify all three choices of Hawaii, Jamaica, and Tahiti.
	Radio Button tool	Add radio buttons when you want the user to make a single choice among two or more items. An example is a customer service form that lets the user choose among a range of responses, from "terrific" to "terrible."
	List Box tool	Create a list of items from which your user can select; usually list boxes are designed to allow for multiple selections. For example, when building your dream car at an online site, you can choose any or all items from a list of accessories.
	Combo Box tool	You can offer a list of items in a pop-up menu or let your user enter a custom value. For example, your order form can include several choices of countries where you commonly ship your products, as well as an option for customers to type their country name.
	Button tool	Use a button to initiate actions for anything from printing a document to submitting a form. A Button tool is also included on the Advanced Editing toolbar—learn more in Chapter 15, "Controlling Action and Interaction."
	Digital Signature tool	Use this tool to add a special type of field for applying a digital signature to the document. Learn more about digital signatures in Chapter 16, "Making Your Documents Secure."
	Barcode tool	Use this tool to add specialized codes used by hardware and software readers.

#88 Drawing and Customizing Form Fields

Add more fields and change existing ones in Form Edit mode during the form creation process, or by choosing Forms > Add and Edit Fields. In Acrobat 8, you'd have to configure a form field using its multi-tabbed Properties dialog. Now, in Acrobat 9 Extended and Extended Pro, fields are placed almost like a stamp on the page, and you can do most of the configuration right on the page in the small pop-up dialog that displays as you add fields.

In this example, see how a set of radio buttons is added to a sample file.

Follow these steps to add and configure a new field:

1. On the Form Edit toolbar, click Radio Button ⊙ and move the pointer over the page. You'll see crosshairs and an outline of the field.

2. Click when the field outline is at the right location to place the field on the page. In the example, the field overlays the first radio button image included in the form document.

3. In the pop-up dialog that opens when you placed the field on the page, click to select the default name "radio" in the Radio Group Name field, and type a new name for the button group—"priority" is used in the example (**Figure 88a**).

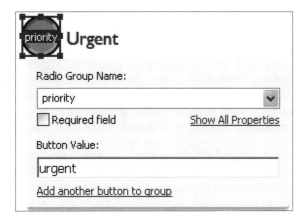

Figure 88a Name the radio button group and specify the button's value.

4. Type a new value in the Button Value field in the pop-up dialog, such as "urgent" in the example. The default is "yes."

(continued on next page)

Batching a Change

You don't have to select and change properties for one field at a time. To make some changes to a collection of fields, select the fields in the Fields pane or on the form and then open the Properties dialog. You won't be able to do some tasks, such as assigning actions, but you can make changes such as modifying the appearance or format selections that are applied to all.

5. Click "Add another button to group" at the bottom of the pop-up dialog to reactivate the Radio Button tool and place it in the location for the next button. You can use the dotted guidelines to line up the button on the form. Again, the properties pop-up dialog displays. Type a new entry in the Button Value field, and repeat adding and configuring the buttons until the set of buttons is finished (**Figure 88b**). Click anywhere on the form to deselect the Radio Button tool.

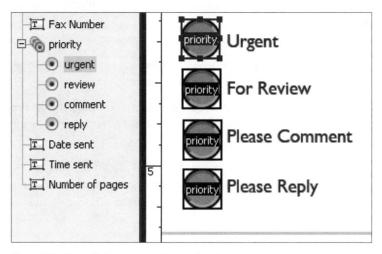

Figure 88b The radio button group is completed.

Tip

If you are building multiple fields of the same type, you can click "Keep tool selected" on the Form Edit toolbar to place all the fields without reselecting the tool. You won't have the mini-properties dialog display and will have to configure the options in the Radio Button Properties dialog.

Form fields share many features regardless of the type of form tool you use, although some configuration options are used for only certain types of fields. Rather than using the pop-up dialog that displays when you add a field, you can make the choices in the Properties dialog, which is named according to the type of field you're configuring.

To open the Properties dialog for a field, choose Properties from a field's shortcut menu.

Here's a brief rundown of the configuration tabs you can use with form fields in Acrobat 9, and how the example uses the features:

- **General tab.** This tab is common to all types. You add a name and tooltip in this tab of the dialog, as well as define whether the field is visible or invisible. In addition, you specify whether a field is required (an entry is mandatory) or whether the field is read only. You may want to make the user's name field required, for example, or specify calculated text fields as read only. In the example shown in Figure 88b, each button is visible and has its own tooltip.

- **Appearance tab.** This tab is common to all types of form fields. You configure the color of the border and fill, as well as other characteristics, such as text. In the example, the form contains an image for each button already, so the radio buttons should be invisible. To do that, click Border Color and choose No Color; click Fill Color and choose No Color (**Figure 88c**).

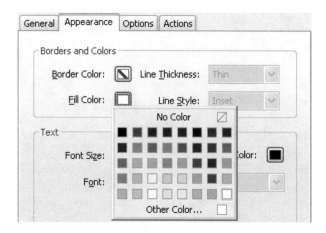

Figure 88c Configure the colors used for the radio button in this tab.

- **Options.** All form fields have an Options tab; the contents vary according to the type of field. Buttons, for instance, contain options for choosing labels and images for their display (see how that's done in Chapter 15, "Controlling Action and Interaction"); a Check Box field allows you to choose the appearance of the object, such as a check

(continued on next page)

Submit Your Form

In the past, you'd have to include a Submit button on a form, or trust that your recipients would take the time to send you an e-mail with their form attached. In Acrobat 9, due to the changes in the Form Tracker, receiving form results is much simpler. When you open the form to complete it, you'll see that the Document Message Bar includes a Submit button, which uses your Acrobat.com file's tracking information to submit the form for you. How convenient!

mark or a star; Combo Box and List Box fields include areas where you can insert lists of items; and a Radio Button field offers button style and selection status choices in the Options tab.

- **Actions.** All form fields have this tab, and it looks and works the same in all types. Actions are activities Acrobat performs in response to some sort of interaction, such as typing a number in a form field that then shows a calculation in another form field. Actions are described in Chapter 15. The example doesn't use an action associated with the radio button choice.

Note
Four additional tabs display according to the type of form field selected. For example, the ListBox Properties dialog includes the Selection Change tab, which lets you set the behavior that occurs when the list box's selected item changes. Read more about the other types in the following technique.

#89 Adding Calculations and Field Behaviors

Everybody uses forms, and Acroforms makes it simpler than ever to create, distribute, and manage forms. Aside from the usual information-type form, such as attendance, surveys, and so on, a large number of the forms commonly used have some type of calculations. Basic calculations using form fields aren't that difficult, once you get the knack.

Before you start, evaluate the names of the fields Acrobat adds automatically and change them as necessary, following the steps described in #87, "Working in Form Edit Mode." Review the names as well, and rename if necessary (check out the sidebar "What's in a Name?" for some tips).

There are several situations you'll commonly encounter when building a form. In all cases, let's assume the fields are added and named, and you're working in the Form Edit mode:

Using a special format. You want your form information to appear in the correct format, and using the proper range of values, such as a Zip Code field. In the Text Field Properties dialog, click Format. Formatting can range from numbers to currency to dates.

From the "Select format category" pop-up menu, choose Special to display a list of *masks* (structured field inputs having a preconfigured arrangement of characters and spacing), and click Zip Code. In the form, if a user tries to tab out of a field without adding the correct number of digits, a JavaScript warning displays (**Figure 89a**).

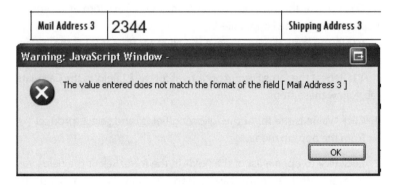

Figure 89a Use a special format to decrease errors in the form.

Validate the content added. You can restrict what your user enters in a field, such as a number or characters added in Text Box fields. In many fields, you need to make selections in more than one tab in order to be able to validate the field's contents. A Tax ID# on an invoice is a

---

What's in a Name?

When it comes to form fields, the answer is, "Plenty." If you are using a simple form, it's no big deal to reference the fields visually and associate them with their labels and purposes. By contrast, a poorly named set of 200 form fields is a migraine waiting to happen.

Decide on the naming structure based on the purpose of the form. For example, if you are building an order form, each row of the form usually relates to the item being ordered. So, you might use *item01* in **row01** to identify the product, *item02* in **row02** for the second product, and so on. The color for the first item could be *color01*, and its size named *size01*, and so on.

Similarly, look for totals that make sense. Using the same example, if there are different prices for *item01* based on the customizations offered, the **Total** column may contain *item01-total* as the price for the first item and its extras.

good example. Suppose in your area, the ID numbers are five characters, all above 30000 and below 90000. To ensure that the user enters the proper range of numbers within the proper range, you have to choose several settings in the Text Field Properties dialog:

- In the Options tab, enter *5* in the "Limit of [n] characters" field.

- In the Format tab, select Number from the "Select format category" pop-up menu, and set the Decimal Places to 0.

- In the Validate tab, click "Field value is in range" and enter *30000* and *90000* in the From and To fields, respectively.

When you test the form, you'll receive different JavaScript warnings, depending on which error is encountered.

Calculations. Many forms include calculations. Fortunately, most simple calculations can be done using the Text Field Properties dialog. In my example invoice, there are several fields required for calculating the costs for each item:

```
Quantity of an item (Q1) x unit price (P1) = total for
that item (T1)
```

To configure the fields to do the calculation of the total price, I need to do the following:

Q1: Choose the Number format from the "Select format category" pop-up menu in the Format field.

P1: In the Format field, choose the Number format from the "Select format category" pop-up menu, and leave the Decimal Places set at 2.

T1: Repeat the same Format options as for the P1 field. In the Calculate tab, follow these steps:

1. Click "Value is the [n] of the following fields," and select "product (x)" from the pop-up menu.

2. Click Pick to open a list of the fields in the form. Select the fields you want to calculate, in this case, Q1 and P1, and click OK to close the dialog. The selected fields are shown in the dialog (**Figure 89b**).

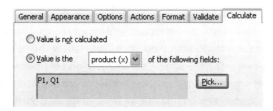

Figure 89b Specify the fields and operator for the calculation.

3. Click Close in the Text Field Properties dialog to return to the form. When you exit Form Edit mode and test the fields, you'll see the calculation at work.

#90 Organizing and Ordering a Form

Tweaking the Fields

You can select a group of fields and then use commands from the shortcut menu to organize their layout. For aligning, distributing, and sizing fields, move your pointer over the field that shows the correct configuration before opening the shortcut menu (like the Phone Number field in Figure 90a), and then do the following:

- Use Align options to line up selected objects according to a certain feature, such as the top or bottom.

- Use Distribute options to space objects evenly either horizontally or vertically.

- Use Center options to move the selected fields to the center of the page horizontally and/or vertically.

Adding and testing form fields is only the first part of the process. By its very nature, a form is an organized structure—fields for accumulating data are placed on the form along with their identifying labels; the fields and labels are often arranged on the page in some sort of grid-like pattern. Our approach to forms is generally systematic as well—we usually start filling a form at the top left, and keep going until we finish at the bottom right.

To achieve these worthy goals, Acrobat 9 offers tools and features designed to enhance the visual, organizational, and functional aspects of a form.

Note
You can select fields to work with on the document page or in the Fields pane, which is often easier to do. However, the shortcut menu items differ depending whether you right-click (Control-click) the selection in the Fields pane or on the page.

Visual aspects. Large numbers of the same type of field in similar arrangements are common on forms. Acrobat offers a method for spacing and sizing the fields on your form. Select the fields you want to work with on the form or in the Fields pane, and right-click (Control-click) on the document to open the shortcut menu. Select Align, Distribute, or Center and then an option from the submenu.

For sizing a group of fields, choose Set Fields to Same Size and then choose Height and/or Width choices from the submenu (**Figure 90a**).

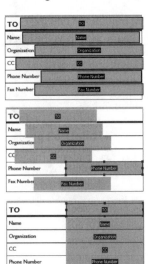

Figure 90a The layout of the fields needs improvement (top), after resizing (center), and finally after aligning and distributing (bottom).

Organizational aspects. In Form Edit mode, the fields added to your form are shown in the Fields pane sorted by their tab order. In forms containing dozens or hundreds of fields, it's often easier to locate a group of fields you want to change by ordering them alphabetically. To do so, click Sort in the Fields pane and choose Alphabetic Order.

Many complex forms, such as human resources, financial, or engineering forms, contain numbered fields, which are also ordered sequentially when you use the Alphabetic Order option. Read about examples of numbered fields in #116, "Building a Batch of Buttons," and in the sidebar "Duplicating Buttons," also in #116.

Functional aspects. It's common knowledge that you can press the Tab key to move through a form from field to field. This sequence, called *tab order*, can be modified in the Fields pane if you have selected the Tab Sort option.

There are several ways to adjust tab order:

- The Default Tab Order option is chosen by default, and is assigned to your form when Acrobat defines the form fields.

- Order Tabs By Row is commonly used for forms that collect hundreds of pieces of data. Tabbing in rows allows the user to tab across from left to right.

- Order Tabs By Column is commonly used when you are assembling data for comparison. For example, a form lists sale quantities of different items (values added in rows) according to a particular salesperson (defined by column).

- Choose Order Tabs Manually if you want to redefine the order yourself. Drag a field's label in the Fields pane up or down to change its order. You may need to order fields manually when you are dealing with calculated fields.

(continued on next page)

Making Form Fields More Visible

It can be difficult to visualize form fields on a stylized form if they aren't colored or identified in some way. Fortunately, Acrobat offers preferences to set form field visibility.

In a distributed form, your users can toggle the Show Highlight check box on the Document Message Bar to show or hide the highlight colors, or show a border when the mouse passes over a field, with or without highlighting the form fields:

1. Choose Edit > Preferences > Forms (Acrobat > Preferences > Forms).

2. Click the "Show border hover color for fields" if you want to show a border around a field as you pass the mouse over its location on the page.

3. Click the "Fields highlight color" color swatch to choose a custom color when you have the "Highlight fields" option selected on the form's Document Message Bar.

4. Click OK to close the Preferences dialog.

(continued on next page)

The form fields on the document are now identified by the selected background color when the Highlight Fields option is selected on the Document Message Bar, and show a border when the mouse moves over a field.

- Choose Show Tab Numbers to see the tab order on your form. If you delete extraneous fields, your tab order remains intact, but you see the remaining fields don't renumber themselves (**Figure 90b**).

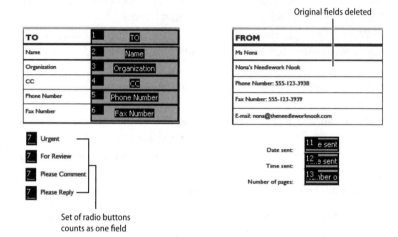

Figure 90b The tab order for the fields is numbered, excluding those fields that were deleted from the form.

#91 Simplifying a Visually Complex Form

Some forms are fancy—period. There's little chance that Acrobat 9, regardless of its intelligence level, is able to identify and build form fields on a page that uses a lot of graphic content, or one in which it's hard to make out what might be the fields.

Visually complex forms are generally made in a layout or imaging program, but you don't have to start from scratch or add the fields manually. Here's how to use an interesting form built in InDesign in combination with the power of the form field recognition process in Acrobat to add fields.

1. In your source program, configure the layers so the field labels and their structures are on one layer, and export two versions of the form:

   • Export the form layer as PDF to use for placing the fields.

   • Export the entire publication as PDF to replace the single-layer form after fields are added.

2. In Acrobat, choose Forms > Start Form Wizard to open the Create or Edit Form dialog. Leave the default selection "An existing electronic document" (Windows) or "Start with a PDF document" (Mac) and click Next.

3. Locate and select the PDF containing the form layer, and then click Next. Acrobat processes the file, and the results are shown in the Form Edit mode. As you can see, all the text fields have been inserted automatically (**Figure 91a**).

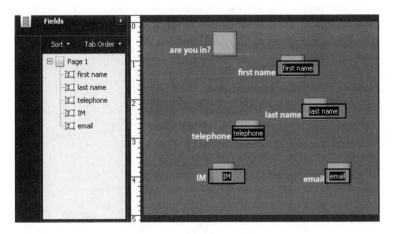

Figure 91a The form field layer contains nearly all the required fields.

(continued on next page)

Is It Worth the Time?

Good question. A few factors are involved, but as a general principle—yes. Whether to use two versions of the form must be based on its overall complexity. Unless you are confident the form's appearance will wreak havoc on the recognition process, it may not be worth the time involved to export two versions from your source program. In the example, Acrobat assigned over a dozen form fields to the full form layout, only two of which were actually the correct fields in the right locations.

Your choice is also based on how quick you are. If you are a whiz in your source program and not so fast in Acrobat, making the extra version may take far less time than fixing fields. The inverse scenario also applies.

248

LiveCycle Designer on Mac

Although you won't find LCD available for the Mac in Acrobat 9, here's a convenient workaround: Use VMware Fusion™ on an Intel Mac and install Acrobat on XP or Vista OS. It's the best of both worlds!

4. Modify the fields as required. In the example, which uses five text fields and one check box, only the check box was inserted manually.

5. Save the file, and close the Form Editing mode window.

6. Choose Document > Replace Pages to open the Select File With New Pages dialog. Locate and select the full version of the form. Click OK; click OK in the subsequent Replace Pages dialog.

The full form structure replaces the simplified form structure without affecting the fields (**Figure 91b**). Read about replacing pages in #50, "Changing Pages and Their Contents."

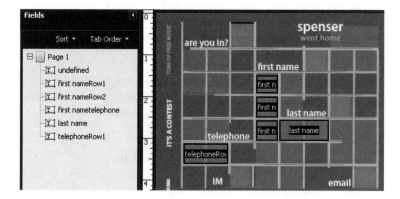

Figure 91b The revised form shows different content but the same field structure.

#92 Distributing Forms

Once you've finished building and testing your form, you have to get it to your respondents. Acrobat 9 offers three methods for distribution. You can use an e-mail distribution process, which has been extended to Acrobat 9 Standard users. As with other collaborative efforts, you can store and manage your form process from Acrobat.com. You can also use your own intranet to serve the forms and collect the data.

> **Note**
> *If necessary, be sure to add security or digital signature information to the form before distributing it. For details on setting permissions for using form fields, see #119, "Using Security Levels and Passwords for a Document"; read about using signatures in #121, "Signing a Document."*

In this technique, read how to distribute a form using e-mail and Acrobat.com. If you are distributing and collecting forms by e-mail, and intend to include respondents using older versions of Adobe Reader, choose Advanced > Extend Features in Adobe Reader. Read more about enabling a document for use in Adobe Reader in the sidebar "Including Adobe Reader Users." However, if you are working with an Acrobat.com distribution method, only Adobe Reader 9 users can access the file, so you don't need to enable the form manually.

Regardless of the distribution method, you initiate the process the same way. Choose Forms > Distribute Form from the menu or Forms task button. If you have a form file open, click Distribute 🖳 on the Document Message Bar to open the Distribute Form wizard.

To set up a form for e-mail distribution, follow these steps:

1. In the Distribute Form wizard, choose "Manually collect responses in my email inbox" from the pop-up menu. The screen shows a graphic representation of the process (**Figure 92a**). If you usually use the same distribution method, select the "Remember my choice" check box at the bottom of the screen. Click Next.

(continued on next page)

Automating Return Storage

When Acrobat prepares a file for distribution, part of the process is creating a PDF portfolio to manage the returns. By default, the returns file is stored in the same folder as your form, and uses the form's name with "_responses" appended to the name.

Preferences for Easier Form Completion

Try some of these preferences—you may find that they increase your form's processing speed and make working with forms simpler.

Choose Edit > Preferences > Forms (Acrobat > Preferences > Forms) and look for these options:

- "Automatically calculate field values" lets you calculate the content of numerical fields when you enter the data. Often this feature is programmed into the form (see some simple calculations in #89, "Adding Calculations and Field Behaviors").

(continued on next page)

250

- "Show focus rectangle" shows which form field is currently active (or has focus). This is a useful preference in forms with a great number of fields on one page.
- "Show text field overflow indicator" displays a plus sign when you try to type too much text into a text field. The number of characters allowed in a field is defined by the form's designer.
- When "Show field preview when creating or editing form fields" is selected, you see the field highlight under the field's name in Form Edit mode.

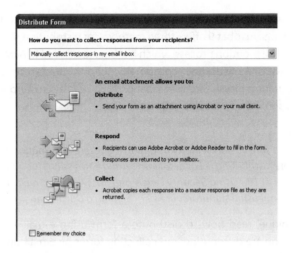

Figure 92a The wizard shows you a summary of the distribution process.

2. Choose an option for distributing the form, either "Send it automatically using Adobe Acrobat" or "Save a local copy and manually send it later." If you choose to save the form locally, click Browse to locate and select a storage location. Click Next.

Tip
Choose the automatic option if you have an e-mail client configured to work with Acrobat, and follow the wizard prompts to select recipients and review the default text added to the outgoing e-mail message. If you use an online e-mail client, save a local copy that you attach to an e-mail and send at your convenience.

3. On the third and final screen of the wizard, your delivery method is listed at the top of the window as an active link. If you want to revise the settings, click the link to return to the start of the wizard. Also, select the "Collect name & email from recipients to provide optimal tracking" check box at the bottom of the screen to help in your form tracking.

4. Click Finish to close the wizard and save the file (if you are sending the file manually), or Send (if you are sending the file automatically) to pass the file to your e-mail client, depending on your choice in step 2.

Use the same wizard for uploading a form to Acrobat.com for distribution. Again, open the wizard and then follow these steps:

1. On the first screen of the wizard, choose "Automatically download & organize responses with Acrobat.com"; click Next.

2. Type your Adobe ID and Password into the appropriate fields on the screen, and click Sign In to authenticate your Adobe ID.

3. The Distribute Form dialog opens. In this dialog, you configure the invitation for your distribution list:

   • Click To in order to display your Outlook e-mail address book, or type the addresses in the field.

   • Leave the default subject and message or type your own. The message invites you to complete the form and click Submit to return it to the sender.

   • Choose an Access Level from the pop-up menu. The option is "Open access: Anyone who knows the URL can fill out and submit the form." To restrict the form's recipients, choose "Limited access: Only my specific recipients can fill out and complete the form."

   • Select the "Collect name & e-mail from recipients to provide optimal tracking" check box to maintain up-to-date records of your form cycle.

4. Click Send. Acrobat processes the form. First, a PDF portfolio file is created in the form's folder for storing results; then the form is prepared and sent on its way.

5. The form file closes in Acrobat, and the Tracker opens. (Check out the Tracker in #93, "Tracking Forms.")

(continued on next page)

Including Adobe Reader Users

A form can be distributed for completion by those working with Adobe Reader if you enable the usage rights. As in the commenting and reviewing process, specify the rights that users are given to allow them to work in Adobe Reader. Choose Advanced > Extend Features in Adobe Reader. The usage rights include the following:

• Saving form data from a fill-in PDF form

• Using commenting and drawing markups

• Signing an existing signature field

• Digitally signing anywhere on a document (for Adobe Reader 8 or 9 users only)

Click Save Now to resave the file. Enabling form fill-in rights is limited to 500 copies of a form. By the way, you can't enable features if you are in Form Edit mode.

When a recipient receives the e-mail, the information provided is included, along with links to the file at Acrobat.com (**Figure 92b**). The link opens a Flash image of the form at Acrobat.com—not an actual interactive copy of the form itself. Click the Download button above the form to download a copy to the hard drive for completion.

Instruction from distribution process

Thumbnail of form   Notification re: form origination

Figure 92b The invitees receive the e-mail and links to the online file.

#93 Tracking Forms

Follow the progress of a form distribution and collection cycle using the Form Tracker. Choose Forms > Track Forms, or click the Forms task button and choose Track Forms to open the Tracker. You'll see both Review and Form sections at the left of the dialog (**Figure 93**).

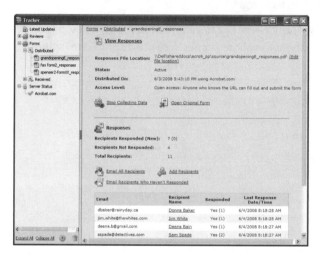

Figure 93 Use the information on the Tracker to see what's happening with your forms.

The Tracker is a highly interactive dialog, where you can do the following:

- Click Distributed or Received in the Forms listing at the left to view a list of the forms you're working with.

- Click View Responses to open the PDF portfolio generated when you started the form distribution.

- Change the file location for the responses file.

- Click Stop Collecting Data to terminate the form process, something you may do when you reach a capacity for some event or survey.

- Click Open Original Form to see the form used for the review.

When you receive the responses, you can do the following:

- Track the response data, including new responses and those who haven't responded.

(continued on next page)

Stay in the Loop

If you are waiting for form returns, you don't have to keep the Tracker open to wait for form returns to show up. Instead, click Latest Updates in the Tracker and choose "Turn on notification icon in system tray." You'll see the Tracker icon on the taskbar , and a pop-up notifies you when a new form is received.

Coordinating with QuickBooks

Acrobat 9 offers new Acrobat > QuickBooks features. Now you can do the following:

- Collect form data using your QuickBooks templates

- Use one of seven new QuickBooks-enabled templates in Acrobat

- Use a wizard to get your template ready for - distribution

- Export forms data back to QuickBooks

- Send e-mail to all your respondents, or just those who haven't responded to the form.

- Add Recipients to open the Form invitation and distribution described in the previous technique.

- Click the Recipient Name link to view their data on the Responses PDF (read about the automatic responses in #94, "Handling Form Returns").

#94 Handling Form Returns

If you distribute your form from Acrobat, data from your returned forms is compiled in a PDF portfolio, created as part of the distribution process (read about distribution in #92, "Distributing Forms"). As the data starts to flow in, use the PDF Portfolio feature to sort or filter the returns, edit data in-line, and add more data as additional returns are received.

To open your returns file, you can do the following:

- Choose Track Forms from the Forms task button's menu.

- Choose File > Open to locate and select the PDF returns file.

- Click View Responses on the Tracker (shown in Figure 93).

The responses PDF Portfolio opens with a welcome page, explaining the tasks you can complete in the file. Click Get Started to close the Welcome window, and open the PDF portfolio, shown in Home mode view as a table listing the fields from your form and returned responses (**Figure 94a**).

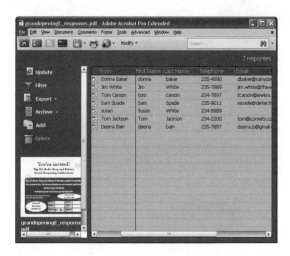

Figure 94a The returns are listed in the PDF portfolio.

You can do several maintenance and management tasks with your form returns:

Update returns. Click Update to have Acrobat look for new responses online and include them in the portfolio returns, or show a message saying there are no new responses.

Adding E-mail Form Returns

Sometimes a recipient of your form may attach the form to an e-mail to return to you. You can easily add those returns to your other returns in your PDF Portfolio using program commands. Follow these steps:

1. Choose Forms > Compile Returned Forms to open a dialog. Click Browse to locate and select the response file.

2. Click Add File.

3. Repeat as necessary until you have selected all the returns.

4. Click OK to close the dialog, and add the return data to your PDF portfolio.

Filter the returns. Click Filter  to show a list of your form's field names. Click the field name you want to use for filtering, such as *Radio Button1* (used in the example form for the recipients to state whether they were attending an event). Choose a condition from a pop-up menu, such as contains (in the example), does not contain, is blank, and so on. Finally, type the condition in the field, such as *No*. The returns are filtered and your results displayed, as shown in the example in **Figure 94b**. When you're done, click Clear All to remove the filter; click Done to return to the full Home mode view.

Figure 94b Filter the returns based on your own criteria.

Archive responses. Click Archive to move responses into an archive file for storage. You can select rows in the responses and choose Archive selected from the Archive pop-up menu, or archive all your responses (read more in the sidebar "Who Needs an Archive?").

Add additional returns. Click Add to open the Add Returned Forms dialog, where you can manually locate and select files to add to the PDF portfolio's list of returns. Once you've located and selected the returns, click OK to close the dialog and include the new returns.

Export results. Click Export to export the results in a CSV (comma-separated value) format for use in a spreadsheet. You can select rows in the responses and choose Export selected from the Export pop-up menu, or export all your responses. The Select Folder to Save File dialog opens. Locate and select the folder, then choose the export format, either XML or CSV. Click Save to export the data and close the dialog. The file is now available to use in a spreadsheet or database (**Figure 94c**).

E	F	G	H	I
Last Name	**Telephone**	**Email**	**Radio But**	**How Many**
baker	235-4890	dbaker@rainy	Yes	2
White	235-7889	jim.white@the	Yes	3
carson	234-7897	tcarson@ewk	Yes	4
Spade	235-9011	sspade@dete	No	
White	234-8989		Yes	4
Jackson	234-2200	tom@comets.	Yes	2
bain	235-7897	deena.b@gma	Yes	3
				18

Figure 94c Export the data to a spreadsheet to use for calculations such as number of attendees.

Delete results. If you have a results processing plan in place, such as forwarding comments to a salesperson, you can delete the results when you are done with them, again to decrease the volume of returns you have to manage.

CHAPTER THIRTEEN

Using Flash Video and 3D Media

Acrobat 9 Pro lets you incorporate media in PDF documents to bring your documents to life. You can use different types of media, such as sound and movie files, Flash movies, and 3D models and animations.

Tailor your projects to your users' playback options by providing different renditions of a movie compatible with different players. All versions of Acrobat 9 and Adobe Reader are able to play Flash content without a separate Flash player, as there is a player embedded in the Acrobat and Adobe Reader programs. However, only Acrobat 9 Pro Extended (Windows) can format and embed a SWF file as a Flash video file.

Flash is used and integrated with Acrobat in other ways. PDF portfolios use a Flash navigation interface (read about portfolios in Chapter 4, "Producing a PDF Portfolio"). Also, Adobe Presenter, a PowerPoint plug-in for Acrobat 9 Pro Extended, uses a Flash interface for displaying content and configuring quizzes (read how in Chapter 9, "Building Content with Adobe Presenter"). Acrobat.com, featured in Chapter 11, "Live Reviewing and Collaboration," uses Adobe Air and Flash to build rich Internet applications (RIAs).

Multimedia in general requires configuring some trust and security settings—read about your options in #124, "Managing Multimedia and Security Trusts."

#95 Inserting Flash Media in a PDF File

You can embed media files directly into PDF documents within Acrobat, or you can add the media to a source document—such as a Word document or an Excel spreadsheet—and then convert the file (Windows). Read how in #14, "Adding Specialized Media Content."

In Acrobat 9 Pro and Pro Extended, add a movie to a PDF document by embedding the movie or linking to it. An embedded movie is integrated into the PDF document itself, while a linked movie simply has a programmed link from the PDF document to the original movie, stored in its original location.

Tip
Choose the linked option if you intend to use the PDF file online and store the FLV file online as well for streaming and faster display.

To include a movie file in your PDF document—regardless of its format—Acrobat automatically uses the Insert Video dialog, whether you've started with the Flash or Movie tools.

To insert an FLV (Flash video) movie file, follow these steps:

1. Open the PDF file you want to use, and choose Tools > Multimedia > Show Multimedia Toolbar.

2. Select the Flash tool 🔳 on the Multimedia toolbar, and draw a marquee or double-click the page to open the Insert Flash dialog.

3. Click Browse to locate and select the file you want to use (shown in the File field).

   If you use the Flash tool and select an FLV (Flash Video) movie file, the dialog automatically changes to the Insert Movie dialog, although some of its settings are specific to Flash video, rather than other types of video.

Note
When you select the file, notice that the "Snap to content proportions" check box appears in the dialog and is selected by default, maintaining the width/height ratio of the movie file on the page.

4. Select the Show Advanced Options check box to display three tabs of additional settings.

5. In the Launch Settings tab, choose from these options:

- Activation Settings for starting and stopping the movie; and the playing location—either on a fixed page location or in a floating window

- Appearance settings for choosing a Border Width and Color

- Poster Image—from a frame of the movie or a separate file

6. In the Controls tab, specify the playback controls from these options:

- Select a Skin that provides a set of controls ranging from none to a full set (**Figure 95a**).

- Choose a color and opacity for the skin.

- Leave the Auto-hide controls check box selected to hide the controls when your mouse moves away from the movie's area, or deselect the check box to have the controls display at all times.

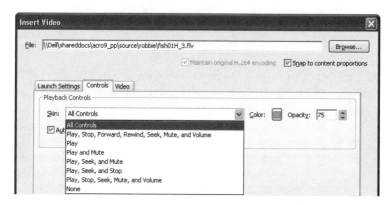

Figure 95a Configure the appearance and behavior of the video in the dialog.

7. In the Video tab, select a frame to use as a poster image (as mentioned in Step 5) and trim the video's In and Out points if desired. Also in this tab, you can add and configure chapter points, described in the sidebar "Make Your Point."

(continued on next page)

Multimedia Preferences

To set general multimedia preferences, choose Edit > Preferences and click Multimedia in the left column.

From the Player Options menu at the upper section of the dialog, choose a player option. The preferences do not identify the versions of the chosen players. For example, the latest Flash Player is version 9; if users choose Flash as their player option but have version 6 installed on their computers, they won't be able to see your work unless it is playable on a version 6 player.

At the lower portion of the dialog are the Accessibility Options. If you use assistive devices, enable the appropriate options.

Make Your Point

Make Your Point

A *chapter point* is a marker added to a video that defines a frame where you can launch an action. In a travel video, for example, you could use a chapter point to add a link to online reservation, information, and tourism sites; or even launch a form to solicit feedback.

Drag the slider under the video preview to the frame where you want to add the chapter point. Click the Chapter Points plus sign to add the notation. Then, select the notation and click Actions. For more on actions, check out Chapter 15, "Controlling Action and Interaction."

Floating Along

You can have a multimedia file inserted in your PDF file float in a window. The window can be positioned in any location and isn't tied to a particular page. You might want to use a floating window for holding contact information, a movie with links to other resources, and so on.

8. Click OK to close the dialog and insert the video on the page (**Figure 95b**).

Figure 95b The inserted Flash movie shows a poster image, and includes a full set of playback controls in a color that coordinates with the movie's content (shown as an overlay on the figure).

9. If you want to make adjustments, click the movie with the Select Object tool to activate the frame; drag the movie to reposition it on the page, or drag a handle to resize the movie's play area.

Note
The adjustments apply to SWF, FLV, other movies, and sound files.

#96 Inserting SWF in a PDF File

Inserting a SWF file into a PDF document starts in the same way as inserting a Flash movie, but offers different configuration options to take advantage of the programming potential in the SWF file.

Follow these steps to insert and configure a SWF file:

1. Select the Flash tool on the Multimedia toolbar, and double-click the page to activate the tool and open the Insert Flash dialog.

2. Select Show Advanced Options to display three additional tabs in the dialog.

3. In the Launch Settings tab, choose from the same features as for configuring movies—that is, Activation Settings, Appearance, and Poster Image options.

4. Click the Flash tab to display settings for using content from the SWF file:

   • Select the "Pass context menu click to Flash movie" check box to replace the default Acrobat shortcut menu with the SWF file's shortcut menu (**Figure 96a**).

   • Insert ActionScript variables for the file in the Flash Vars field.

Fix It!

Whether you add a Flash or other movie file in Acrobat or in an Office document prior to conversion to PDF, you can make changes to your settings in the same way.

Follow these steps:

1. Click the Select Object tool on the Advanced Editing toolbar, and right-click (Control-click) the movie to open the shortcut menu.

2. Choose Properties to reopen the Edit Movie dialog. You'll find the same settings and options, with the exclusion of the file selection field at the top of the dialog.

3. Make the changes as necessary, and click OK to close the dialog.

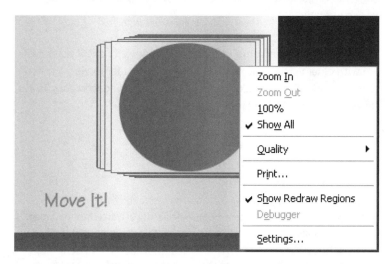

Figure 96a Use the SWF file's shortcut menu items rather than the default Acrobat context menu items, such as the Show Redraw Regions command.

(continued on next page)

5. Click the Resources tab to include accessory files required by the SWF file. Click Add or Add Directory to locate and include external files in the PDF file. To check your resource files, click the name in the list at the top of the dialog, and review the path in the Name field.

6. Click OK to close the dialog, and run your SWF content (**Figure 96b**).

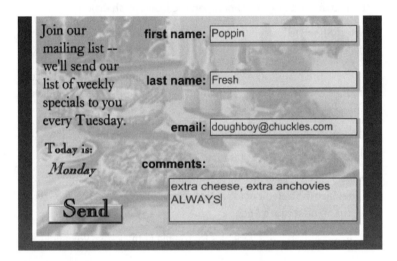

Figure 96b Inserted SWF content retains its interactive features.

You can use a number of versions of the movie to allow users working with older versions of Acrobat and Adobe Reader to view your content. Read about including other movie versions, called *renditions*, in #97, "Inserting Movies and Legacy Versions."

#97 Inserting Movies and Legacy Versions

Prior to Acrobat 9, movies were embedded in different movie file types, such as MOV and AVI formats. In Acrobat 9, movies are generally stored as a FLV movie, since Acrobat 9 and Adobe Reader 9 include an integrated Flash Player.

Follow these steps to add a movie to a PDF file:

1. Click the Video tool [icon] on the Multimedia toolbar, and double-click on the page to open the Insert Video dialog.

2. Click Choose to locate and select the movie file. A preview is loaded into the dialog (**Figure 97a**).

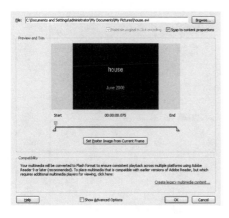

Figure 97a Select a movie file to convert to FLV and embed in your document.

3. Drag the endpoints on the slider below the preview to establish a trim length. Display the frame you want to use as a poster for the movie, and click Set Poster Image from Current Frame.

4. Click the Show Advanced Options check box to display a set of four tabs in the dialog and make your choices from the Launch Settings, Controls, and Video options, described in the previous two techniques.

   Inserting a Movie also includes a Quality tab, where you can specify the video and audio quality, as well as resizing options.

5. Click OK to close the dialog. The movie is converted to FLV format and embedded in the document.

Using Multiple Movie Versions

Follow these steps to add multiple movie renditions to your document:

1. Double-click the movie with the Video tool to open the Multimedia Properties dialog, displaying the Settings tab.

2. You'll see the Annotation Title, a name assigned by Acrobat to identify the object; for accessibility purposes, type a description for an alternate text tag.

3. Select an action from the List Renditions for Event pop-up menu, or leave the default Mouse Up action.

4. Click Add Rendition, and then select a location:

   - Using a File to locate and select another movie version

   - Using a URL, and then typing the URL in the resulting field

   - By Copying An Existing Rendition, to select the rendition you want to copy

(continued on next page)

5. Select a rendition from the list and click Edit Rendition (described in the sidebar "Play It Again, Sam").

6. Add and edit as many renditions as needed.

7. Use the arrow keys on the right side of the pop-up menu to arrange the renditions in the appropriate order. Renditions are played in the order listed.

8. When you finish adding and editing renditions, click Close.

Considering Accessibility

One of the cornerstones of designing accessible content is including alternate versions of visual content. For users working with screen readers or other assistive devices, you have to provide the text equivalent of your visual content and captioning (if required). The media you're using determines your ability to embed text, verbal commentary, and captions, and you can't control this ability from within Acrobat.

To add legacy media files that you don't want to convert to FLV format, follow steps 1–3 of the previous set of steps and then do the following:

1. Click the "Create legacy multimedia content" link in the lower-right corner of the Insert Video dialog to open the Add Movie dialog.

2. Choose either Acrobat 6 (and Later) Compatible Media or Acrobat 5 (and Earlier) Compatible Media.

   Selecting the Acrobat 6 version offers more configuration options; selecting the Acrobat 5 version works only with media that plays in QuickTime Player (**Figure 97b**).

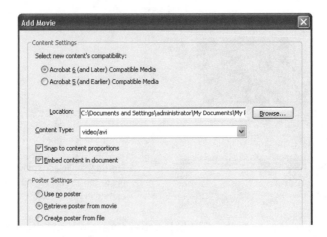

Figure 97b Configure a movie file to add to the document in various formats.

3. For Acrobat 6 (and Later) Compatible Media, choose further selections:

   • Specify a format from the Content Type pop-up menu.

   • Use or deselect the "Snap to content proportions" and "Embed content in document" check boxes.

   • Choose a poster setting.

4. Click OK to close the dialog and insert the movie.

After you add the video to the PDF, you can specify additional properties that determine how the clip appears and plays—read more in the sidebar "Using Multiple Movie Versions."

Play It Again, Sam

You can modify the characteristics of any of the renditions you add to a movie. Click a rendition in the Multimedia Properties dialog and then click Edit Rendition to open the Rendition Settings dialog. Use this five-tab dialog to tweak your movies as necessary:

- In the Media Settings tab, make a rendition accessible to JavaScript, choosing options similar to those in the basic Add Movie dialog.

- In the Playback Settings tab, define looping, specify players and how long the player remains open, and add controls.

- In the Playback Location tab, choose to play your movie in a floating window or full-screen.

- In the Systems Requirements tab, specify languages and playback requirements such as screen resolution and subtitles.

- In the Playback Requirements tab, review the settings chosen in other tabs.

#**98** Working with 3D Content

There are a number of ways to change the appearance of your model in Acrobat using the tools on the 3D toolbar:

- Specify the type of projection—either orthographic or perspective—for viewing the model.

- Choose a Render Mode from the Model Render Mode pop-up menu—the model in the figure is shown in Shaded Illustration mode.

- From the Enable Extra Lighting pop-up menu, choose supplementary lighting for the model ranging from night lights to headlamps—the model in the figure uses Bright Lights.

- Select a background color for the model from the color swatches.

- Show or hide cross sections.

In Acrobat 9 Pro Extended, you can use 3D content exported from various 3D modeling programs in several common 3D formats in a PDF file, or in a source Microsoft Office file. You embed a 3D model in the same way you embed movies or sounds.

Follow these steps to embed a 3D model in a Word document:

1. Click the 3D Tool ⬚ on the Acrobat PDFMaker toolbar to open the Add 3D Data dialog. A marquee is placed on the page automatically.

2. Select the model file and scripts. Click OK to close the dialog and insert the model.

3. Position the model's marquee on the page. Save the file and convert to PDF.

4. In Acrobat, click the model on the page with the Hand tool to display the toolbar and run any animations associated with the file (**Figure 98**). Move the Hand tool away from the model's location to hide the toolbar.

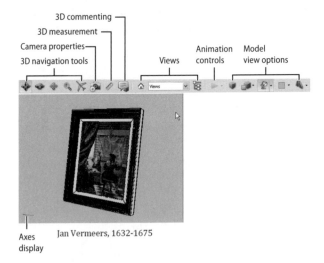

Figure 98 Moving the Hand tool over the model activates the toolbar automatically.

Several categories of tools are available for working with a 3D model:

- **3D navigation tools.** With these tools you can turn and spin, pan and zoom, and fly by to view the image. From the shortcut menu, add a

Walk tool for walkthroughs in a model. As you move the model with the tools, notice that the three-dimensional axes displayed at the bottom left of the window move as well.

- **3D Measurement tool.** This measures objects and distances in the model (read about 3D measurements in #100, "Measuring 3D Objects").

- **Toolbar view controls.** View or hide different objects in the model; return to the Home view, the default view set for the model.

- **View the model tree.** Toggle to display the Model Tree pane, which lists the objects in the model.

- **Animation controls.** Play or pause animation (the example isn't an animated model).

- **Viewing the model.** Choose from a collection of options for the type of projection, coloring, and other features (read more in the sidebar "Adjusting the Model's Appearance").

Editing an Embedded 3D Model

If you'd like to edit the model once it's embedded in a PDF, right-click (Control-click) the 3D model and choose Enable Content. Then right-click (Control-click) the model again, and choose Edit In 3D Reviewer. If the file has security preventing changes, you can't edit it, of course.

Create a PDF Template for 3D Files

To give 3D PDFs a consistent layout and structure, create a PDF template that contains a placeholder for a 3D model. Create the template in any Microsoft Office application in which PDFMaker is available. After you create a template, select it in the Acrobat Pro Extended Conversion dialog whenever you convert a 3D file to PDF.

1. In an Office 2003 document, click the Insert Acrobat 3D Model button on the PDF toolbar. In an Office 2007 document, click Embed 3D on the Acrobat ribbon.

2. In the Add 3D data dialog, click OK without selecting a 3D model to create a placeholder for your 3D conversion.

3. Move and resize the 3D placeholder to accommodate your 3D models.

4. Add any other information you want and save the file.

5. Click the Convert To Adobe PDF button on the PDF toolbar (Office 2003), or select Create PDF on the Acrobat ribbon (2007). Then save the file as a PDF.

To use this template when you convert a file, click the Document tab in the Acrobat 3D Conversion dialog. If the template name is not displayed in the Template PDF section, click Browse to find and open it.

#99 Editing in Adobe 3D Reviewer

What Is Universal 3D?

The format supports animations and is editable in Adobe 3D Reviewer.

U3D allows the use of computer-aided design (CAD) models with progressive detail, allowing viewers to see the underlying structure of the design as well as the finished product or model. U3D settings are for most CAD files created in digital content creation applications and many CAD files created in mechanical engineering applications.

The 3D Industry Forum developed the Universal 3D (U3D) format to serve as an open, extensible 3D visualization and repurposing format. The 3D Industry Forum has various industrial members, including Hewlett-Packard, NVIDIA, Intel, and Adobe.

Adobe 3D Reviewer is a separate application that is installed with Acrobat Pro Extended. To open 3D Reviewer outside Acrobat Pro Extended, choose Start > Programs > Adobe 3D Reviewer. If you are working with a model in Acrobat Pro Extended, you can right-click the model and choose Edit in 3D Reviewer.

You can use Adobe 3D Reviewer to work with 3D files in many ways:

- Merge CAD files

- Compare and measure exact geometry

- Calculate bounding box and physical properties

- Move and delete parts

- Add animations

- Create exploded views and bills of material

- Export to common 3D formats such as Universal 3D (U3D) and raster and vector 2D image files

In the example shown in **Figure 99**, the model is being animated, using one of the Adobe 3D Reviewer default animation routines.

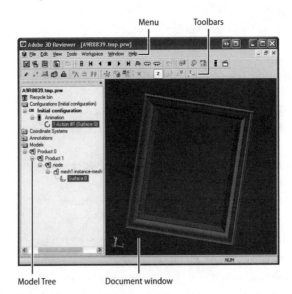

Menu   Toolbars

Model Tree   Document window

Figure 99 Use the features in Adobe 3D Reviewer to modify an existing model, such as adding an animation.

Making Your Way Around

At first glance (and even second and third!) Adobe 3D Reviewer can seem rather daunting. Fortunately, the program offers a number of workspaces designed for different types of workflows. To select one, choose Workspace > Toolbar Presets and then select an option. Choose from these layouts:

- **Visualization.** This is the default set of toolbars, which includes tools used for viewing 3D assemblies and parts. This configuration displays the Standard, 3D Controls, Default Views, Display Mode, Selection Filters, Hide/Show, and View/Configuration toolbars.

- **Design Review.** This layout contains tools used for reviewing design projects, such as bounding boxes, markups, and dimensioning tools. This configuration displays the Design Review, Positioning, and Axis toolbars.

- **Technical Documentation.** This layout is chiefly used by technical writers for building illustrations and animations for manuals and guides. The Play Animation and Snapshot tools display.

#**100** Measuring 3D Objects

Use the 3D Measurement Tool to measure 3D models. You can create measurements between combinations of points or edges, by moving the pointer over the 3D model, or by highlighting specific points and edges. The 3D Measurement Tool supports four types of measurements: perpendicular distance between two straight edges, linear distance between two points, the radius of circular edges, and the angle between two edges (or three points).

You can associate 3D measurements with specific views. If the default view is active when a measurement is added, a new measurement view is created. This view is added to the view hierarchy in the Model Tree. The measurement is associated with that view only, and displays as a child of the view.

You can also display comments while taking measurements. These comments (also called *measurement markups*) are preserved after the document is closed.

Follow these steps to measure and annotate an object in your 3D model:

1. Click the model on the page to activate it and display the 3D toolbar.

2. Click the 3D Measurement Tool on the toolbar. You'll see another palette of tools open in the Document pane that offer a variety of snap and measurement options (**Figure 100**).

Tell Me More

You don't have to leave the default measurement as is. You can add a text label as well. With the measurement still selected, right-click anywhere on the model background and choose Change Markup Label. In the pop-up field that appears, type the text you want to display and click OK. The field closes, and your label includes the text and the measurement.

Moving and Measuring

You often need to move around the model as you are measuring. Keep these keyboard shortcuts in mind:

- Press Alt to rotate the view.

- Press Shift to pan the view.

- Press Alt+Shift to zoom the view.

- Press Ctrl to disable the snap feature.

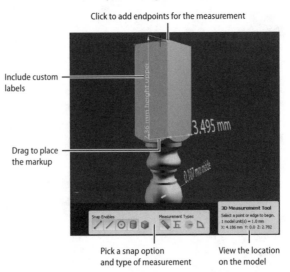

Figure 100 Choose from a wide range of measurement options.

3. Add measurements to the model. To move around the model as you are measuring, check out the keyboard shortcuts in the sidebar "Moving and Measuring."

To measure distance, click to establish a starting point, move the pointer to an edge or other area of the model, and click again to measure the distance.

Tip
If you want to stop a measuring process, right-click and choose Cancel Measurement or press Esc. If you finish a markup and want to remove it, click it with the 3D Measurement Tool and press Delete.

4. After you've set the endpoint for the measurement, click again and drag to set the location for the measurement's label. Read how to customize the measurement's label in the sidebar "Tell Me More."

Temporary Measures

If you want to check on some feature's dimensions, disable the measurement markup. That way, the measurement is visible only as long as it is active. If you change to another tool or start another measurement, the temporary markup disappears.

Converting 3D Measurements to Comments

Unlike with the other forms of commenting, you convert measurements to comments in the Model Tree pane. Right-click the plus sign for the measurement view you want to work with to open its list of measurements. Right-click the measurement to display the shortcut menu, and choose Convert to Comment. Read more in #101, "Inserting Multimedia Comments."

If you decide to convert the measurement to a comment as you are measuring your drawing, select the Hand tool, right-click the measurement, and choose Convert to Comment from the shortcut menu.

#101 Inserting Multimedia Comments

Keep It in View

If you delete one of the automatically generated views inserted when you place a comment on a model, the associated comments are still available. You can view and select them in the Comments panel or in the Model Tree, where they are listed under the views.

Selecting a comment switches the 3D model to the same viewing configuration it had when the comment was added.

3D comments behave in different ways, depending on how you add them, and where:

- Comments added using the 3D Comment tool are associated with the view displayed when you add the comments. If the view is changed, the comments are no longer visible.

- If you don't want a comment to be associated with a 3D view, add the comment outside the 3D object area.

- A new view is added to the Model Tree when you add 3D comments to the default view of a model, called *3DcommentView*.

(continued on next page)

Trying to identify a specific location in a model or movie in writing can be difficult, not to mention time-consuming. With Acrobat 9, those days are gone. Now, you can add comments to individual video frames or a particular 3D object view. Adobe Reader users can add comments to a PDF if the document is enabled for commenting. Adding comments to 3D model views requires version 7.0.7 or later of Acrobat or Reader.

Note
For a general overview of working with comments, check out Chapter 10, "Commenting in a PDF Document."

To add a comment to a video, use the tools on the Comment & Markup toolbar. Play the video, and pause the playback where you want to comment. Add the comment to the frame.

The comments are shown in the Comments List like any other sort of comment. Select the comment in the Comments List to display the video frame with the comment automatically (**Figure 101a**).

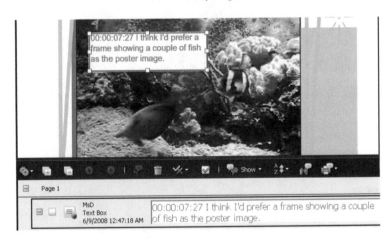

Figure 101a Acrobat shows the video frame automatically when you choose the comment.

Adding comments to a 3D model is a bit more involved than commenting in a video or movie. Instead of adding a comment to a frame as in a movie, you coordinate the information in the model with settings in the Model Tree pane. Read about the changes made in the Model Tree when you add comments in the sidebar "Keep It in View."

You can create views for comments themselves or associate them with views you set in the Model Tree, or by clicking the Views pop-up menu on the 3D toolbar and choosing Manage Views.

Follow these steps to associate actions with named views in the Model Tree:

1. Using the 3D navigation tools, position the view of the model.

2. In the Model Tree, click Create View 🖼 to add a new view.

3. Select the default *NewView#* label and type a different name for the view.

Note

Check out #102, "Using Actions to Show Multimedia Views," to see how a named view is used in a button action.

You add a comment in one of three ways:

- If you want to add a comment to a specific part of a model, use the 3D Comment Tool on the 3D toolbar.

- If you want to add basic comments about the model in general, use the tools on the Comment & Markup toolbar.

- If you have made measurements on a model, you can convert the measurements to comments.

3D Comment Tool. The 3D Comment Tool adds comments associated with the model's geometry, just like measurements. To add a comment, follow these steps:

1. Click the Add Multimedia/3D Comment tool on the 3D toolbar.

2. Display the part of the model where you want to add the comment.

(continued on next page)

- When you add comments using tools on the Comment & Markup toolbar, a new view is created in the Model Tree called *CommentView*.

- 3D comments added to other views are listed as components of that view in the Model Tree (like the examples shown in Figure 101b.)

Where to Add More Comments

To add another comment in a view, select the commenting view in the Model Tree and then click inside the 3D object area.

If you want to add a comment in a new commenting view, check that there are no selected commenting views in the Model Tree. Click inside the 3D object area and add your comment.

3. Type the comment in the Enter Comment String dialog (**Figure 101b**).

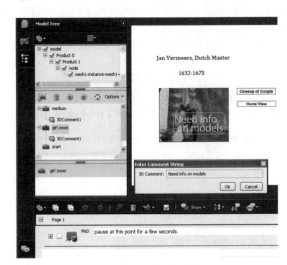

Figure 101b Add a comment to a particular part or view of a model.

Note

In Figure 101b, the dialog shown overlaying the Acrobat window is a duplicate of the comment added—the comment is shown in the Comments List and Model Tree.

Comment & Markup tools. Choose a tool from the Comment & Markup toolbar, and click inside the 3D area. Add your comment.

#**102** Using Actions to Show Multimedia Views

Rather than assuming your viewers can understand and manipulate the Comments List or the Model Tree to view your comments or special features in a movie or 3D model, give them some buttons. Everyone knows that a button on a page is made for clicking, which takes a lot of the mystery out of interacting with your PDF file.

In this example, see how buttons are constructed to let the user easily view a closeup of an area of a painting, and then return to the default Home view (you can see the buttons in place on the page in Figure 101b).

Follow these steps to associate a button with a 3D view:

1. Add and name the views you want to work with, following the steps described in #101, "Inserting Multimedia Comments."

2. Select the Button tool ⬛ on the Advanced Editing toolbar and click the page where you want to place the button. In the Field Name dialog that displays, click Show All Properties to open the Button Properties dialog.

3. Configure the button:

   • Name the button in the General tab.

   • Specify the button's color and text in the Appearance tab.

   • Choose the button's layout features in the Options tab.

   Tip
   Read about configuring options and working with buttons in detail in Chapter 15, "Controlling Action and Interaction."

4. In the Actions tab, select "Go to a 3D/Multimedia view" from the Select Action pop-up menu and click Add to open the Select a 3D View dialog.

5. Click Named view to activate the list of views added to the model, and then click to select one of the named views, such as *start,* shown in **Figure 102a**.

(continued on next page)

Multimedia Action

There are three multimedia-specific actions in Acrobat:

• Play a Sound plays a specified sound file. The sound is embedded in the PDF document in a cross-platform format that plays in Microsoft Windows and Mac OS.

• Play Media (Acrobat 5 Compatible) plays a specified QuickTime or AVI movie that you created as Acrobat 5 compatible. A media object using Acrobat 5 Compatible options is automatically embedded in the PDF document.

• Play Media (Acrobat 6 and Later Compatible) plays a specified movie that you created as compatible with Acrobat 6 and Acrobat 7. Again, a media object must already be embedded in the PDF document for you to be able to select it.

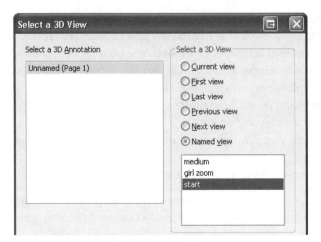

Figure 102a Choose one of the views added to the model.

6. Click OK to close the dialog and return to the Button Properties dialog, where you'll see the new action listed in the Action tab in the dialog.

7. Click OK to close the Button Properties dialog and return to the document.

8. Click the Hand tool and then click your button to display the view you set earlier. Add other buttons as needed (**Figure 102b**).

Figure 102b Add buttons to show different views of your model. Left shows the close-up of the couple; right shows the default model view.

CHAPTER FOURTEEN

Using Drawings, Maps, and Layers

Over the last few years, Acrobat has made great strides in the architecture/ engineering/construction (AEC) arena. Many Acrobat features are perfectly suited for AEC functions. For example, the hundreds of drawings and specifications needed for a project are readily brought together in a PDF portfolio, where they can be searched, organized, and presented (read about the PDF Portfolio feature in Chapter 4, "Producing a PDF Portfolio"). Individual drawings produced in CAD/CAM programs offer usable layers when imported into Acrobat.

The AEC features available in Acrobat aren't just for engineers or architects. The measurement tools, for example, work equally well for measuring the width of a text box on an InDesign page as they do for measuring the width of a parking lot.

A layered file, whether a schematic or a brochure, can be imported into Acrobat, where you can continue to work with the layers. In Acrobat 9, you can even add more layers, and use some new preflight profiles that split the objects on a page into different layers.

Acrobat 9 Pro offers tools and processes designed for working with specialized documents. The new Analysis toolbar brings together the measuring and object data tools from the past, and adds new mapping tools in Acrobat 9 Pro Extended.

#103 Converting Visio, InDesign, and Illustrator Documents

Using the AutoCAD PDFMaker

Acrobat 9 Pro includes a Windows-only PDFMaker for AutoCAD. Here are some tips for working with the AutoCAD PDFMaker:

- Page size and plotting information transfers from AutoCAD to the PDFMaker automatically to specify the right page size.

- Click PDF Layer Settings to open a menu listing settings previously created and saved. Choose the setting you wish to use and click OK to return to the Acrobat PDFMaker dialog, where you see the selected settings displayed.

- After you convert an AutoCAD drawing to PDF, you have to resave the AutoCAD drawing again to actually store the PDF settings.

- Use the Named layer filters options in the Acrobat PDFMaker dialog to select a filter fitting specific criteria. If you want to use all layers except those filtered on your named criteria, click the Invert option.

(continued on next page)

Microsoft Visio and Adobe InDesign and Illustrator are popular source programs for producing layered PDF files. Visio gives you the power to use one document structure and layer the information and data as needed.

InDesign and Illustrator offer collections of PDF presets for export, and you can specify separate layers in most of those presets.

Note
Acrobat 9 Pro also installs a PDFMaker in AutoCAD. Read some hints on using it in the sidebar "Using the AutoCAD PDFMaker."

Layered Visio files. Layers convert using the settings you choose in Visio's Layer Properties dialog, such as visibility, locks, and names. In the Adobe PDF program menu, choose Adobe PDF > Convert all Pages in Drawing to include all layers, including the background. Select basic conversion options as with the other PDFMakers.

The Visio PDFMaker settings include options for embedded data. Choose Adobe PDF > Change Conversion Settings to display the Acrobat PDFMaker dialog. In the Application Settings area of the General tab, look for options to include Visio properties, as well as how to manage objects without custom properties (**Figure 103a**).

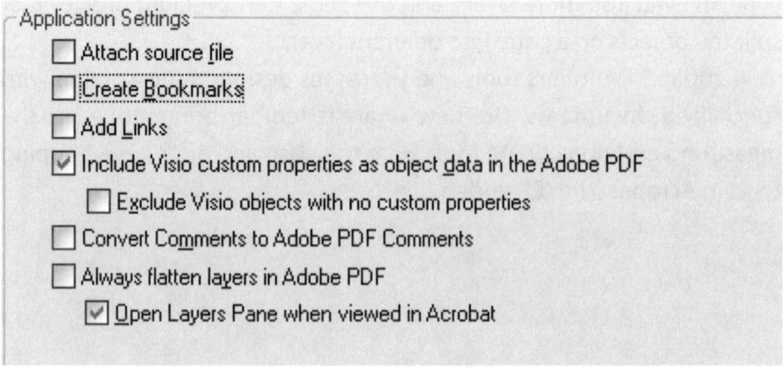

Figure 103a Specify how to handle objects and their data in the dialog.

The conversion process in Visio uses a multipanel PDFMaker. As you step through the PDFMaker, be sure to identify how you want to manage the exported layers. For ease of use in the exported PDF, consider grouping layers into layer sets (you can see an example of layer sets in #104, "Working with a Layered Document").

Layered InDesign documents. You can export documents from InDesign (CS and newer) with retained layers that display as PDF layers in Acrobat.

Choose File > Export and select PDF from the "Save as type" pop-up list in the Export dialog. The Export Adobe PDF dialog opens automatically (**Figure 103b**).

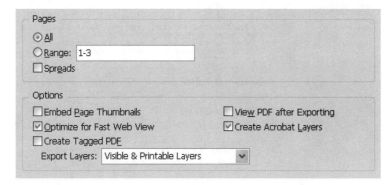

Figure 103b Define layer settings when exporting a PDF from InDesign.

Keep these ideas in mind as you prepare for a PDF export:

- Compatibility must be set to Acrobat 6.0 (PDF 1.5) or higher to support the layers.

- Make sure that Create Acrobat Layers is selected in the Export Adobe PDF dialog.

- Select the layer options from the Export Layers pop-up menu—choose from Visible, Printable, and Visible & Printable options.

- Click Create Layer Set to add a folder to the Layers in PDF list, and then add layers to the folder. After you convert the document to PDF, when you open it in Acrobat, you see the layers in the original AutoCAD drawing arranged in layer sets, which makes it much simpler for users to view specific parts of a drawing.

Why Bother with Layers?

In some cases, you should always flatten a document, such as a drawing certified by an engineer, to preserve its integrity. In other cases, feel free to layer away. A layered PDF document can be a terrific advertising tool. Instead of showing your customer one product image and some color swatches, put the alternate colors on different layers and let your client click through bookmarked layers, viewing the product in its varying colors.

Flattening Layers

If you work with Visio drawings that are converted to PDF on a regular basis and don't need to preserve the layers, select "Always flatten layers and don't show this dialog again" in the second panel of the PDFMaker dialog. The default option is to flatten the drawing; choosing the "Always flatten layers" option saves you one step in your conversions.

Layered Illustrator documents. As in InDesign, you choose a preset for converting to PDF; unlike in InDesign, you don't export the file but simply choose the File > Save As command. The default Illustrator Adobe PDF Preset includes exporting layers (**Figure 103c**).

Note
Since the AI format is a derivative of PDF, you are changing format characteristics rather than converting to a different format type.

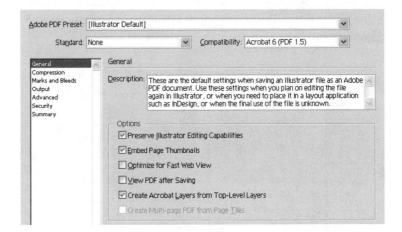

Figure 103c Choose layering options in a PDF file saved from Illustrator.

#104 Working with a Layered Document

In Acrobat 9 you can work with layered documents created in several programs, including InDesign, Visio, and AutoCAD. Acrobat doesn't support layers created in Photoshop.

Manipulate layers in Acrobat for different purposes, such as hiding layer content in different languages, or showing corporate information on a printing layer.

The Layers icon displays in the Navigation pane when you open a document containing layers. Click the Layers icon in the Navigation pane to open the Layers pane (**Figure 104a**).

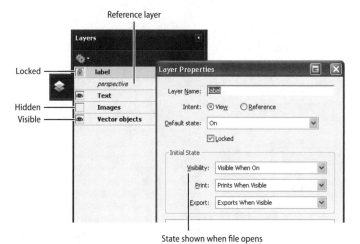

Figure 104a View layers and access their properties in this pane.

The Layers pane shows different types of layers and statuses:

- Toggle a layer's visibility on and off by clicking the eye icon—when the eye is visible, the layer is visible.

- Lock a layer in the source document before conversion to PDF or in the Layer Properties dialog if security settings permit.

- A reference layer is indicated in the Layers pane in italics. The reference layer works like a background in that it is always visible and can't be modified. The reference layer is specified in the source program, or in the Layer Properties.

(continued on next page)

Taking Action with Layers

Acrobat does not allow you to author layers that change visibility according to the zoom level. However, you can highlight a portion of a layer that is especially important by creating a bookmark that magnifies or hides the layer using page actions. You can also add links that let users click a visible or invisible link to navigate to or zoom in on a layer. Read about using links and bookmarks in Chapter 15, "Controlling Action and Interaction;" check out #110, "Bookmarking Drawings, Maps, or Layers," for more information on bookmarking drawings, maps, and their layers.

Changing Layers

As with other documents, you may be able to make changes to the content depending on the rights granted by the document's author. If a layered document doesn't contain security, you can add comments to it, print it, or export it in another file format from Acrobat.

Keep in mind that settings applied to the original layered document cannot be changed. For example, if a document layer is assigned the Prints When Visible setting, only a blank page prints unless the layer's eye icon is toggled to visible.

Showing the Layers Pane

To specify that the document appear with the Layers pane and Document pane automatically, choose File > Properties and select the Initial View tab; choose Layers Panel and Page from the Navigation pop-up menu. Refer to the sidebar "Crafting Your Readers' Viewing Experience—Part 1: Navigation" in #31, "Finding Information about Your Document."

- To see what a layer contains, right-click (Control-click) it in the Layers pane and choose Layer Properties to open the dialog (also shown in Figure 104a). The Layer Properties dialog lists information about the layer, including its original name, visibility, print status, and export status.

Layer groups hold multiple layers, and can be collapsed or expanded in the Layers pane. Programs such as Visio and AutoCAD can produce layer groups, where a number of layers are nested within a heading (**Figure 104b**).

Name	Locked On
▼ 🗀 Plantings	
Existing planti...	☐
New planting	☐
New Plants	☐
New Trees	☐
Plant	☐
▼ 🗀 Hardscaping	
Decks	☐
Door	☐
Site Improve...	☐
Wall	☐
Window	☐

Figure 104b Layers may be organized in groups before converting to PDF.

Use the commands in the Options menu to rename, flatten, rearrange, merge, and lock/unlock layers.

Different Types of Layers

What you see in the Layers pane depends on how the original document was constructed and converted. In some cases, a document is converted with preserved layers. In other cases, the document layers may be flattened or locked. In a flattened document, you see a single layer as in a regular PDF document. A locked document, on the other hand, displays the layers individually, but they can't be edited in any way.

#**105** Adding New Layers

In Acrobat 9, you can add new layers from another document, or split your current PDF file into layers. Add new layers to an existing PDF file using layers from another PDF file, or an image in BMP, GIF, JPEG, JPEG 2000, PCX, PNG, or TIF format.

Open your target PDF file and follow these steps to add a new layer:

1. Choose Import As Layer from the Layers pane's Options menu to open the Import as Layer dialog (**Figure 105a**). Click Browse to select the file you want to add, and click OK. The file is listed in the Source area of the dialog.

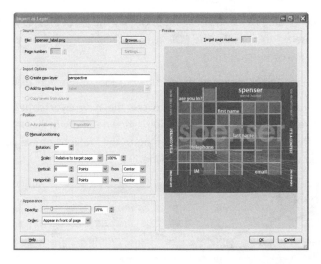

Figure 105a Specify the file and its appearance before adding the new layer to your document.

Tip
If the source document has multiple pages, indicate the page to import; if your target file contains multiple pages, specify the Target page number in the Preview area of the dialog.

2. Choose an import option; read about the options in the sidebar "Adding On the Layers."

3. Adjust the Position and Appearance settings as needed. In the example, the imported content is scaled to fit the page, and its opacity is decreased.

(continued on next page)

Adding On the Layers

Acrobat offers several ways to import content for layering from the Import as Layer dialog. Here are your options:

- "Create new layer" adds a single layer from the source document.

- "Add to existing layer" adds the content of the new layer to a selected layer in your document. If you have existing layer groups, you can select one from the pop-up menu.

- "Copy layers from source" imports the layers from the source document—you won't be able to choose this option unless the selected source document contains layers.

4. When you are pleased with the appearance shown in the preview, click OK.

But what if you have a single-layered InDesign PDF file and your client wants to see the layout without text? Or graphics? In Acrobat 9 Pro, you can use one of the new layer manipulation Preflight profiles and show clients what they want to see. You can read more about Preflight in Chapter 6, "Complying with PDF and Accessibility Standards."

Follow these steps:

1. Choose Advanced > Preflight to open the Preflight dialog.

2. Click the Create PDF Layers heading to display the list of profiles, and click to select the profile. The PDF layer options are based on your document's contents.

3. Click Analyze and fix to process the document. Close the Preflight dialog.

4. Save, close, and reopen your file to see the new layer structure (in **Figure 105b** the open Preflight dialog is shown along with the Layers pane). The new layer is named according to the Preflight profile you selected, and appears in the Layers pane.

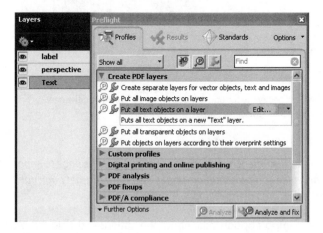

Figure 105b Add new layers to your document using Preflight profiles.

#106 Using Data Embedded in a Document

A number of programs produce PDF files that contain metadata converted from custom information embedded in the source files.

To view custom metadata embedded in a PDF file, choose Tools > Analysis > Object Data Tool, or select the Object Data tool ⬚ on the Analysis toolbar.

Move the Object Data tool over the page. When you mouse over an object that contains metadata, the pointer changes to crosshairs. Click to select all the objects containing data in the drawing; double-click to select just the object beneath the tool.

The Model Tree pane opens once the object selection is complete, and the content of the embedded data is shown in the lower section of the pane (**Figure 106**).

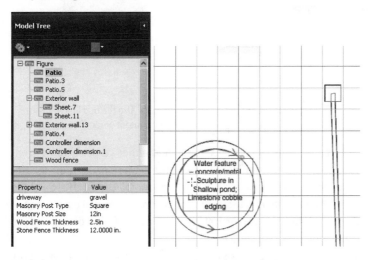

Figure 106 Display an object's data embedded into the document.

Tip
If you are using a document that also contains layers, you are in luck—open the Layers pane and hide the layers you don't need to work with at the moment. That way, there are fewer objects to select using the Object Data tool.

From the Options menu in the dialog, you can choose different ways to use the data, including the following:

• Export the data as XML from either the selected node or the entire model tree.

• Copy the content of an object's data to the clipboard.

More Object Actions

Here are some more ways to work with the object data in a drawing from the Model Tree pane:

• From the Highlight Color pop-up menu, you can open a color picker and choose another color to highlight or identify a selected object.

• Choose Previous View from the Options menu to go back to content viewed at the previous magnification.

Up Close and Personal

To check out an object close up, select it from the Model Tree pane and choose Zoom to Selection from the Options menu. The Document pane shows just the selected object.

How Many?

Choose an object from the list at the top of the Model Tree pane and then choose Count from the Options menu. The resulting information dialog lists the number of objects that have the same data associations. Some objects are single objects, whereas others are created in multiples.

#**107** Applying Positioning Features

If you have worked with image, illustration, or layout programs, you know about grids and guides. Acrobat 9 Standard and up includes both these handy features, along with rulers to help you position content precisely, and to assist in measuring and examining drawings.

Grids are sets of vertical and horizontal lines that overlay a document. The lines of the grid, which use spacing that you specify, aren't printed.

Choose View > Grid to display the grid. If you want to be able to move an object and have it "snap" to the grid (align itself automatically with the grid lines), choose View > Snap to Grid. As you drag an object or click with a Measuring tool, you see it jump to align with the grid lines horizontally or vertically (**Figure 107a**).

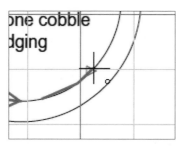

Figure 107a Use the grid lines to assist in placing content or for measuring.

Guides are custom lines that you can add either vertically or horizontally to help with positioning. Before using the guides, turn on the rulers by choosing View > Rulers. Click the horizontal ruler at the top of the Document pane with any tool and drag downward to place a horizontal guide; drag right from the vertical ruler at the left of the Document pane with any tool to place a vertical guide.

Both grids and guides can be customized in the Preferences dialog. Choose Edit > Preferences (Acrobat > Preferences) and then choose the Units and Guides option in the list at the left of the dialog to display the customization settings (**Figure 107b**). Choose an option from the Units pop-up menu other than the default inches, if required. Select options for grid spacing, color, and position of the grid. Use the arrows for each setting to increase or decrease the values, or you can type a value in the text boxes.

Figure 107b Modify the appearance and positioning of the grid and guides.

When Objects Misbehave

Whether or not the grid is displayed, the Snap to Grid feature can still be active. If you are moving content on your page—images, text, form fields, drawings—and you can't seem to nudge it into position smoothly, click the View menu, and see if the Snap to Grid option is checked. Uncheck the setting and you can nudge to your heart's content.

#**108** Measuring Objects

Acrobat 9 Pro includes several tools for measuring the distance and area of objects in a PDF drawing. You most often use these tools with drawings, PDF maps, or documents being sent to a printer.

Open the Analysis toolbar by choosing Tools > Analysis > Show Analysis Toolbar. You can also right-click (Control-click) the toolbar well at the top of the program window and select Analysis.

To measure on a document, click the Measuring tool 🖉 on the Analysis toolbar; the Measurement toolbar opens. Choose one of four ways for the Measuring tool to align with page content or snap—read about the Snap Types in the sidebar "Make It Snappy."

Before you start measuring, check the scale the tool uses. The Scale Ratio for the measurement tools is 1:1 and set in inches—that is, moving your pointer 1 inch on the page equals 1 inch in actual size. You usually have a 1:1 ratio for pages destined for print, but that's not the case for drawings or blueprints.

Note
The default is to use the scale and units from the document, if they are present. The scale and unit values are embedded in the file's metadata when you create the PDF file in programs like Visio and AutoCAD. In georegistered maps, the scale and unit values are taken from the map's metadata (see #109, "Commenting and Measuring on a PDF Map").

To reset the ratio, follow these steps:

1. Select a tool from the Measurement toolbar and right-click (Control-click) the page with the tool to open the shortcut menu. Choose Change Scale Ratio to open the dialog.

2. Type a value in both of the Scale Ratio fields, and select the unit of measure from the pop-up menus. A common ratio on floor plans is 1/8 inch to 1 inch, shown in **Figure 108a**. Notice that 1/8 inch is entered as a decimal value, as the dialog doesn't accept fractions.

3. Click OK to close the dialog.

Make It Snappy

The Measurement tool uses different methods of aligning itself to content on the page, which helps with accurate measurement. Choose from four Snap Types, located on the Measurement toolbar. With an active measurement tool, when you click the document, the pointer automatically moves to the nearest location specified by the active Snap Type.

Here are your choices:

- Snap to Paths ⬉ moves your pointer location to the closest drawn path or line.

- Snap to Endpoints ⬉ moves the pointer location to the end of the closest drawn line.

- Snap to Midpoints ⬉ moves the pointer location to the center of the closest drawn line.

- Snap to Intersections ⬉ moves the pointer location to the nearest intersection of two drawn lines.

If you don't want to use any snap options, right-click (Control-click) with the measurement tool to open the shortcut menu, and choose Don't Snap to Page Content.

Figure 108a Set the ratio according to your project's scale.

Once your Scale Ratio is set, start to draw points on the page with the selected measurement tool. As you draw, information is displayed in the Measurement Info widget (**Figure 108b**). You can read the values set with mouse clicks, angles, and delta values (the location of the point on the X-Y axes of the page).

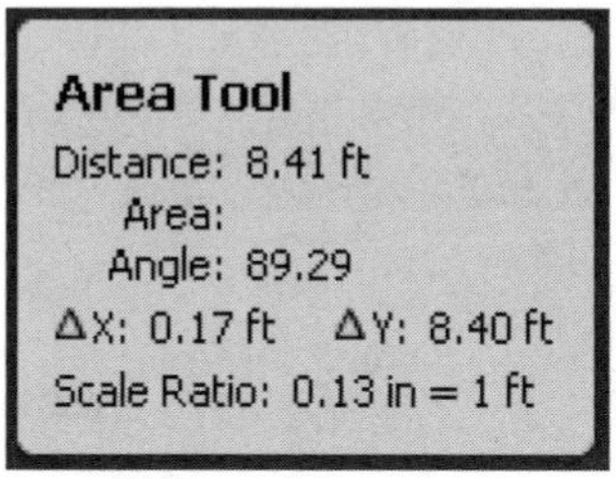

Area Tool

Distance: 8.41 ft
  Area:
  Angle: 89.29
ΔX: 0.17 ft   ΔY: 8.40 ft
Scale Ratio: 0.13 in = 1 ft

Figure 108b Read information about your measurement.

Note
To stop the drawing process before completing a shape, press Esc on your keyboard or select another tool from the toolbars. To constrain the segments to straight lines as you draw, hold down the Shift key as you click and drag the mouse.

Each tool measures in a different way:

- Click the Distance Tool to measure the distance between two points. Click the location for the first point, drag to the second point, and click the mouse again.

- Click the Perimeter Tool to measure the distance between several points. Click each point you want to measure and then double-click the last point to finish the measurement.

- Click the Area Tool to measure the area within line segments. With the tool, click each point you want to measure and then click the first point again to complete the measurement area.

Move It Around
You can adjust the paths and points you draw for a measurement. Make sure either the Hand tool or the same tool you used for the measurement is active and move your mouse over the measured shape:

- To move the measurement on the page, drag when you see the Move tool over one of the measurement's paths.

- To adjust one of the endpoints on the measurement, drag when you see the Direct Select tool over an endpoint of the measurement's shape.

Once you've finished drawing the measurement, the value is shown in the Measurement Info widget and inserted as a comment (**Figure 108c**). The shape can be reconfigured (read how in the sidebar "Make It Snappy"), and the values in the comment and Measurement Info widget automatically update.

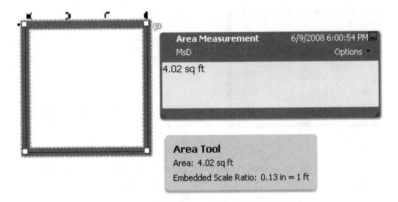

Figure 108c The measurement appears in a comment.

#**109** Commenting and Measuring on a PDF Map

Acrobat 9 Pro Extended (Windows) offers two new features for dealing with *georeferenced* maps, that is, maps that have longitude/latitude, coordinate systems, and other mapping data embedded in them. As you'll see in this technique, you can mark geographic locations, search for a map location, and add georeferenced measurement markups.

You can open a PDF map in Acrobat 9 Pro Extended and add geospatial referencing data to it—read how in the sidebar "Building a PDF Map."

To add a point of interest on a georeferenced map, follow these steps:

1. Select the Geospatial Location tool on the Analysis toolbar—the pointer changes to crosshairs.

   Tip
   If you don't see crosshairs, the map you are using hasn't been georeferenced, and you won't be able to identify or mark locations as described in these steps.

2. Move the cursor over the map, using the Latitude and Longitude values shown in the Info widget at the bottom of the document window to help pinpoint a location.

3. Right-click the tool at the point of interest to open the shortcut menu and choose Mark Location. A Sticky Note comment is added at the map location you click, and the latitude and longitude values are automatically added to the comment (**Figure 109a**).

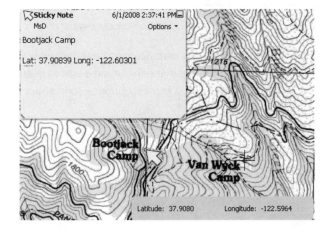

Figure 109a Identify geographic locations that are stored in a comment.

Building a PDF Map

With Acrobat Pro Extended (Windows), you can import a map image and create geospatially enabled PDFs. You can georegister a map by using its boundary coordinates and the projection scale on which the map is based. Select the Geospatial Registration tool 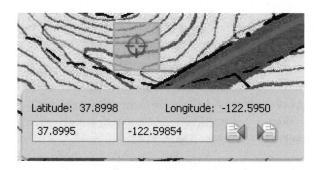 on the Analysis toolbar, and right-click an area on the map to start the Geospatial Registration wizard.

1. Type a name for the map. Click Next.

2. Define the *neatline* (boundaries) for the map you want to produce. Click at each of four corners to add an indicator and continue to draw the shape; double-click to end the neatline. To use the entire page, select "Use page bounds as neatline."

3. The Input Registration Points screen of the wizard displays automatically. Click a point on your neatline and type the latitude and longitude values in the Input points fields for the point. Repeat for the other three boundary points. Click Next.

(continued on next page)

Tip

As with other comments, you can customize the content and appearance. Read about comments in Chapter 10, "Commenting in a PDF Document."

Search for specific coordinates rather than scrolling the maps for a location, a handy approach if you have several pages of maps showing different features such as topography and rainfall distribution. To use the coordinate searching, you need a georeferenced map.

Right-click the Geospatial Location tool on the map to open the shortcut menu and choose Show Location Search. In the Info widget, type the positioning values in the two blank fields and click Next ▶. The location is shown on the map in a special icon (**Figure 109b**). If you like, identify the location with a comment. Continue adding reference data and identifying map locations as required. When you're done, choose Hide Location Search from the shortcut menu to close the Search widget.

Figure 109b Identified geographic locations are stored in a comment.

The Measuring tools can measure distance, area, and perimeter on a map. The tools measure map content in much the same way as measuring any other type of content, with a few exceptions—read about the differences in the sidebar "Measurable Differences." The values shown in the measurement are inserted into a comment using the map data (**Figure 109c**). Read instructions for using the tools in #108, "Measuring Objects."

Figure 109c Locations on a map are measured using the map's data as units of measurement.

4. Select a registration system from the drop-down list, and specify default units of measure.

5. Click OK to move to the end of the wizard; the Geospatial Location tool and Measurement tool are now enabled to interact with geospatial content in the document.

Measurable Differences

The measuring tools work much the same way in map and non-map PDF files, with exceptions:

- On a PDF map, the measured value is stored in a drawing markups comment, such as a line or polygon.

- On a PDF map, the shortcut menu for the measurement types includes options to specify distance units and area units.

#**110** Bookmarking Drawings, Maps, or Layers

Why Use Bookmarks?

Acrobat lets you attach bookmarks to layers, which you can use in different ways. For example, you can distribute the same information using different languages without having to provide documents in different languages, or you can show customers samples in different colors in the same document. Use bookmarks in conjunction with layers to give readers control over what they see and print. Use actions to extend the function of a bookmark beyond just pointing to a location in your document.

Say you have a document made up of several pages, some containing layers, some containing maps with georeferenced locations, and still others containing content with headings that you want to hyperlink with bookmarks. You can make the document easier to work with by navigating from one pane only.

The process of adding a bookmark to a drawing or map is the same as for adding a basic bookmark—that is, add and name the bookmark, display the correct view, and set the destination. The process for bookmarking a layered document requires more document manipulation.

Note
For the inside scoop on working with bookmarks, refer to Chapter 15, "Controlling Action and Interaction."

Follow these steps to bookmark a layered document:

1. Open the Bookmarks pane and add default bookmarks corresponding to the layers you want to link (**Figure 110a**). At this point, if you click any bookmark, it displays the same location on the same page.

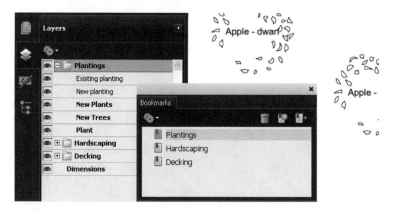

Figure 110a Add the bookmarks used to initiate the action.

2. Select the first layer bookmark and name it. To minimize confusion, it's sometimes easier to name the bookmarks and arrange them in the same order as the layers listed in the Layers pane.

3. In the Layers pane, toggle all layers' visibility off but the one associated with the first bookmark.

4. In the Bookmarks pane, right-click (Control-click) the bookmark to open the shortcut menu. Choose Properties to open the Bookmark Properties dialog and then select the Actions tab.

5. From the Select Action pop-up menu, select "Set layer visibility" **(Figure 110b)** and then click Add. The action automatically appears in the Actions section at the bottom of the dialog.

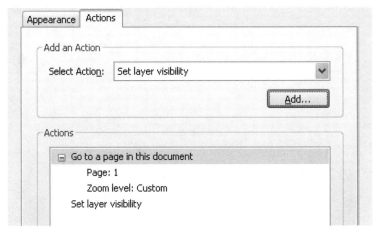

Figure 110b Specify the bookmark's link to the displayed layer in the Actions tab.

6. A notification dialog appears to tell you that the target layer state of the selected actions will be set to the current state. In other words, set the destination layer you want to see as a result of clicking a bookmark and leave the rest hidden. Click OK. The action is added to the Actions list.

7. Repeat these steps with the other layers. Be sure to hide all layers except the one you are attaching to the bookmark.

The Same Goes for Links

You don't attach a link to a specific layer in a PDF file. Instead, the link basically floats, remaining on top of whatever layer or layer group is visible. However, if you add and configure a link, you can specify the layers that are shown or hidden.

CHAPTER FIFTEEN

Controlling Action and Interaction

The most common type of form field is a button—so common, in fact, that in Acrobat 9, the Button tool is included on the Advanced Editing toolbar.

Buttons aren't the only type of common action feature used in PDF files. Links can be set using a variety of elements, including text or images. Although Bookmarks display in the Bookmarks pane, they also function as a type of link since they respond to the "Go to a page view" action, taking you wherever you want to go within a given document.

Speaking of action—whether you use buttons, links, or bookmarks, you can generally perform the same sorts of actions. In this chapter, you'll learn how to use these versatile objects to control content and activity in your PDF masterpieces.

And, if you thought you could apply actions only to specific items in a document, think again. You'll see how to apply actions to the document as a whole, providing invaluable orientation for large and complex documents.

#**111** Linking Content in a Document

Linking to a PDF Page from a Web Site

You can specify that a hyperlink on a Web page open a particular page in a PDF file by using an open parameter along with the URL. For example, if I want a user to view page 3 of my report, the link is written as `myreport.pdf#page=3`.

The greatest convenience of using links in a PDF file is that you don't have to prepare anything in advance, like a button shape or underlined text. Instead, use the settings in Acrobat to make a link appear distinctive on a page following these steps:

1. Choose Tools > Advanced Editing > Show Advanced Editing Toolbar to display the tools.

   Tip
   If you're working with several editing activities, it's easier to have the toolbar open.

2. Click the Link tool ![link icon] to select it, and then draw a marquee around the text you want to associate with the link. The Create Link dialog opens (**Figure 111a**).

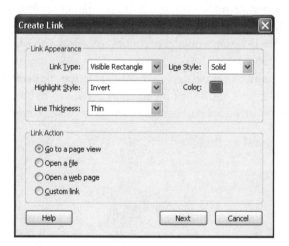

Figure 111a Specify how you want the link to look and function in this dialog.

3. Choose whether you want the link to be visible or invisible, and specify characteristics for the link's frame. You can draw a dashed or solid rectangle around the text, like the example in Figure 111a, or underline the text.

4. Choose an action by selecting one of the radio buttons at the bottom of the dialog and click Next. The dialog that appears depends on the option you choose:

- "Go to a page view" opens the Create Go to View dialog in place of the Create Link dialog (**Figure 111b**). Use the scroll bars and Zoom tools to set the view. Once you have the view set, click Set Link to close the dialog and finish the link.

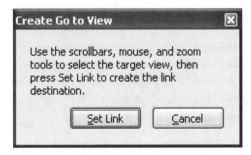

Figure 111b Follow the instructions in the dialog to position the content you want to display when the user clicks your link.

- "Open a file" opens a browse dialog for you to select the file you want to display. If you choose a PDF document, the dialog closes and another one opens for you to choose a window open preference. Select "Window set by user preference," New window, or Existing window, and click OK to finish the link. If you're linking to a non-PDF file, when you click Select, the dialog closes and the link is finished.

- "Open a web page" opens the Edit URL dialog. Type the Web address you want to open from the link and click OK to close the dialog and finish the link.

- "Custom link" opens the two-tab Link Properties dialog, and shows the options selected earlier in the Appearance tab. Click Actions to display the tab, and choose an option from the Select Action pop-up menu. Configure the action, which is displayed in the bottom area of the dialog. Links have only one state—that is, the action occurs when the link is clicked.

5. Click the Hand tool on the Select & Zoom toolbar to deselect the Link tool—you can't see your link in action as long as the tool is selected. Click to test the link.

The Perfect Link

You can apply Acrobat's Link tool function to a feature that serves as a button in another program to produce a custom appearance. For example, you may have converted a document to PDF and want to use the logo in your footer as a link in Acrobat. Draw the link box over the logo image. From the Link Type pop-up menu in the Create Link dialog, choose Invisible Rectangle. You then get the link action without any lines or frames detracting from the beauty of your logo.

Once you add a link (or a bookmark or button) you can change the settings easily. For a link, double-click the link with either the Link tool or the Select Object tool ▶ on the Advanced Editing toolbar to open the Link Properties dialog. The dialog contains the Appearance and Actions tabs. The radio button options for common link actions, shown in the Create Link dialog when you start a new link (shown in Figure 111a), don't appear in the Appearance tab.

You can use a special type of link or bookmark process to display a particular location, called a *destination*, on a numbered page, in either the same or another PDF document. If you then add or remove pages, the link or bookmark still points to the original page, not to the original content. Read how to use destinations in #114 , "Naming Destinations."

#112 Creating Bookmarks in a Source Document

The Windows PDFMaker lets you assign bookmarks in Microsoft Office programs quickly and easily if the source document is constructed properly using styles or headings. However, if you aren't that well versed in the source document's program, you may find the process of converting headings or styles to bookmarks a bit confusing—and your results will be less than optimal.

Note

Instead of using structural elements, as in this technique, check out #113 ("Adding Bookmarks in Acrobat") to learn how to add bookmarks visually in Acrobat. You must use the technique in #113 if you are working in Mac as Acrobat 9 doesn't offer PDFMaker for Mac.

The bookmarks in a sample document converted to Acrobat PDF are shown in **Figure 112**. You can see that there are many, many bookmarks, and their organization is rather chaotic—the sample uses every option available in the PDFMaker, and the document uses too many styles and headings.

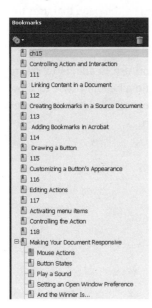

Figure 112 Only choose the styles or headings you need for bookmarks, or your results may be virtually useless, like this set of bookmarks for a three-page document.

Jumping Bookmarks

Be sure to click the bookmark's name in the Bookmarks pane to activate it before setting the destination view. If you position the document in the desired location and set the magnification, as soon as you click the bookmark you want to change, Acrobat jumps to the original view—which means you have to start all over again.

Using Destination Options Correctly

As with many other settings, a magnification option applies until you change it. In other words, every time you add a new bookmark, it inherits the destination or magnification last specified. Take advantage of the inheritance when you are adding a set of bookmarks to a document. But be careful if you add bookmarks during a different session—if the settings you use for some bookmarks are different from the settings used with other bookmarks, readers will find the progress through your document jumpy and distracting.

Cut and Paste

Cut and paste bookmarks rather than trying to reorder and nest them in the Bookmarks pane. Click the bookmark you want to remove, and choose Cut from the Bookmarks pane's Options menu. Then click the bookmark preceding the location where you want the bookmark moved, and choose Paste After Selected Bookmark.

To convert a document resulting in logical bookmarks, keep these points in mind:

- Choose the option that is most convenient for your purposes. If you use a template, use its styles.

- If your document already contains a table of contents, simply select the Convert Word Bookmarks option in the Bookmarks tab of the Acrobat PDFMaker dialog. That way, content that is included in the Table of Contents is automatically mirrored in the Bookmarks pane in Acrobat.

- If you aren't constrained by policy or other business-related issues, and you aren't an advanced user of Office products, use the Word headings conversion option. It is simple to attach a Heading1 style to major document headings, a Heading2 style to subheadings, a Heading3 to lower-level headings, and so on.

- In the document, don't use headings or styles for any text but the text you intend to use for bookmarks. Anything on the page that uses the heading or style is converted to a bookmark regardless of whether it contains any text.

- You will produce blank bookmarks if you use headings to create blank space on your page. Instead of using a heading style to show a blank space, create a custom style for your templates that includes extra space before and after the paragraph.

#113 Adding Bookmarks in Acrobat

Acrobat lets you add new bookmarks to a document using different methods. The option you choose depends on the number needed. It's easy to add two bookmarks manually, but not so simple to add 200. Choose one of these methods:

- Add blank bookmarks to the Bookmarks pane and fill them in manually.

- Select text from the document to create your bookmarks.

- Base bookmarks on the document's structure.

Click the Bookmarks icon 📖 to display the Bookmarks pane.

To add a blank bookmark, click the existing bookmark in the list above where you want to add a new bookmark. Click New bookmark 🔖 on the Bookmarks pane toolbar to add a blank bookmark to the Bookmarks pane (**Figure 113a**). Type the text for the bookmark to replace the default "Untitled" label.

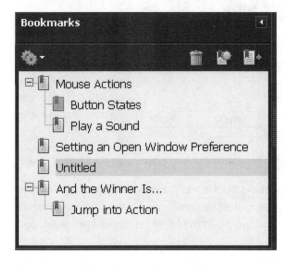

Figure 113a Add new bookmarks using default text or text copied from the document.

Tip
You can add a new bookmark by using the Ctrl+B (Command+B) shortcut keys when the Bookmarks pane is active.

Defining Your Workflow

Some people like to complete their work in one area—that is, they want to add the list of bookmarks in the Bookmarks pane and then add the actual text—whereas others prefer to complete one bookmark at a time and make their way through the document from start to finish. For either method, you need to start with the document and the Bookmarks pane open in Acrobat.

Bookmarking an Image

You don't have to stick with boring old text to define a bookmark location—you can use an image as a bookmark location instead. Click the Select tool on the Select & Zoom toolbar. Then, click an image or draw a marquee around a portion of an image on your document. Right-click (Control-click) the image and choose Add Bookmark. A new bookmark named Untitled appears at the bottom of the list (or below a selected bookmark). The "Untitled" label is active; click to delete the label and type a name for the bookmark.

Save some time typing by using the document's text. Click the Select tool 🔧 on the Select & Zoom toolbar and then click and drag with the tool to select the text that you want to use for the bookmark label. Next click New bookmark on the Bookmarks pane toolbar to add a bookmark using the selected text.

If you are working with a tagged document, use its structure to create your bookmarks. From the Options menu in the Bookmarks pane, choose New Bookmarks from Structure. The Structure Elements dialog opens (**Figure 113b**). Select the elements you want to convert to bookmarks: Shift-click to select a range; Control-click to select noncontiguous elements. Click OK to close the dialog and make your bookmarks.

Figure 113b Use a tagged document's structure to create a set of bookmarks quickly.

Click a bookmark in the Bookmarks pane to test its action. The part of the document shown in the Document pane is the *destination*, which may or may not be what you want to see. To set the proper destination, follow these steps:

1. Select the bookmark in the Bookmarks pane.

2. Place the document and set the magnification as you'd like to see it when the bookmark is used.

3. Right-click (Control-click) the bookmark to display the shortcut menu and select Set Destination. In the resulting confirmation dialog, click Yes to set the destination and dismiss the dialog.

#114 Naming Destinations

There are two parts to the destination process: First, define the destination in the target document, and second, make the link from the source document.

To specify a destination in a target document, follow these steps:

1. Choose View > Navigation Panels > Destinations to open the Destinations pane.

2. Set the page view and magnification as required using any combination of scroll bars, Zoom Levels, moving the page with the Hand tool, and so on.

3. In the Destinations pane, click New Destination ⊙ and name the destination (**Figure 114a**).

4. Repeat for all the Destinations required, and then save the file.

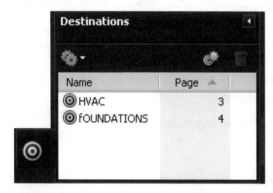

Figure 114a Define a Destination in a document to maintain an anchored location.

Follow these steps in the source document to complete the link:

1. Draw the link on the page with the Link tool; the Link Properties dialog opens.

2. Specify the link's appearance. Select Custom link in the Link Action buttons at the bottom of the dialog, and click Next to open the two-tab Link Properties dialog.

3. Click Actions to display the tab, choose "Go to a page view" from the Select Action pop-up menu, and click Add. The Create Go to View dialog opens.

(continued on next page)

Everything in Its Right Place

Before you start organizing the contents of your bookmark list into a hierarchy, make sure the heading levels are in the right order. Depending on how methodical you were when you created the bookmarks, they might not accurately reflect the order of the contents. To fix the sequence, first select the bookmark you want to move. Drag it up or down in the list to position it in its proper place. You'll see a dotted indicator line with a small black arrow below or above each title as you drag the bookmark up or down the list. Drop the bookmark when the indicator shows the correct location. Reordering the list of bookmarks doesn't change the heading levels in any way.

Handling Bookmarks

Build a nested bookmark structure to declutter the Bookmarks pane. As you build a nested structure, a level indicator appears to the left of the parent bookmark. Click the plus sign to expand, and the minus sign to collapse the bookmark.

Nested bookmarks are dependant on their parent bookmark. When you move the parent bookmark, Acrobat includes any child bookmarks and levels in the move. If you delete a parent bookmark, all nested levels are deleted, too.

4. Open the target document's Destinations pane, and double-click the destination's listing. Acrobat takes you back to the Link Properties dialog, where you see the listed action contains the document and the destination names (**Figure 114b**).

Figure 114b The action's details include the Destination name.

5. Click OK to close the Link Properties dialog, returning you to the link on the source document.

6. Test the link and save the source document.

Nesting Bookmarks

Bookmarks form an interactive table of contents that lets your readers quickly see an outline of your document's contents. To move bookmarks, remember these points:

- If you want to nest a bookmark, select it and drag it by the icon. Again you'll see the horizontal black line. When you are below the bookmark you are designating as the parent, drag slightly to the right. When you see the horizontal line move below the parent bookmark's text rather than its icon, release the mouse to nest the bookmark.

- If you want to move a bookmark out of a nested position, drag the bookmark icon to a position below the parent bookmark and drag left. When you see the horizontal black line below the parent bookmark's icon, release the mouse to promote the bookmark.

#**115** Drawing a Simple Button

Everybody knows what buttons are—digital ones, not the kind sewn on your shirt. Acrobat offers four different button behaviors. The Push behavior lets you configure different states and appearances (see #117, "Configuring a Push Button," to learn about Push buttons).

Follow these steps to configure the button:

1. Select the Button tool ⬚ on the Advanced Editing toolbar and use the placement guides to add the button shape to the page (**Figure 115a**). Release the mouse and the button appears on the page.

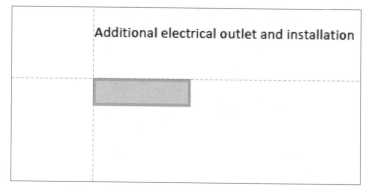

Additional electrical outlet and installation

Figure 115a Use the automatic guides to help place the button.

2. The Field Name dialog opens, naming the button "Button1" by default; click Show All Properties to open the Button Properties dialog.

3. Change the button's name and type a tooltip if you like.

4. Select the Appearance tab, and define how the button will look by choosing background and text color, borders, font, and line styles.

5. Select the Options tab and define how the content on the button should look. You have numerous choices:

   • In the Layout pop-up menu, you can select from a list of layout options. If you choose any options that include labels, the Label field becomes active; if you choose any options that include images, the Icon field becomes active.

(continued on next page)

Converting Program Actions to PDF Actions (Windows)

Acrobat 9 on Windows lets you bring along PowerPoint objects and structures—like links and buttons—into the PDF version of the presentation. You can use overlapping shapes and graphics, action buttons, action settings, and speaker notes.

Before you make the conversion, choose Adobe PDF > Change Conversion Settings to open the Acrobat PDFMaker dialog. Be sure the appropriate options are selected—such as converting notes, links, and so on. Then convert the presentation to PDF and open it. If you then open a link or the Button Properties dialog, you'll see the included action.

If you have other actions you want to add once a document is converted to PDF from a PowerPoint presentation, see if you can reuse the actions you've already imported. In the Link Properties dialog, you can add, modify, remove, or reorder actions that are imported, as well as those you create in Acrobat.

- From the Behavior pop-up menu, choose an option. None shows no change when the button is clicked; Push buttons use different appearances in relation to the mouse location (such as a paler appearance when the mouse moves over the button, or darker when the mouse clicks the button); Outline highlights the button's border when it is clicked; and Invert reverses the dark and light colors in the button when it is clicked (**Figure 115b**).

- Type text for the button in the Label field. To add an icon, which can be an image or a PDF file, click Choose Icon to open a browser dialog. Locate the file and select it. A thumbnail appears in the Button Properties dialog.

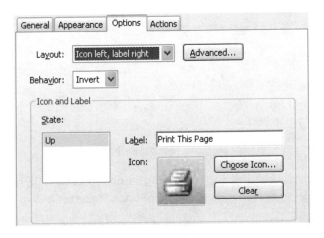

Figure 115b Specify the button's appearance using images, text, or both.

Tip

Click Advanced to choose scaling and placement options in the Icon Placement dialog.

6. Select the Actions tab and specify what you want the button to do when it's clicked. Read about using actions in #118, "Editing Actions."

7. Click Close to dismiss the dialog and complete the button.

8. Click the Hand view to deactivate the editing mode, and click to test your button.

#**116** Building a Batch of Buttons

Acrobat lets you quickly add multiple buttons to a page. Start by drawing the first button and configuring its appearance. See the sidebar "Action—Now or Later" for when to add the actions before you make multiples. Once the button is ready, follow these steps to add a batch of buttons to a single page:

1. Right-click (Control-click) the button (named *Button0* in the example) and choose Place Multiple Fields from the shortcut menu; the Create Multiple Copies of Fields dialog opens.

2. Specify the numbers of rows of buttons you want to display in the document. In the example, there are three buttons across and two rows of buttons. You can also resize the buttons in the dialog.

3. Use the positioning buttons to nudge the group of buttons on the page—you'll see a preview on the page as you make changes.

4. Click OK to close the dialog.

5. The buttons are named according to the original buttons' names (**Figure 116**). In the example, the original button was named Button0 and is renamed Button0.0.0. The button next to it in the row is named Button0.0.1; the second row starts numbering at Button0.1.0. Adding buttons to the collection continues the numbering sequence.

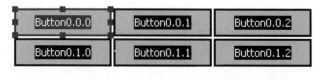

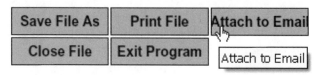

Figure 116 The series of buttons are named using the original buttons' names and their positions (top), and then renamed and reconfigured (bottom).

6. Double-click each button to open its respective Button Properties dialog and make changes to the name and action. The completed set is shown at the bottom of Figure 116.

Duplicating Buttons

Do you want a Back button that appears on every page of your document? Build your button and add the appropriate action. For example, to use a Back button applied to the document's pages, draw the first button, and in the Button Properties dialog, set an action to go to a page view. Setting the action before you make the duplicates saves a lot of time later. To add the duplicates:

1. Move the button to the correct location on the page, and right-click (Control-click) the button to open the shortcut menu. Choose Duplicate to open the Duplicate Field dialog.

2. The default selection is All pages; you can click From and type the page range to use instead if you prefer.

3. Click OK and the buttons are added. Just like that. When you duplicate the button, it is merely a copy of the original—the buttons' names aren't changed.

Action—Now or Later

Consider the buttons' actions—in some cases (such as a set of buttons that open a series of documents), it's simpler to have the action set for the first one, and then make simple modifications to the others. At other times—if the actions are very different—create the buttons and then add the actions to each. The example used here offers different File commands, including Save File As, Print File, Attach to Email, Close File, and Exit Program. The final button in row 2 was deleted. It's simpler to add the command to the first button and then revise the duplicates.

What if you want the same button, such as a Back button or Print button, on every page? No problem. See how to make duplicate buttons in the sidebar "Duplicating Buttons."

Those Annoying Mistakes

Suppose you create a set of buttons by copying and pasting. Then you click the Hand tool and realize your border should be thinner—and the whole batch of buttons uses the wrong appearance. Not to worry. Select all the buttons and then change the appearance on the Properties bar. The changes are applied to all selected buttons.

P.S. The same process applies to links.

#117 Configuring a Push Button

Buttons commonly change appearance when you move the pointer over them, and they may change yet again when you click them. These changes are called *button states*. Acrobat offers four different button behaviors, and one behavior, Push, allows you to configure different states for the buttons.

Select the Button tool 🔲 on the Advanced Editing toolbar and click when the guides show the button at the correct location. Click Show All Properties on the Field Name dialog to open the Button Properties dialog.

Once you are in the Button Properties dialog, follow the instructions in #115, "Drawing a Simple Button," earlier in this chapter for naming and setting the Appearance. The real action takes place in the Options and Actions tabs.

- From the Layout pop-up menu, you can select from a list of layout options. If you choose any options that include labels, the Label field becomes active; if you choose any options that include images, the Icon field becomes active.

- Choose Push from the Behavior pop-up menu to include Down and Rollover on the State menu, along with Up, the only state available for the other behavior options (**Figure 117a**).

- Click the appropriate State in the list at the left of the dialog and then type text in the Label field. To add an icon, which can be an image or a PDF file, click Choose Icon to open a browser dialog. Locate the file and select it. A thumbnail appears in the Button Properties dialog.

Tip
Click Advanced to choose scaling and placement options in the Icon Placement dialog.

Mouse Actions

Buttons can cause different actions depending on where your pointer is in relation to the button, as well as the mouse action itself. These mouse movements are called *triggers*.

Choose from a number of different triggers in the Options panel of the Button Properties dialog. Choose one of these triggers from the Trigger pop-up menu:

- **Mouse Down.** The mouse button is depressed.

- **Mouse Up.** The mouse button has been depressed and is released.

- **Mouse Enter.** The pointer moves over the button.

- **Mouse Exit.** The pointer moves away from the button area.

There are several other triggers as well used specifically for forms and media, such as the on Blur and on Focus triggers for form fields, and Page Visible/Invisible for media clips. Refer to Chapter 13, "Using Flash Video and 3D Media," for information on using multimedia.

Belly Up to the Toolbar

All of the tools used for modifying buttons, links, and toolbars are on the Properties toolbar. Right-click the toolbar well at the top of the program window and choose Properties Bar or use the shortcut Ctrl+E (Command+E). If you are working with a large number of items, drag the toolbar into the toolbar well to dock it. When you click a link, bookmark, or button, the item's Properties bar is active—click More on the toolbar to open the two-tab dialog if you want to set actions for the selected item.

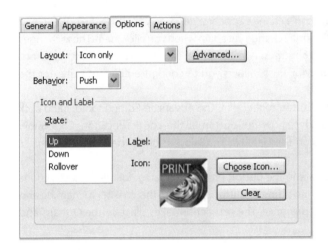

Figure 117a Specify the appearance for each state of the button using images, text, or both.

Once you've set the appearance for each state, select the Actions tab and specify both triggers and actions that you want to associate with the button. If you want to use separate actions for separate triggers, repeat the process and choose the appropriate trigger from the Triggers pop-up menu.

Tip
Triggers are described in the "Mouse Actions" sidebar.

Click the dialog when you've finished, and test the button (**Figure 117b**).

Figure 117b Test the button and its states—in the figure, the left image is the static button, the center button shows the Mouse Enter state, and the right image shows the Mouse Down state.

#**118** Editing Actions

Using buttons and other interactive objects like links or bookmarks is a rather pointless exercise unless something happens when the user clicks the object. In the Button Properties dialog, click Actions to display the options you can choose and customize.

You can add any number of actions you like to a link, button, or bookmark (**Figure 118a**). But be careful that the sequence is correct—you probably don't want an action that opens a pop-up explaining that another document is going to open after the file is already displayed, for example.

Figure 118a Add several actions to the same bookmark or other interactive object such as a link or button.

One large category of actions lets you apply menu items to your interactive button, link, or bookmark from the Properties dialog. In the Actions tab, notice that "Execute a menu item" is the default action shown in the Select Action list. Click Add to open the options available (**Figure 118b**).

Figure 118b You can use many menu items as actions attached to buttons.

Jump into Action

Experiment with the options available in the "Execute a menu item" action. You may be surprised how interesting and functional your documents become. Here are a few of the things you can do:

- Send a document by e-mail.
- Save copies of the document.
- Open other documents or digital media.
- Zoom to various magnifications.
- Show different toolbars and Navigation panels.

Making Your Document Responsive

Apply actions to individual elements of a document or to the entire document. You can use actions applied to your document for a variety of purposes—for example, to display instructions or thank visitors for completing a form.

To set document actions using Acrobat JavaScript, follow these steps:

(continued on next page)

1. Choose Advanced > Document Processing > Set Document Actions. The Document Actions dialog opens, showing a list of actions that refer to different states of a document.

2. Select an action from the list at the left of the dialog. Then click Edit to open the JavaScript Editor dialog.

3. Type the text for your script in the JavaScript Editor dialog.

4. Click OK to close the dialog and list the script in the Document Actions dialog—the selected action shows a green circle next to its listing, meaning it has an active script.

5. Click OK to close the Document Actions dialog.

6. Save the document. To test the script, close the document or print it, depending on the chosen action.

As you can see, there are many menu commands you can attach to your buttons and links.

Keep these tips in mind:

- When you are editing link actions, click the action itself, not the details (such as a filename) that are listed for some actions.

- If you are editing a button action, click the action itself, not the trigger or the details—remember, only buttons have triggers.

- You don't have to plan a sequence of actions ahead of time. Add the actions you want to use and then select an action you want to reorder, and click Up or Down to move it in the execution list.

- If you change your mind about using an action, select it in the Actions area of the dialog and click Delete.

Note

You can also add actions to the entire document. Read about document actions in the sidebars "Making Your Document Responsive" and "Get in a State."

Get in a State

Documents have five scriptable states, including the following:

- Document Will Close (when a document closes)
- Document Will Save (before a document is saved)
- Document Did Save (after a document is saved)
- Document Will Print (before a document is printed)
- Document Did Print (after a document is printed)

Take note of the different states. For example, an action used in the Document Will Save state takes place before the document is saved, whereas the Document Did Save action occurs after the document is saved.

Scripting Assistance

There are many resources available to help you learn how to write JavaScript, including the form of JavaScript used in Acrobat. For example, check out the Adobe JavaScript Scripting Guide available at http://www.adobe.com/devnet/acrobat/javascript.html.

CHAPTER SIXTEEN

Making Your Documents Secure

Many of the PDF files you create on a regular basis need some sort of protection—to prevent unauthorized access to, or manipulation of, your files. It isn't necessary to secure every document you create, but for those you share or distribute, it's a good idea.

Acrobat 9 offers several types of security. The option you choose for your document depends on the material involved, as well as on your intended audience:

- Use passwords to prevent unauthorized access to documents. Restrict opening of your document with a password, and further restrict any types of changes with another password. You can also specify whether to allow users to copy, print, or extract content from a document.

- Digitally sign your document, which defines the contents of a document at the time of signing and restricts editing of those contents. You can identify the first signature applied to a document as a certified signature.

- E-mail PDF documents and attachments securely by wrapping them in Security Envelopes.

- Restrict access to your document to a specific user list, based on digital signatures, and assign different rights to different users using security policies.

#**119** Using Security Levels and Passwords for a Document

The simplest way to protect your document is to use passwords, which can be applied in any version of Acrobat 9. Acrobat offers two levels of passwords. You can use one or both types of passwords in the same document. Choose from the following:

- The user level, or Document Open password, which requires the user to type the correct characters in order to open the file

- The master-level password, or Permissions password, which allows you to specify the document restrictions

The default setting is a high level of security compatible with Acrobat version 7 and later. To change to a lower level of security for readers using older versions of Acrobat, or a higher level of security to use more features, you have to reset the Compatibility level.

Follow these steps to apply a password to a document in Acrobat 9:

1. Choose File > Properties to open the Document Properties dialog; click the Security tab to display the settings.

2. Select Password Security from the Security Method pop-up menu to display the Password Security – Settings dialog.

3. Select a program version from the Compatibility pop-up menu. The level you choose defines what options are available when you're setting passwords.

4. You can add one or two passwords:

   - Select the "Require a password to open the document" check box to activate the field. Type in the password.

   - Select the "Restrict editing and printing of the document" check box. Type in the password. Then specify the restrictions you want to add to the document (**Figure 119a**).

About Metadata

Metadata is descriptive information about a file that can be searched and processed by a computer. Adobe's Extensible Metadata Platform (XMP) lets you embed metadata into a file to provide information about a document's contents. Applications that support XMP can read, edit, and share this information across databases, file formats, and platforms. If you use Acrobat versions 6 to 9 compatibility options, you can choose to enable Metadata in the security settings.

Give Your Permission

Here's a rundown on the permissions you control using password security at the Acrobat 7 or newer level:

- Disallow (or allow) low- or high-resolution printing.

- From the Changes Allowed pop-up menu (shown in Figure 119a), choose a level of permission for the user with regard to form fields, signatures, and page orientations.

(continued on next page)

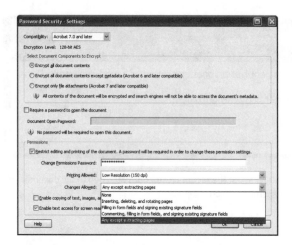

Figure 119a Choose the restrictions to apply to the document from the options based on the compatibility level chosen earlier.

5. Click OK to close the Password Security – Settings dialog. In the confirmation dialog, retype the password and click OK. Click OK again to dismiss the encryption information dialog.

Tip
When you set both passwords, you must confirm both in separate dialogs.

6. Save the document to set the security settings.

After you convert the document to a PDF, you must enter the password in a Password dialog to open it in Acrobat if you used a Document Open password.

When the document opens, you see a security icon at the upper left of the Navigation pane. Click the icon to open the Security Settings dialog, which explains that the document has attached passwords (**Figure 119b**). Click Permission Details to open the Securities tab of the Properties dialog.

- To prevent users from accessing items in your file, deselect the "Enable copying of text, images, and other content" check box.

- Choose "Enable text access for screen reader devices for the visually impaired" to allow reading of the content in your document.

Removing Security

Regardless of the method you use to encrypt or secure a document, you can change or remove the protection from within Acrobat if you have the rights:

1. Choose File > Properties > Security.

2. From the Security Method pop-up menu, choose No Security, and then click OK.

3. Click OK to confirm that you want to delete the security and remove the passwords from the document, and close the dialog.

Tips on Building Passwords

Here are a few things to remember about Acrobat passwords:

- A PDF file with both Document Open and Permissions passwords can be opened by using either password.

- Passwords can use any characters, but they are case sensitive.

- You can't use the same characters for both Document Open and Permissions passwords.

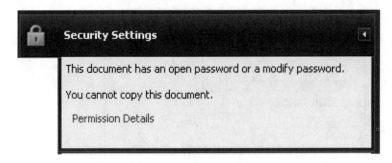

Figure 119b Information about the security restrictions attached to the document is shown in the Security Settings dialog.

#**120** Creating a Digital ID Profile

Acrobat—along with numerous document and process management systems—uses a digital signature (also known as a digital ID or digital profile) to secure content. A digital signature, like a handwritten signature, represents you.

A digital signature has two parts: a public key and a private key. Fortunately, you don't have to decide which key to use when. Here's how it works.

You use your private key to apply your digital signature to a file, which encrypts the data using the public key. The public key is contained in a certificate that you exchange with your colleagues and contacts to verify your identity. Others use your public key to create encrypted information to share with you. This two-way exchange of certificates and keys is the basis for building trusted identities, the subject of the sidebar "Sharing and Importing Digital IDs."

The visual signature applied to a document, either a default or custom signature, is referred to as an *appearance*. The appearance is composed of combinations of information fields (such as dates or text), the Acrobat logo, or imported graphics.

You can create both default and custom signatures. To create a new signature, follow these steps:

1. Choose Advanced > Security Settings to open the Security Settings dialog. Click Digital IDs in the left of the dialog to display your existing ID files in the upper-right pane of the dialog (**Figure 120a**).

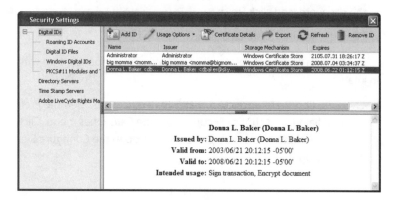

Figure 120a Digital ID files, along with other types of security servers and IDs, are listed in the Security Settings dialog.

(continued on next page)

Sharing and Importing Digital IDs

In order to open a document signed by someone else, you need a copy of his certificate, called a *trusted identity*. Choose Advanced > Manage Trusted Identities to open the Manage Trusted Identities dialog. Your identities list can be displayed as either certificates or contacts in the dialog. Contacts are the FDF (file data format) files exchanged via an e-mail request, while a certificate is the public key included in an encrypted document.

There are several important tasks you can perform in the dialog:

- Click Add Contacts to open a dialog in which you can select, search, or browse for contacts and certificates on your computer.

- Click Request Contact to open the E-mail a Request dialog. Address it to the person from whom you'd like to receive the contact.

- Click Edit Trust to open the Edit Certificate Trust dialog and change the policy features assigned to a specific contact.

(continued on next page)

2. To build a new signature, click Add ID on the dialog's toolbar. The Add Digital ID dialog opens, giving you four options. The first three deal with existing IDs: You can find an existing ID from a file, a roaming ID stored on a server, or a device connected to your computer (like a smart card). To build a new ID, click "A new digital ID I want to create now" and then click Next at the bottom of the dialog.

   On Windows, the next dialog asks where you want to store the Digital ID. You have two choices: The default is to create a new PKCS#12 digital ID file, or you can add the Digital ID to your Windows Certificate Store (Windows). Click an option, and then click Next.

3. In the next dialog, add the information you want to include in the certificate, such as Name, Organization Name, and E-mail Address. At the bottom of the dialog, make these choices:

   - Choose a Key Algorithm, which defines the level of encryption (and the version of Acrobat that can open the file)—2048-bit RSA for Acrobat 9, or 1024-bit RSA for Acrobat 7 or 8.

   - From the "Use digital ID for" menu, choose Digital Signatures, Data Encryption, or Digital Signatures and Data Encryption; click Next.

4. In the final pane of the dialog, click Browse to choose a storage location for the certificate, or leave the default location in the Security subfolder of the Acrobat program's installation folders so that you don't lose track of your certificates. Type a password and a confirmation of the password, and click Finish.

5. Close the Security Settings dialog.

Instead of using the default signature appearance, sparkle it up with an image:

1. Choose Edit > Preferences (Acrobat > Preferences) to open the Preferences dialog, and choose Security from the Categories menu. Click New in the Digital Signatures preferences to open the Configure Signature dialog.

2. Enter the new signature's description and information (**Figure 120b**):

Figure 120b Specify the features for the custom signature appearance.

- Type a title for the appearance—use a descriptive name to make it easier to recognize.

- Select a Configure Graphic option. You can choose to use no graphic, an image from a file, or your name. To use an image, click Imported graphic and then File to open a Select Picture dialog. Locate the file and click OK to close the dialog; click OK to close the picture's preview.

- Specify the text options you want to display in the Configure Text section of the dialog. All options are selected by default. Any choices that are deselected, such as the Reason or Date, don't appear in the finished signature.

- If applicable, select a text direction and digits (not shown in the figure).

3. Click OK to close the Configure Signature Appearance dialog. The new signature appearance is added to the Appearance list. Click OK to close the Preferences dialog.

- Click Export to open the Data Exchange File-Exporting Contact Information wizard. Step through the wizard and specify the destination (e-mail or export), add an optional digital signature, choose a storage location, and review the results; click Finish to exit the wizard and export the data.

- Click Delete to remove a selected contact or certificate.

- Click Show Certificate to display the certificate contents for a selected contact or certificate name.

Pick the Defaults

Save time when you are working with secured documents by specifying default signatures in the Security Settings dialog. Pick one of your signatures and click Usage Options to open the list. Specify the signature as the default for these purposes:

- Signing a document by selecting Use for Signing

- Certifying a document by selecting Use for Certifying (the same icon displays if you choose both signing and certifying options)

- Encrypting a file by selecting Use for Encryption

- Attaching a descriptive name to the file, by clicking Personalize

Policy Servers

There are three types of policy servers you can use with Acrobat. All are available by choosing Advanced > Security Settings to open the Security Settings dialog. Settings and access to these servers are controlled by your systems administrator:

- **Directory server.** The VeriSign Internet Directory server is a system used for third-party signatures and encryption. Rather than through an exchange of certificates among individuals, your content is managed by the server.

- **Time Stamp server.** If your network or system allows for a timestamp server, you can use the server's capabilities to authenticate time displayed in your documents' signatures.

- **Adobe Policy server.** This Adobe-hosted server controls access to your document using named users, and can track document access and versions, set dates on documents, and apply watermarks and expiration dates.

#121 Signing a Document

One way to apply a digital ID to a PDF document confirming the file as a legally correct document is to certify it. This affirms the contents as correct and specifies the types of changes allowed to the document. For example, a form may be certified and allow the user to fill in the fields; however, if the user tries to delete or replace pages, the document will no longer be certified at the document level.

Here's what you do for a visible signature (read the sidebar "Here a Click, There a Click" for details on dialogs not included in the following technique):

1. Click the Sign Task button to open its menu and choose either Certify with Visible Signature or Certify Without Visible Signature to activate the Digital Signature tool.

2. Draw a rectangle on the document with the tool. When you release the mouse, the signature icon displays where you drew the rectangle, and the Certify Document dialog opens (**Figure 121a**).

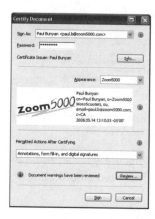

Figure 121a Specify how you want the document certified using these options.

3. In the Certify Document dialog, decide how the signature will appear and work by choosing options from the pop-up menus:

   • Select the Digital ID and type in the password for the signature.

   • Choose one of your signature appearances from the Appearance pop-up menu. If you don't have the right appearance, design a new one.

(continued on next page)

Certify It or Sign It?

Decide when you need to certify a document and when you need to sign it. If you create a lot of documents for secure distribution, you may want to certify each document as you generate it.

Be aware of the restrictions added to a document when you certify it. If you intend any of your recipients to make changes, such as additions or deletions, sign it and specify a reason, such as *"I am the author"* rather than certifying it. For specifying modification rules in a multi-signatory workflow, however, certifying is definitely the way to go.

Signing and Certifying Convenience

Acrobat 9 brings some simplifications to the signing and certifying workflow that you're sure to appreciate. In the Certify Document dialog, choose New ID from the Sign As pop-up menu. Don't have the right appearance for the signature? No problem—create a new appearance (read how in #120, "Creating a Digital ID Profile"). Voilà!

- If the signature includes the Reason option, specify why the document is being certified using choices from the Reason pop-up menu (see #120, "Creating a Digital ID Profile").

- Specify the rights you want to grant the user from the Permitted Actions After Certifying pop-up menu. You have three options: You can prevent any changes from being made; allow users to fill out forms and sign the document; or allow users to add comments, fill out forms, and sign the document.

- Click Review to check the document for issues that can interfere with certification, such as a preexisting signature.

4. To certify the file, click Sign to open the Save As dialog.

5. Name the document and click Save. The document is saved, and the Document Message Bar displays basic information about the signature (**Figure 121b**).

Figure 121b The finished signature is drawn on the page, and the Document Message Bar shows information and contains a link to signature properties.

Instead of adding a single certifying signature, you can add a blank signature field, a specialized type of form field used for collecting signatures from others.

To add a signature field, do the following:

1. Click the Sign Task button to open its menu and choose Sign Document to activate the Digital Signature tool. Draw a rectangle for the field on your document.

2. Release the mouse to open the Sign Document dialog, which contains the same choices for selecting a signature and appearance as the Certify Document dialog. Choose signature and appearance details.

3. Select Lock Document After Signing if you want to prevent changes after the document is signed and saved.

4. Click Sign to open the Save As dialog. Name the file and select its storage location; click Save to close the dialog. You'll see your signature in the field and listed in the Signatures pane, which displays automatically when the document is saved (**Figure 121c**).

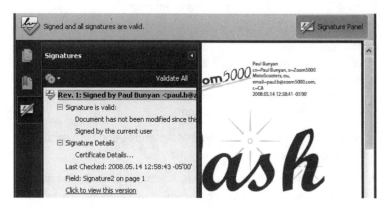

Figure 121c Read details about the signature in the Signature Panel.

To check a signature's validity, select it in the Signature Panel and choose Options > Validate Signature in the panel. The signature is tested, and Acrobat displays the results in a dialog. Click Close to dismiss the dialog. If you have several signatures to validate, click Validate All in the Signature Panel.

Make It Valid—and Quick

If your work includes a lot of signature validation, it can be time-consuming to choose commands repeatedly to validate a signature or signatures in each document you open. Instead, set a preference to have signatures validated automatically when the document opens. Choose Edit > Preferences (Acrobat > Preferences) and click the Security category in the list. Click the "Verify signatures when the document is opened" check box at the top of the dialog and click OK. Next time you open a document that contains signatures, they are verified automatically.

Preview Before Signing

Acrobat offers a Preview Document mode, where you can see what items (if any) may compromise the document's security, such as 3D models, layers, or Flash video. Choose Edit > Preferences (Acrobat > Preferences) and select Security. Click the Select View Documents in Preview Document Mode When Signing check box and click OK.

When you click a signature field, the Document Message Bar opens and describes the status. Click View Report to show a list of items that can affect the status, then click Close to dismiss the dialog. Click Sign Document to proceed with signing.

If you work with a lot of dynamic content and signatures, the Preview Document mode likely won't explain anything you don't already know, and simply adds extra mouse clicks.

#122 Tracking Changes

Acrobat 9 Pro offers the ability to monitor a document containing multiple signatures and view the history and changes made at a particular point in the workflow. Rather than add multiple signatures using the Sign or Certify tool, work with the Digital Signature forms tool (read all about forms in Chapter 12, "Creating and Handling Forms").

Note
The changes described in this technique relate to options allowed by the certifier of the document, such as adding annotations and signing the document. To read about comparing documents for changes in general (and you can compare much more than in earlier versions of Acrobat!) check out #84, "Comparing Documents."

Here's how you add fields for several signatures, and then certify/sign the document yourself:

1. Choose Forms > Add or Edit Fields. Acrobat displays an information dialog, asking if you'd like the document scanned for existing form fields. Click Yes to dismiss the dialog and process the file.

2. Once the file is processed, another dialog notifies you about any fields that are found; click OK. Another copy of your document opens in the Form Editing window.

3. Click Add New Field on the Form Editing toolbar, and choose Digital Signature.

4. Move the pointer over the page and click when the field is in the right location. The signature block is drawn on the page, and the Field Name dialog appears (**Figure 122a**). The field is named by default with the type of field and a number; enter a replacement in the Field Name field.

Check It Out Another Way

Choose Options > View Signed Version from the Signatures panel's menu to open the document in another Acrobat window. You'll see a message in the Document Message Bar that you're viewing a signed version. Click View Report on the Document Message Bar to open the PDF Signature Report, which lists any problems in displaying the document, such as external dependencies or dynamic content, as well as details.

A Multiple Signature Workflow

The basic workflow for building and collecting multiple signatures works like this:

- Add fields for signatures using the Digital Signature forms tool.

- Sign or certify the document.

- Distribute or share (check out the new reviewing features in #11, "Merging Word Files in PDF").

- Evaluate the changes by comparing histories.

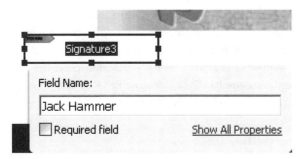

Figure 122a Use the Digital Signatures tool to add and configure the fields on your document.

Note

Click Show All Properties to open the full Digital Signature Properties dialog, where you can include a tooltip, choose an appearance for the field, and specify actions that occur when the field is signed. Click Close to return to the document. Read all about field properties in #87, "Working in Form Edit Mode."

5. Continue to add additional signature fields as required. Click Close Form Editing to close the window and return to the document in the original Acrobat window.

Next, sign or certify the document. Click the Sign task button to display its menu and choose either Sign Document or Place Signature, depending on how you want to add your signature:

- **Sign Document.** If you choose Sign Document, an information dialog opens, explaining that you can use an existing unsigned field. Click OK to close the dialog, click the field you want to use, and add your signature.

- **Place Signature.** If you choose Place Signature, an information dialog opens, explaining how to draw a new field. Click OK to close the dialog, then click and drag to add the new signature field.

Make sure the members of a review group all have the same sets of certificates; a missing certificate results in an unknown signature. You can get certificate information directly from a signature to use to validate that signature.

Verify that the reason the signature isn't validating is not simply that the certificate is missing. In the Signatures panel, select the signature's listing and then choose Options > Show Signature Properties to open the Signature Properties dialog. Click Show Certificate at the right of the Summary tab (shown by default when the dialog opens). When the Certificate Viewer dialog opens, select the Trust tab, and then click Import Contact to open the Import Contact Settings dialog. Follow the prompts to add the certificate to your list and verify the signature.

Continue as described in #121, "Signing a Document."

Finally, after the reviewing or distribution process is complete, you can check out the document at any point. When you open the file, Acrobat automatically validates the signatures for you and displays the results in the Document Message Bar. Click Signature Panel to open the panel. You'll see a number of items listed (**Figure 122b**).

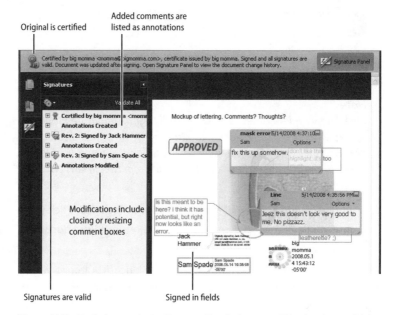

Figure 122b Track changes in the Signature Panel when a workflow involves multiple digital IDs.

Compare the current version of the file with its contents at the time a signature was applied using the historical information stored with the signatures. Select the signature in the Signature Panel, and then choose Options > Compare Signed Version to Current Version to process the file.

The differences are shown in a new window (**Figure 122c**). If you like, you can save the results document, or close the signed document's window to return to the parent document.

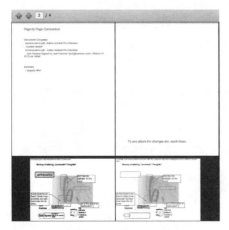

Figure 122c View differences in a document between the time a selected signature was applied and the current state of the file.

You can also use the history to check out one particular version. Read how that's done in the sidebar "Check It Out Another Way."

#123 Creating and Managing Security Policies

Security policies work in a similar way to building and using styles for text, and you can create policies for passwords and certificates. If you work in an enterprise environment, you may have Adobe Policy Server, a separate Adobe Server product that manages security policies.

1. Click the Secure task button and choose Manage Security Policies or choose Advanced > Security > Manage Security Policies to open the Managing Security Policies dialog (**Figure 123**).

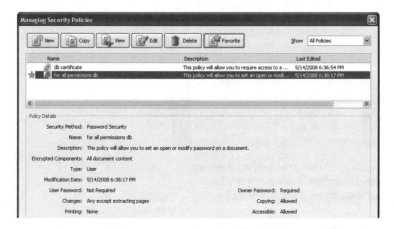

Figure 123 Add, remove, edit, and otherwise manage your security policies in this dialog.

2. Click New to open the New Security Policy wizard. The steps involved in creating each type of policy are listed at the left of the window. All types use the same initial screen for choosing a security type, all use a General settings screen, and all have a Summary screen at the end of the wizard.

3. Follow through the wizard to complete the policy. Click Cancel at the bottom of the window at any time to exit the wizard.

Here are some tips to keep in mind as you construct and work with policies:

- When you are creating password policies, be aware of the password inclusion option in the General settings. Deselect "Save passwords with the policy" if you want to specify a password and restrictions each time you use the policy.

Naming Names

When you are creating certificate policies, decide in advance if you want to generate policies for a specific group of people on a regular basis, or if you need to send documents to different people at different times. When creating or editing a Public Key certificate policy, check the option "Ask for recipients when applying this policy" in the General settings window of the wizard to generate a different list of recipients each time you apply the policy.

Make It a Favorite

In many workflows, you often use the same policy over and over. Rather than opening the dialogs and choosing the policy each time, save a couple of mouse clicks and define a policy as a favorite. In the Managing Security Policies dialog, click the policy in the listing at the top of the dialog, and then click Favorite on the dialog's toolbar. Any policies you define as Favorites show a star at the left of their listing in the dialog. When you close the policies

(continued on next page)

- Choose an encryption method in keeping with both your users and what you need to secure. For example, unless your users have Acrobat or Adobe Reader 7–9, they can't use the 128-bit AES encryption option that lets you secure only attachments. If you choose the 256-bit AES encryption, your users need Acrobat or Adobe Reader 9 to view the contents.

- From the Show menu, displayed in Figure 123, filter the list by displaying only organizational or user policies.

- Click a policy from the list in the top pane of the dialog to view its details in the bottom pane of the dialog. Click Apply to Document, and follow the sequence of dialogs and prompts to secure the document.

dialog, the next time you need to secure a document, your favorite is listed in the Secure task button's menu.

Who Are You Today?

When you are choosing a digital ID for an encryption policy, select one of these three options to specify the persistence of the Digital ID:

- "Ask me which Digital ID to use next time" is the default. When you choose this option, each time you click a signature field, the Apply Digital Signature dialog opens.

- "Use this Digital ID until I close the application" is a useful option if you are in a workflow where you are reviewing, commenting, modifying, and signing documents.

- Choose "Always use this Digital ID" if you work with one signature all the time.

#124 Managing Multimedia and Security Trusts

In Acrobat there are several types of security and trusts that you can access in different locations. In addition to managing your trusted identities, you need to establish trusts for using multimedia. New to Acrobat 9, you can choose and export your security settings to share with recipients, take to another computer, and so on.

Note
Many of the preferences are available for Windows only, as the Pro Extended features aren't available for Mac.

Multimedia Trust (legacy). You need to specify how to manage multimedia documents and how the document behaves. To get started, choose Edit > Preferences (Acrobat > Preferences) to open the Preferences dialog. Click Trust Manager to display the Trust Manager settings (**Figure 124a**).

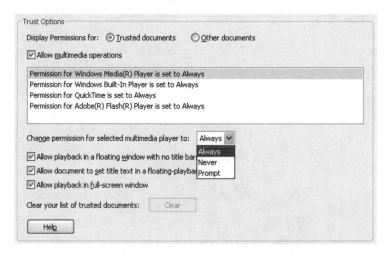

Figure 124a Specify how different media players and displays are used in Acrobat.

At the top of the dialog, select the "Allow multimedia operations" check box and then choose an option from the "Change Permission for selected multimedia player to" pop-up menu. You can select different options for the listed players (see the sidebar "Pick Your Player" for details). At the lower part of the dialog, select various options for playback, such as floating windows or full-screen views.

Trusted Identities. Trusted authors come to you via the digital ID you hold for an identity. To add someone to your list, open the Signature Panel for a document that includes the signature and follow these steps:

1. Select the signature in the Signature Panel, and choose Options > Show Signature Properties to open the dialog.

2. In the Summary tab, which shows by default, click Show Certificate to open the Certificate Viewer dialog.

3. Click the Trust tab to display the digital ID's Trust Settings (**Figure 124b**). Click Add to Trusted Identities. You'll see an information dialog that explains you'll have to validate signatures again if you change trust settings. Click OK.

Pick Your Player

In the Multimedia Trust (legacy) preferences, you can specify whether to allow multimedia to play in trusted documents. Assign a permission level for multimedia operations from these choices:

- "Always" plays content in the player at all times.

- "Never" prevents the player from being used.

- "Prompt" asks for a decision when a nontrusted document that contains media is open. You decide whether to add a nontrusted document to your list of trusted documents or authors.

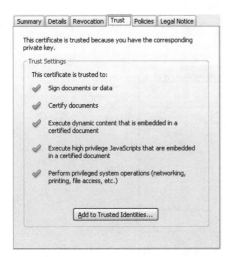

Figure 124b Include a digital ID in your list of trusted identities.

4. Next, the Import Contact Settings dialog opens, so you can select/deselect the trust items shown in Figure 124b. Click OK to return to the Signature Properties dialog; click Close to return to the program.

Trust Manager. With all the different sorts of trusts in Acrobat, it stands to reason that there's a trust manager in place! In the Preferences, click Trust Manager to display the settings. Define options in these three areas:

- Select the "Allow opening of non-PDF file attachments with external applications" check box to launch a source program if you want to open a Microsoft Word or Excel file attached to your PDF document.

(continued on next page)

#124: Managing Multimedia and Security Trusts

Enhancing Security

As if password, certificate, and other forms of security weren't enough, Acrobat 9 includes an Enhanced Security feature. In the Preferences, click Security (Enhanced) to display the settings. The recommendation is to maintain the security level, and the Enable Enhanced Security check box is selected by default. You may have problems with a high level of security in some workflows, which you can specify in the dialog. To define a location exempt from the enhanced security feature:

- Click Add File to locate and include a single file.

- Click Add Folder Path to define a folder location to exempt.

- Click Add Host to display a field where you type the URL for the hostname to be excluded from the security level.

- Specify how PDF files access the Internet. The default option is "Unless explicitly permitted, PDF files cannot send information to the Internet." Read about your options in the sidebar "Whom Do You Trust?"

- Let Acrobat handle automatic updates for root certificates from an Adobe server. The default action includes asking you first before installation. How considerate!

Managing All Your Security Settings. Acrobat 9 includes an interesting new feature that lets you pack up all your security settings into one convenient package you can export and save as an external file, ready to share with others or move to another computer. Follow these steps:

1. Choose Advanced > Security > Export Security Settings to open the dialog shown in **Figure 124c**. As you see in the dialog, the list includes settings you've collected and created in many dialogs, preferences, and tasks.

Figure 124c Choose groups of settings to export.

2. Click OK to open an expanded version of the dialog, where you can select each category of setting and specify what components are exported.

3. Click Export 🡒 to open a small encryption dialog and choose how you want to secure the settings file. Choose password, certificate, or no security, and then click OK. Proceed with the next dialogs according to the selected security type.

4. In the final Save Security Settings dialog, name the file and click Save. The settings are stored in an AXML (Adobe XML) file using the file type .acrobatsecuritysettings.

If you want to import security settings, choose Advanced > Security > Import Security Settings and follow the prompts.

Note
Exporting the collection of settings is different from exporting a certificate. You export a certificate to share with recipients who can then validate your signature and send encrypted documents to you.

#125 Using Secure ePaper

Acrobat 9 Pro offers an efficient way to wrap documents and attached files—PDF and otherwise—in a Security Envelope for distribution. Security Envelopes even look like envelopes!

Simply embed the attachments in a Security Envelope, encrypt the Security Envelope using a password or certificate security method, and then e-mail it. Only the person with rights to open the Security Envelope can see the contents. Once opened, the recipient can extract the file attachments and save them, although they are no longer encrypted. The encryption doesn't modify the attachments in any way.

You apply a Security Envelope by stepping through a wizard:

1. Choose Advanced > Security > Create Security Envelope, or choose the command from the Secure task pop-up menu.

2. Work through the steps in the wizard:

   • Select documents to attach.

   • Choose a template. **Figure 125a** shows examples of each of the three default templates.

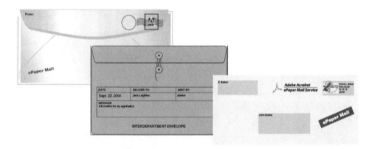

Figure 125a Choose from one of three provided templates to use for the Security Envelope, or create your own.

   • Choose either to complete the process manually or complete the Security Envelope and e-mail it. The default is to mail it later, which is necessary when the template contains fields you have to complete.

   • Specify a security policy (Click Show All Policies on this screen of the wizard to display your list of certificate or password options).

- Specify identity information in the fields, which show the identity you establish in Acrobat when you perform different functions, such as creating certificates, signing, and so on. If you like, select "Do not show again" to bypass this screen.

- Review the summary—the file(s) included in the Security Envelope, the template, and your choice for distribution.

- Click Finish to close the wizard.

3. The next step depends on the policy and delivery options you selected:

- If you choose a password, for example, you see the Password Security—Settings dialog (described in #119, "Using Security Levels and Passwords for a Document").

- If you attach a certificate, the Certificate Security Settings dialog opens for you to choose and apply a policy.

- If you intend to e-mail directly, type your recipient's e-mail address in the e-mail dialog that opens, and click Send to send it on its way.

- If you choose "Send the envelope later" as your delivery method, the Envelope opens in Acrobat after you click Finish. The files you included in the wizard are listed as attachments to the Security Envelope PDF (**Figure 125b**).

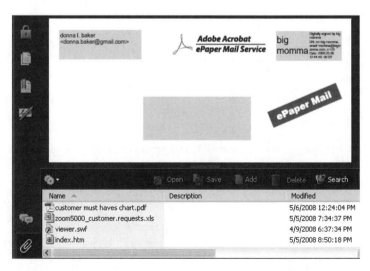

Figure 125b The files included with the Security Envelope are listed in the Attachments pane.

Make It Personal

You can create other templates to use for the Security Envelope. Create and save a document as a PDF. Then store it in this location: Program Files\Adobe\Acrobat\DocTemplates\ENU. The next time you want to create a Security Envelope, your custom template is included in the list; select it as you work through the wizard.

Once your recipient receives the e-mail, the Security Envelope appears as an attachment. The recipient can't open the attachment without the proper permissions and must enter the password used to encrypt the Security Envelope.

Index

Symbols

+ (plus) sign
  changing magnification with, 11
  comments indicated with, 197
  opening nested Help with, 4
- (minus) sign
  changing magnification with, 11
  opening nested Help with, 4

A

Access, 31–32
accessibility
  about, 101
  considering embedded movie, 266
  correcting document, 120
  enhancing PDF, 123–125
  forms and, 238
  keystrokes for, 125
  planning PDF, 118
  reporting on document, 121–122
  specifying requirements for, 117–118
Accessibility Full Check dialog, 121–122
Accessibility Setup Assistant, 117–118
Acrobat. See also Acrobat PDFMaker
  adding tags from, 120
  advanced search options in, 15–16
  attaching source files to PDFs, 61–63
  building and applying index, 17–20
  converting file from source program vs., 53
  creating PDFs outside, 21
  customizing display in, 5–6
  ensuring standards compliance, 104–105
  file formats convertible to PDFs within, 52
  Flash Player in, 259
  help for, 4
  layered documents in, 283–284
  navigating interface for, 2–3
  Organizer in, 10–11
  policy servers for, 324, 338
  Portfolio commands in, 75–76
  preference settings for, 7–9
  printing options for, 94–95
  QuickBooks features in, 253
  scanning documents into, 56–58
  Snapshot tool, 60
  types of security, 317
  Web pages converted to, 38–39, 54–55
Acrobat PDFMaker
  adding video files from, 35–37
  dialog for, 25
  merging and mailing Word PDFs, 29–30
  operating system and application support for, 21

restoring defaults for, 27
Security tab of, 28
tabs of, 25–27, 28
using in Word, 25–28
Acrobat.com
  about, 207
  Air and Flash integration with, 259
  Buzzword in, 209, 222–224
  collaborating live on, 208–210
  distributing forms via, 251–252
  meeting with ConnectNow, 219–221
  MyFiles feature, 209, 216–217
  system requirements for, 218
  using files with Web pages, 217
Acroforms, 233, 234
actions. See also bookmarking; buttons; links
  adding buttons to portfolios, 76
  associating with Model Tree views, 275
  configurable, 141
  converting from source file to PDF, 310
  editing, 315–316
  form field, 240
  magnifying or hiding layers with, 283
  mouse, 309, 313
  showing multimedia views with, 277–278
  specifying bookmark link to layer with, 297
  types of, 277, 299
activating bookmarks, 303
Add Attachment dialog (Presenter), 173
Add Movie dialog, 266
Adobe Acrobat. See Acrobat
Adobe Acrobat Comments dialog, 200–201
Adobe Air, 259
Adobe Distiller. See Distiller
Adobe Illustrator, 282
Adobe InDesign, 281
Adobe PDF Document Properties dialog, 22–24
Adobe PDF printer driver, 22
Adobe PDF Settings dialog, 45–46
Adobe PDF standard option (Accessibility Full Check dialog), 121
Adobe Policy server, 324, 338
Adobe Presenter. See Presenter
Adobe Reader. See Reader
Adobe 3D Reviewer, 270–271
advanced search options, 14, 15–16
AEC (architecture/engineering/construction) functions, 279
AICC (Aviation Industry Computer-Based Training Committee), 176
Air, 259
aligning form fields, 244
Analysis toolbar, 279, 290
Appearance Options dialog, 137
appending Web page to PDF, 55
applications. See also specific applications

embedding special media in PDFs, 35–37
file conversion from, 31–32, 53
generating PDFs in PowerPoint, 33–34
merging and attaching Word PDFs to e-mails, 29–30
printing PDFs from Windows, 22–24
rich Internet, 259
using PDFMaker in Word, 25–28
archiving
  e-mails as PDFs, 40–42
  form returns, 255, 256
  PDF files, 8
  PDFMaker options for, 27
art crop, 132
Attach a File tool, 61
attachments
  advantages of PDF, 63
  attaching source files to PDFs, 61–63
  converting document to PDF, 41
  files listed in Security Envelope as, 339
  merging Word files and mailing as, 29–30
  not copied to split component, 130
  presentation, 166, 173–175
  presentation links vs., 174
  sending documents for e-mail reviews as, 214–215
audio
  adding to movies, 264
  adjusting presentation quality, 182
  ConnectNow features for, 220
  making comments in, 196
  recording, 170
Audit Space Usage dialog, 85
audit trails in preflight profile, 109
AutoCAD PDFMaker, 280, 281
automatic scrolling, 114
autosaving documents, 8
Aviation Industry Computer-Based Training Committee (AICC), 176

B

backgrounds
  adding, 139–140
  configuring portfolio image, 68–69
  removing from PowerPoint presentations, 34
  removing while scanning documents, 56
batch processing
  building buttons with, 311–312
  changing multiple fields with, 237
batch sequences, 141–144
  building for project, 143
  organizing, 142, 144
  planning for, 142, 144
  preparing for, 142
  stopping script of, 141
Bates numbering, 135–136
bleeds, 132

bookmarking
  Access files, 32
  actions and, 299
  adding, 305–306
  advantages of, 296
  drawings, 296–297
  Help pages, 4
  images, 153
  layers, 283, 296–297
  maps, 296–297
  naming destinations for, 307–308
  nesting bookmarks, 308
  Office source files, 303–304
  organizing bookmarks, 307
  PDF locations, 80
  tagged documents, 306
  Word documents, 27, 28
Bookmarks pane, 303–304, 308
branding portfolios, 70–72
browsers
  problems using with PDF files, 39
  using Acrobat.com from, 109–110
buttons
  actions and, 299
  associating with 3D view, 277–278
  batch assembly of, 311–312
  button states, 313–314
  configuring and grouping form
    field, 237–238
  configuring states for push,
    313–314
  drawing, 309–310
  duplicating, 311
  editing in batch, 312
  mouse actions triggering, 309,
    313
  showing/hiding labels for, 5
Buzzword, 209, 222–224

C

CAD files, 270–271
calculations, 242–243, 249
callouts, 196
Case Sensitive option (Find toolbar),
  12
Categories pane (Organizer), 10
centering form fields, 244
certificates
  certifying PDF documents,
    325–327
  missing results for, 329
  naming policies managing, 332
Certify Document dialog, 325
Change Scale Ratio dialog, 290
chapter points, 262
clipboard
  copying Acrobat.com link to, 217
  creating PDFs from, 59–60
collaborating
  allowing screen sharing, 221
  checking for shared review
    comments, 211
  ConnectNow meetings, 209,
    219–221
  live on Acrobat.com, 208–210
  online, 216–218
  starting shared review, 211–213
collections, 11

color
  customizing portfolio, 69
  selecting for vision-impaired, 118
  simulating paper and ink, 93, 112
color modes, 155
color separation, 99
columns in Portfolio, 73
Combine Files wizard, 52
comments, 185–205
  accessing tools for, 185
  adding to doodles, 195
  adding with drawings and
    marked up shapes, 195–196
  audio, 196
  checking shared review, 211
  converting 3D measurements
    to, 273
  defining status and summarizing,
    204–205
  e-mail review, 214–215
  enabling files for, 212
  exporting to Word, 200–203
  filtering, 199
  formatting, 186–187
  grouping, 198, 199
  making, 189
  measurements appearing in, 292
  migrating into revised
    documents, 203
  multimedia, 274–276
  PDF map, 293–294
  preference settings for, 188–189
  preserving in converted Word
    PDFs, 27
  searching, 199
  stamps in, 192
  sticky notes, 186
  summaries of, 204–205
  text editing, 190–191
  viewing while scrolling pages, 189
  working with in Comments list,
    197–199
Comments List toolbar, 199
comparing
  signed documents, 331
  unsigned documents, 225–227
configurable actions, 141
Configure Presets dialog, 56
Configure Signature Appearance
  dialog, 323
ConnectNow, 209, 219–221
ConnectPro Server LMS, 176
content. See also documents; images
  authoring frame rates for
    Presenter, 170
  capturing image document,
    157–159
  changing, 128–131
  copying from clipboard to PDF,
    59–60
  editing portfolio, 73–74
  linking in document, 300–302
  managing from Pages pane, 128
  Presenter default settings for, 165
  redacting, 160–162
  replacing text in comment box,
    191
  searching for diacritical marks

in, 14
  setting preferences for hidden, 84
  validating form, 241–242
  working with 3D, 268–269
  X/Y coordinates for placing, 133
Conversion Settings dialog, 28
copying. See also cutting, copying,
    and pasting
  Acrobat.com link to clipboard, 217
  buttons, 311
  content from clipboard to PDF,
    59–60
  encircled text into drawing
    comment, 195
  existing preflight profiles, 107
  images, 151–154
  tables, 147, 150
Create Go To View dialog, 301
Create Link dialog, 300
Create PDF From Web Page dialog, 54
creating PDFs outside Acrobat, 21–42
  archiving e-mails as PDFs, 40–42
  converting Web pages to PDFs,
    38–39
  embedding media files in PDFs,
    35–37
  Excel, Access, and Project PDF
    conversion options, 31–32
  generating PDFs in PowerPoint,
    33–34
  merging and mailing Word PDFs,
    29–30
  PDFMaker for, 21
  printing PDFs from Windows,
    22–24
  using PDFMaker in Word, 25–28
cropping
  pages, 93, 132–133
  undoing with Revert command,
    133
cross-references in converted PDFs, 26
custom stamps, 192, 193, 194
customizing
  Acrobat display, 5–6
  attachment icon, 61
  Bates numbering, 136
  digital signatures, 322–323
  form fields, 237–240
  portfolio appearance, 68–69
  Presenter preload text, 168, 169
  Read Aloud preferences, 114–115
  redaction tools, 160
  scan presets, 58
cutting, copying, and pasting
  bookmarks, 304
  images, 151–152

D

dates, 137
defaults
  Presenter content, 165
  restoring PDFMaker, 27
  restoring toolbars to, 5
  specifying digital signature, 324
deleting
  files and folders from Watched
    Folders list, 49
  indexes, 17

metadata from document, 83–84
pages, 128, 130, 131
signature fields, 326
descreen option, 56
deskew, 56
despeckle option, 56
destinations
    activating bookmarks before
        setting, 303
    defined, 302
    inheritance of, 304
    naming, 307–308
Details mode (Portfolio), 74, 75
diacritical marks, 14
digital IDs. *See also* digital signatures
    creating for encryption policies,
        333
    including with trusted identities,
        335
digital signatures
    adding to forms, 249
    creating, 321–324
    encryption vs., 326
    invalid, 329
    signing documents with, 325–327
    specifying default, 324
    tracking document changes with
        multiple, 328–331
    uses for, 317
    using, 101, 109
    viewing documents with, 328
DirectX driver, 260
Distiller
    about, 43
    Advanced Setting options for, 45
    distilling files with, 44–47
    illustrated, 44
    starting PDF from blank page,
        50–51
    watching folders via, 48–49
Distribute Form wizard, 249–252
distributing
    form fields, 244
    forms, 249–254
    portfolios, 77–78
DOC file format, 88
document message bar, 2, 3
Document Open passwords, 318, 320
Document pane, 2, 3
Document Properties dialog, 80, 97
documents
    accessibility of, 114–116, 123
    adding signature fields to,
        326–327
    applying actions to, 315–316
    autosaving, 8
    bookmarking, 296–297, 303–304,
        306
    certifying vs. signing, 325
    changing pages in, 128–131
    combined or merged, 127
    comments in, 189, 199, 203
    comparing, 225–227, 331
    controlling reading path through,
        116
    converting Web pages to PDF,
        38–39, 54–55
    creating reports on preflight

status of, 109
cropping and rotating pages in,
    132–133
display options for, 81
examining, 83–84
group conversion to PDF format,
    23
headers and footers in, 137–138
index for, 17–20
inserting pages, 128, 130, 131
layered, 283–284
list and properties of fonts in, 82
magnification options for, 81
making into PDF attachment, 41
merging and attaching Word PDF,
    29–30
metadata embedded in, 287
naming merged PDF, 29
navigation properties for, 80
number displayed on File menu, 7
numbering pages, 134–136
opening and attaching index
    to, 82
optimizing PDF, 85–87
passwords for, 318–320
PDF/A mode for, 8
preparing for PDF conversion, 24
print previews for, 112–113
printing portions of, 98
reading aloud, 114–115
redacting content in, 160–162
reflowing, 114, 115
removing security from, 319
replacing pages, 129–130, 131
reporting on and repairing,
    121–122
saving redacted and full versions
    of, 161
scanning into Acrobat, 56–58
scriptable states for, 316
searching, 12–16
security previews for, 327
sharing from MyFiles, 216
signing, 325–327
splitting, 129, 130
tagging, 119–120
tracking changes to signed,
    328–331
using Buzzword with, 222
viewing and modifying
    information about, 80–82
where to convert, 53
downloading Web pages to PDFs, 55
drawing
    adding bookmarks to, 296–297
    buttons, 309–310
    form fields, 237–240
drawing markups
    placement of exported, 200
    using, 195–196
droplets
    modifying, 111
    storing, 110
duplicating. *See* copying

E

edge shadow removal, 56
Edit Profile dialog (Preflight), 106

Edit Sequence dialog, 143
Edit Video dialog (Presenter), 171
editing
    actions, 315–316
    bookmark color, 306
    buttons in batch, 312
    contents of portfolios, 73–74
    embedded 3D model, 269
    existing preflight profiles, 107
    files within portfolio, 75
    headers and footers, 138
    layers, 284
    marking comments in text,
        190–191
    pages and content, 128–131
    PDF text, 146–147
    quizzes, 179, 180
    round-trip image, 155–156
    text and attributes with TouchUp
        Text tool, 148–150
    3D CAD files, 270–271
e-mails. *See also* attachments
    archiving, 40–42
    distributing forms via, 249–250
    e-mail reviews, 212–215
    incorporating attached forms in
        portfolio, 256
    merging and attaching PDFs to,
        29–30
embedding
    audit trails in preflight profile, 109
    fonts or substituting, 47, 96–97
    joboption files in PDF, 45
    media files in PDFs, 35–37,
        260–262
    metadata in documents, 287
Encapsulated PostScript (EPS) files, 43
encrypting documents, 326, 333
ending reviews, 212, 229
Enhanced Security feature, 336
EPS (Encapsulated PostScript) files, 43
errors
    correcting preflight, 103
    displaying printing, 98
    examining documents, 83–84
Excel, 31–32
Export All Images As TIFF Settings
    dialog, 92
exporting
    comments to Word, 200–203
    file to apply Preflight commands,
        108
    form layers, 247
    form return results, 256–257
    InDesign files, 281
    PDFs in other formats, 88–90
    security settings, 336–337
Extensible Markup Language (XML)
    files, 88, 176
Extensible Metadata Platform (XMP),
    318
extracting pages, 128–129

F

Fast Find preference setting, 14
favorites, 332
FDF (file data format) files, 322

fields
adding and selecting, 234–235
batch changes to, 237
changing properties for, 232
configuring, 239–240
drawing and customizing,
237–240
naming structure for, 241
setting to same size, 244
signature, 326–327, 328–329
tab order for, 245–246
File Attachment Properties dialog, 61
files. *See also* FLV movies; source files;
SWF files
Acrobat formats convertible to
PDFs, 52
Acrobat.com conversion of, 210
adding to collection, 11
Author and Co-authors of, 222
comparing, 227, 331
converting to standards-
compliant, 105
deleting from watched folder, 49
distilling, 44–47
editing within portfolio, 75
embedding in PDFs, 35–37
enabling comments for, 212
exporting to apply Preflight
commands, 108
finding MyFiles, 217
FLV, 260–262
found in index folder, 18
Illustrator files saved as layered
PDFs, 282
joboption, 44, 45, 48
linking portfolio, 76
listed in Security Envelope, 339
managing returns, 249
merging multiple to single PDF,
52–53
naming converted PDF, 24
PDFs saved in other formats,
88–90
preventing user access to, 319
previewing PDF portfolio, 67
previewing without local fonts,
96–97
printing, 98–99
PRN, 43
PS, 43
reducing size of, 85, 87
replacing filenames with Bates
numbers, 135
saving copied image to, 152
saving older Acrobat files as PDF
Portfolio, 40
saving PDF as image, 91–92
splitting into multiple PDFs,
129, 130
supported movie formats, 264,
265, 266
types of PDF formats, 88, 89
U3D format, 270
XML manifest, 176
Files pane (Organizer), 10
filtering
comments, 199
form returns, 256
Find toolbar, 12

fixups for preflights, 106–107
Flash. *See also* FLV movies; SWF files
adding movies to PDF files,
265–267
adding SWF file to PDF, 263–264
features in Buzzword, 223
inserting FLV movie in PDF,
260–262
integration with Acrobat, 259
player installed with Presenter,
165
using multimedia content in
presentations, 170–172
using multiple movies in
presentation, 164
Flash Lite, 166
Flattener Preview dialog, 94
flattening
avoiding patches on layered
images, 94
Photoshop layers copied to
clipboard, 59
troubleshooting printing
problems with, 99
Visio layers, 282
floating media windows, 262
FLV movies
distributing embedded, 36
embedded vs. linked, 260
embedding in PDFs, 35–37,
260–262, 265
folders
adding to portfolio, 74
index, 18
managing droplets in, 110
watched, 48–49
fonts
choosing, 96–97
embedding or substituting, 47,
96–97
locking, 96
optimizing, 86
subsetting options for, 96–97
troubleshooting touchups for, 150
vertical and horizontal, 148
viewing document's, 82
footers, 137–138
form distribution
collecting e-mail responses from,
249–250
handling form returns, 255–257
tracking, 253–254
via Acrobat.com, 251–252
Form Edit mode, 232–236
formatting comments, 186–187
forms, 231–257. *See also* fields; form
distribution
accessibility of, 123, 238
Acroforms vs. LiveCycle Designer
forms, 233
calculations and field behaviors
for, 241–243, 249
creating, 232–233
distributing, 249–252
drawing and customizing fields
for, 237–240
enabling Reader users to receive,
251
Form Edit mode for, 232–236

handling returns, 255–257
naming form fields, 241
options for configuring fields,
239–240
organizing and ordering, 244–246
preferences for easier completion,
249, 250
simplifying visually complex,
247–248
tab order for fields, 245–246
tabbing order of, 123
tracking distribution of, 253–254
using with portfolios, 77
working with, 231

G

georeferenced maps, 293–295
gradient conversions, 45
grids, 288
grouping comments, 198, 199
guests for ConnectNow, 219
guides, 288–289

H

halo removal, 56
headers, 137–138
help
building SCORM manifest files,
176
how to use, 4
viewing printing, 99
hiding. *See* showing/hiding
highlighting
form fields, 245, 246
text, 187
History, 10, 11
hyphenating text, 149

I

Identity Setup dialog, 192, 193
Illustrator, 282
Image Editor, 156
images
adjusting quality of, 182
avoiding white patches in, 94
bookmarking, 305
extracting active text from,
157–159
optimizing, 86
performance when moving, 8
printing file as, 98–99
redacting, 160–162
reusing, 152, 153–154
round-trip editing of, 155–156
saving PDF as, 91–92
selecting before text, 152
watermarking, 140
Import Comments from Adobe
Acrobat dialog, 202
importing
review comments, 214
source file pages as layers,
285–286
InDesign, 281
Index Definition dialog, 17
indexes
building and applying, 17–20

files and folders required for, 18
opening and attaching to
document, 82
tips for, 19
index.pdx file, 18
Insert Video dialog, 261
Internet Explorer
difficulties using presentation
attachments, 175
PDFMaker for, 38

J

JavaScript, 316
joboption files, 44, 45, 48

K

keyboard shortcuts
accessibility keystrokes, 125
navigation keystrokes, 115
PDF Optimizer, 85
searches using, 13
selecting paragraphs with, 148
TouchUp Object tool, 152
using with 3D models, 272
keyword searches, 15, 16
knockouts, 113

L

labels, 235
language options for Presenter, 167
layered document navigation, 80
layered images
flattening, 59
preventing white patches of, 94
layers
about, 281
adding, 285–286
bookmarking, 296–297
converting text image to text,
157–159
converting Visio, 280–281
editing, 284
exporting InDesign files as
layered PDFs, 281
flattening, 282
form, 247–248
magnifying or hiding, 283
working with layered documents,
283–284
Layers pane, 283, 284
layout
customizing Compare pane, 227
inserting pages in, 131
placing exported comments
in, 200
setting comment preferences for,
188–189
working with forms layers,
247–248
layouts
Adobe 3D Reviewer, 271
choosing comment summary, 205
learning management systems (LMSs),
176
legacy versions
of media, 264, 266

multimedia trusts, 334, 335
line breaks, 149
Link Properties dialog, 308
links
actions and, 299
adding to portfolio files, 76
configuring presentation, 174
linking content in document,
300–302
specifying to layer, 297
testing presentation, 173
using thumbnail-sized images
as, 91
LiveCycle Designer forms, 232, 233,
248
LMSs (learning management systems),
176
lock symbol icon, 96
locking
fonts, 96
notes, 187
placement of Search and Acrobat
windows, 13
toolbars, 5
log files, 23
log-in name for author, 193
Lotus Notes, 40

M

Mac operating systems
converting PDF files in, 21
starting forms with, 232
workaround for LiveCycle
Designer for, 248
magnification
changing in File pane, 11
inheritance of, 304
reflow and, 114, 115
setting, 81
Mail Merge, 30
Manage Trusted Identities dialog,
322, 323
Managing Security Policies dialog, 332
maps, PDF, 293–297
margins
checking page, 132
specifying, 133
masks, 241
Measurement Info widget, 291, 292
measurement markups, 272, 273
Measurement tools, 279, 290–291,
294–295
measuring
items on PDF map, 293–294
measurements in comments, 292,
293, 294
objects, 290–292
3D objects, 272–273
menus
about, 2
actions executing commands on,
315–316
illustrated, 3
opening Buzzword, 224
Merge Comments? dialog, 215
merging
and attaching Word PDFs, 29–30

multiple to single PDF files, 52–53
metadata
examining document for, 83–84
using, 318
viewing, 287
microphone, 220
Microsoft Access, 31–32
Microsoft Excel, 31–32
Microsoft Office, 303–304
Microsoft Outlook, 338
Microsoft PowerPoint. See PowerPoint
Microsoft Project, 31–32
Microsoft Visio, 280–281, 282
Microsoft Word. See Word
migrating comments to revised
documents, 203
minus (-) sign
changing magnification with, 11
opening nested Help with, 4
Missing Folder icon, 49
mobile devices
running Flash Lite on, 166
viewing presentations on, 165
Model Tree, 274, 275, 287
modifying
Adobe PDF printer driver, 22
document information, 80–82
droplets, 111
objects with TouchUp Object,
151–152
text in PDF, 146–147
text with TouchUp Text tool,
148–150
More Tools dialog, 6
mouse
selecting text with, 147
triggering button states with,
309, 313
movies
accessibility and, 266
adding multiple renditions of, 265
adding sound file to, 264
distributing embedded, 36
embedded vs. linked, 260
file types used in Acrobat
versions, 265
including multiple presentation,
164
inserting in PDF file, 260–262, 265
tweaking renditions of, 267
types of multimedia actions for,
277
using legacy versions of, 264, 266
moving
guide lines, 288
images, 8
Multimedia Properties dialog, 265
multimedia trusts, 334, 335
multiple file optimizing, 86
multiple page cropping, 133
MyFiles feature, 209, 216–217

N

naming
archived PDF files, 42
certificate policies, 332
converted PDF files, 24

naming *(continued)*
destinations, 307–308
form fields, 241
merged Word PDF documents, 29
navigating
Acrobat's interface, 2–3
from bookmarked image, 153
documents with accessibility
options, 114–116
portfolio breadcrumb menu, 73
setting properties for, 80
to Web Page Conversion Settings
dialog, 54
Navigation pane, 2, 3
neatlines, 294
nested bookmarks, 308
New Document Editor, 50–51
New Form Assistant, 232
New Preflight Profile dialog, 106

O

Object Editor, 156
Object Inspector, 113
objects
measuring 2D, 290–292
measuring 3D, 272–273
positioning with guides and grids,
288–289
touching up, 151–152
viewing metadata for, 287
OCR (optical character recognition),
157–159
online features in Acrobat.com
creating PDFs online, 209, 210
document collaboration, 216–218
online document processing,
222–224
online shared reviews, 213
opening
Buzzword menus, 224
comment pop-up boxes, 189
Search window, 13
Slide Manager, 182
operating systems. *See* Mac operating
systems; Windows operating
systems
optical character recognition (OCR),
157–159
Optimization Options dialog, 57
optimizing
PDF documents, 85–87
PDF viewing on Web, 46
Organizer, 10–11
organizing
batch sequencing, 142, 144
bookmarks, 307
comments in documents, 199
form fields, 245
portfolios, 73–74
reviews in Tracker, 228
stamps, 194
orientation of pages, 132
Output Options dialog, 130, 135, 143
Output Preview dialog, 93, 112
overprinting, 113

P

page cache settings, 8
page margins, 132
Page Number and Date Format dialog,
137
page numbering
adding to header or footer, 137
using, 134–135
Page Properties dialog, 124
Page Setup dialog, 51
page sharing, 217
pages. *See also* Web pages
applying headers and footers to,
137–138
changing, 128–131
cropping and rotating, 132–133
customizing setups for, 51
deleting, 128, 130, 131
inserting, 128, 130, 131
numbering, 134–136
printing noncontiguous, 98
replacing, 129–130, 131
viewing comments while
scrolling, 189
Pages pane, 10, 128
Password Security - Settings dialog,
318–319
passwords
creating security policies for, 332
document, 318–320
tips for, 320
uses for, 317
PDF files. *See also* Acrobat PDFMaker;
PDFMaker
accessibility of, 117–118, 123–125
Acroforms vs. LiveCycle Designer,
233
appending Web page to, 55
archiving e-mail messages, 40–42
attaching source files to, 61–63
converting Visio, InDesign, and
Illustrator files to layered,
280–282
creating from clipboard image,
59–60
creating online, 209, 210
Distiller resolution options for, 46
editing text in, 146–147
examining documents, 83–84
Excel, Access, and Project PDF
conversion options, 31–32
exporting in other formats, 88–90
file format types for, 88, 89
FLV movies in, 36
generating in PowerPoint, 33–34
generating with PDFMaker, 21
inserting Flash movie in, 260–262
joboption files embedded in, 45
linking to Web sites, 300
merging multiple to single files,
52–53
preparing documents for
conversion to, 24
printing from Windows
applications, 22–24
redacting content in, 160–162
special media embedded in,
35–37, 260–262

starting from within Distiller,
50–51
templates with placeholder for 3D
models, 269
Web pages converted to, 38–39,
54–55
PDF maps
bookmarking, 296–297
measuring and adding comments
to, 293–295
PDF Optimizer, 85–87
PDF Portfolio. *See* portfolios
PDF/A compliance profile, 102, 105
PDF/A view mode, 8, 9
PDF/E compliance profile, 102, 105
PDF/X compliance profile, 102, 105
PDFMaker. *See also* Acrobat PDFMaker
AutoCAD, 280, 281
Internet Explorer, 38
Lotus and Outlook, 40
Visio, 280–281
Windows, 303–304
Permissions passwords, 318, 320
Photoshop
correcting pixel aspect ratio, 155
flattening layers copied to
clipboard, 59
maintaining image connections
with, 156
pixel aspect ratio, correcting in
Photoshop, 155
planning ahead
background or watermark for
project, 140
batch sequences, 142, 144
playing presentations, 164, 165
plus (+) sign
changing magnification with, 11
comments indicated with, 197
opening nested Help items with, 4
pods, 220
policy servers, 324, 338
Pop-Up Open Behavior options
Commenting Preferences dialog,
188, 189
portfolios
advantages of, 67
applying Acrobat commands for,
75–76
branding or customizing display
of, 70–72
building, 66–67
combined PDFs vs., 52
compiling returned forms with,
255–257
customizing appearance of, 68–69
defined, 65
incorporating attached e-mail
forms in, 256
managing and distributing, 77–78
managing returns file with, 249
one file per window for, 234
organizing and modifying
contents of, 73–74
saving earlier Acrobat files as
PDF, 40
searching, 15

PowerPoint
building Presenter publication from, 164–166
configuring presentation links, 174
converting presentations to PDFs, 33–34
specifying Presenter theme from, 167–168
preference settings
Buzzword, 224
comments, 188–189
configuring Word PDFMaker, 26
customizing Read Aloud, 114–115
Distiller, 44
Fast Find, 14
hidden content, 84
how to adjust, 7–9
managing Acrobat.com, 208, 209
modifying Adobe PDF printer driver, 22, 23
multimedia, 261
page cache, 8
rendering, 8, 9
search, 14
Preflight dialog, 102
preflight droplets, 110–111
preflight profiles
categories of, 102
editing, 106
editing, duplicating or creating new, 107
selecting standard for, 104
testing compliance with, 102–103
unlocking existing, 106
preflights
about, 101
creating reports about, 109
ensuring standards compliance, 104–105
fixing print and file issues in, 106–107
inserting results as comments, 109
previewing document output, 112–113
testing and fixing documents in, 102–103
tools for, 79
using, 108–109
Presentation Settings dialog (Presenter), 164
Presenter, 163–184
about, 33, 163, 259
adding quizzes to presentation, 176–181
attachments for presentations, 166, 173–175
authoring frame rates for, 170
building publication from PowerPoint, 164–166
capturing video, 170–172
personalizing loading screen for, 168, 169
previewing and publishing presentations, 182–184
quiz boundaries, 176, 177
recording audio for, 170

testing presentation links, 173
theme selections in, 167–169
presets, scanning, 58
preventing file access, 319
Preview and Select Page Range dialog, 53
Preview Document mode, 327
previewing
document output, 112–113
document security, 327
files in portfolio, 67
files without local fonts, 96–97
presentations, 182–183
Print dialog, 94–95
printers, 108
printing
Acrobat options for, 94–95
background text on document, 139
noncontiguous pages, 98
PDFs from Windows applications, 22–24
portions of documents, 98
setting permissions for, 318
troubleshooting, 98–99
printing droplets, 110–111
private keys, 321
PRN files, 43
projects
building batching sequence for, 143
including legacy versions of media with, 264, 266
processing all files uniformly, 111
proofs
producing with Commenting summary feature, 94
soft, 93, 112
Properties dialog (Acrobat), 237–240
PS (PostScript) files, 43
public keys, 321, 322
Publish Presentation dialog (Presenter), 182, 183
publishing presentations, 183–184

Q

questions in quizzes, 177, 178
QuickBooks features, 253
Quiz Manager
about, 176, 177
editing quizzes, 179, 180
questions in quizzes, 177, 178
quiz boundaries, 176, 177
setting user interaction for quiz, 181
writing quizzes, 178–181
Quiz Settings dialog, 178

R

radio buttons, 237–238
Read Aloud feature, 114–115
Reader
distributing forms to users of, 251
features of tracker in, 228–229
Flash player embedded in, 259
updating portfolio in, 77
reading order

about, 124
accessibility and, 123
reading path, 116
recording audio, 170
redacting content, 160–162
reducing file size, 85, 87
reflow, 114, 115
remote control, 221
removing document security, 319
rendering preferences, 8, 9
renditions of movies, 265, 267
repairing documents, 121–122
replacing
filenames with Bates numbers, 135
pages, 129–130, 131
text in comment box, 191
reports
Accessibility, 122
creating preflight, 109
generating repair hints, 121–122
Quiz Manager, 177
quiz results, 179
resolution of Distiller PDFs, 46
responses
archiving from form returns, 255, 256
collecting from form distribution, 249–250
handling form returns, 255–257
Results tab (Preflight dialog), 103
reusing images, 152, 153–154
reviews
adding document comments from Buzzword, 222
checking for comments in shared, 211
comparing vs., 226
e-mail, 214–215
ending, 212, 229
sending invitations for, 212–213
starting shared, 211–213
tracking, 228–229
using online, 213
viewing details of, 228
RIAs (rich Internet applications), 259
rotating pages, 132–133
round-trip editing, 155–156
RSS feeds in Tracker, 229
RTF file format, 88

S

Save As command, 87, 88–90
saving
Acrobat files as PDF Portfolio, 40
copied images, 152
custom headers and footers, 137
Illustrator files as layered PDFs, 282
PDF as image file, 91–92
PDFs in other formats, 88–90
redacted and full document, 161
security policy as favorite, 332
watermarks and backgrounds, 139
scanning
behavior of scanned text, 149
documents into Acrobat, 56–58

scanning *(continued)*
 reasons for page conversion
  with, 158
 unable to append scanned file in
  portfolio, 75
SCORM (Sharable Content Object
 Reference Model), 176
scriptable document states, 316
scrolling
 automatic, 114
 viewing comments while, 189
Search window, 13
searching
 advanced options for, 14, 15–16
 comments, 199
 portfolio files, 77–78
 for redacted content, 162
 from Search window, 13–14
 setting preferences for, 14
 text extracted from scanned
  image, 157–159
 using Find toolbar, 12
 wildcards unavailable for, 13
Section 508 Web-based intranet
 and Internet standards option
 (Accessibility Full Check dialog),
 121
security, 317–340
 creating and managing policies
  for, 332–333
 digital ID profiles, 321–324
 document security levels and
  passwords, 318–320
 exporting settings for, 336–337
 managing security and trusts,
  334–337
 previewing document, 327
 removing document, 319
 restricting portfolio access, 77
 Security Envelopes, 317, 338–340
 settings applied in folder vs.
  Distiller, 49
 signing documents, 325–327
 tracking changes to signed
  documents, 328–331
 types of Acrobat, 317
Security Envelopes, 317, 338–340
security levels, 249, 318
security policies, 332–333
Security Settings dialog, 320
Security tab (Acrobat PDFMaker
 dialog), 28
Select & Zoom toolbar, 191
Select A 3D View dialog, 278
Select Action pop-up menu, 297
Select Image icon, 153
Select Object tool, 146
Select tool, 146
selecting
 application for object editing, 156
 color for vision-impaired, 118
 comments for export, 202
 images before text, 152
 portions of document for
  printing, 98
 standard for preflight profile, 104
 text, 147, 148, 150
 tools from toolbars, 5–6

Send by E-mail for Review wizard,
 214–215
Send for Shared Review wizard,
 211–213
Sharable Content Object Reference
 Model (SCORM), 176
shared reviews. *See* reviews
sharing
 page, 217
 screen, 221
showing/hiding
 attached files, 63
 button labels, 5
 Navigation pane in multiple
  documents, 3
 tools on toolbar, 5–6
signature fields, 326–327, 328–329
Signature Panel, 330
Signatures dialog, 109
simulating
 overprinting, 113
 paper and ink color, 93, 112
Slide Manager dialog (Presenter), 182
slide shows
 navigating in, 80
 previewing, 183
slides
 configuring quizzes using
  PowerPoint, 178
 downloading for presentations,
  164
 including PowerPoint slides in
  PDFs, 34
Snap to Grid feature, 289
Snap Types for Measurement tool, 290
Snapshot tool, 60
soft proofs, 93, 112
sound. *See* audio
source files
 attaching to PDFs, 61–63
 bookmarking, 303–304
 converting actions to PDF, 310
 importing pages as layers,
  285–286
 removing page numbering from,
  134
 standards compliance of
  converted, 105
splitting documents, 129, 130
spreadsheets, 256–257
Stamp tools, 192–194
stamps
 custom, 192, 193, 194
 organizing on Stamps palette, 194
 placement of exported, 200
 using in comments, 192
standards
 accessibility, 121–122
 ensuring PDF compliance with,
  104–105
 selecting for preflight profile,
  104, 105
Standards dialog, 47
Standards pane, 104–105
states, scriptable document, 316
sticky notes, 186
stop words for index, 18, 19

stopping integration of comments,
 202
storing droplets, 110
structure, tags vs. document, 119
Structure Elements dialog, 306
subjects for comments, 186
Submit button, 239
substituting fonts, 47, 96–97
Successful Import dialog, 201, 203
Summarize Options dialog, 204–205
SWF files
 adding to PDF, 263–264
 branding PDFs with, 172
 controlling presentation, 171
 stand-alone presentations as, 163
system requirements for Acrobat.
 com, 218

T

tab order, 245–246
tabbing
 accessibility of forms, 123
 testing form's, 124
table of contents, 27
tags
 bookmarking tagged documents,
  306
 checking for preexisting, 119
 choosing in Accessibility Setup
  Assistant, 116
 copying tables by clicking on,
  147, 150
 using, 101, 119–120
task buttons, 2, 3
templates
 creating with placeholder for 3D
  models, 269
 Security Envelope, 338, 339
testing
 button states, 314
 DirectX driver, 260
 documents with preflight,
  102–103
 merged Word documents, 29
 presentation links, 173
text
 behavior of scanned, 149
 breaking, wrapping, and
  hyphenating PDF, 149
 copying encircled text into
  drawing comment, 195
 editing in PDF, 146–147
 extracting from image, 157–159
 highlighting, 187
 marking editing comments in,
  190–191
 personalizing Presenter loading
  screen, 168, 169
 redacting, 160–162
 replacing in comment box, 191
 selecting images before, 152
 techniques for selecting, 147,
  148, 150
Text Edits tool, 190–191
Theme Editor (Presenter), 167–169
themes
 adjusting, 182
 selecting in Presenter, 167–169

3D
    associating button with view in, 277–278
    editing files in Adobe 3D Reviewer, 270–271
    working with content in, 268–269
3D Comment Tool, 274, 275–276
3D Measurement Tool, 272–273
3D models
    adding multimedia comments in, 274–276
    creating PDF template placeholder for, 269
    inserting in PDFs, 37
    measuring objects in, 272–273
3D Reviewer, 270–271
thumbnail-sized linked images, 91
TIFF files, 92
Time Stamp server, 324
toolbars
    about, 2
    Analysis, 279, 290
    Comments List, 199
    illustrated, 3
    locking, 5
    returning to default settings, 5
    searching from Find, 12
    Select & Zoom, 191
    selecting tools on, 5–6
    tools on Measurement, 290–291
tools
    accessing comment, 185
    customizing redaction, 160
    Highlighting, 187
    Measurement, 279, 290–291, 294–295
    selecting toolbar, 5–6
    setting scale ratio for Measurement, 290
    Text Edits, 190–191
    3D Measurement, 272–273
    used with Form Edit mode, 236
tooltips, 5
TouchUp Object tool
    round-trip image editing with, 155–156
    using, 151–152
TouchUp Properties dialog, 122
TouchUp Text tool, 148–150
Tracker, 253–254
tracking
    changes to signed documents, 328–331
    distribution of forms, 253–254
    reviews, 228–229
triggers, 309, 313
trim crop, 132
troubleshooting printing, 98–99
Trust Manager, 334, 335–336
trusted identities, 322, 323, 335
trusts, 334–337
    legacy versions of multimedia, 334, 335
    Trust Manager, 334, 335–336
    trusted identities, 322, 323, 335

U
U3D format, 270
undoing crops, 133
unlocking existing preflight profiles, 106
updates, tracking, 228
updating portfolios in Reader, 77
user interface
    Acrobat, 2–3
    types of quiz interaction, 181
    views in Portfolio, 66

V
validating
    form content, 241–242
    signatures, 327
VeriSign Internet Directory server, 324
versions
    legacy media, 264, 266
    multimedia trust, 334, 335
    Navigator, 72
video. See also FLV movies
    adding comments to, 274
    capturing for presentations, 170–172
    embedding in PDFs, 35–37
viewing
    comments, 188, 197–198
    details of review, 228
    documents in PDF/A mode, 8
    History, 10, 11
    signed documents, 328
Visio, 280–281, 282
VMware Fusion, 248

W
W3C Web Content Accessibility Guidelines, 121–122
watched folders, 48–49
watermarks, 139, 140
Web Page Conversion Settings dialog, 54
Web pages
    appending to PDF, 55
    converting to PDF documents in Internet Explorer, 38–39
    creating PDFs in Acrobat from, 54–55
    making multiple page conversions for, 38
    specifying site levels for downloading, 55
    using Acrobat.com files with, 217
Web sites
    linking PDF page to, 300
    optimizing PDF views on, 46
Webcams, 220
welcome page for portfolio, 70–72
wildcards, 13
windows
    configuring display options for PDF, 81
    locking placement of Search and Acrobat, 13

Windows operating systems
    adding droplet to Start menu, 110
    converting PDF files in, 21
    exporting comments to Word, 200–203
    hardware acceleration for, 260
    printing PDFs from Windows applications, 22–24
    starting forms with, 232
    Vista's influence on Acrobat, 234
Word
    embedding 3D model in, 268–269
    exporting comments to Windows, 200–203
    merging and attaching PDFs to e-mails, 29–30
    tips for exporting PDFs to new format in, 90
    using PDFMaker in, 25–28
workflow. See also collaborating; comments
    batching tasks to save time, 141–144
    bookmarking, 305
    collaboration, 207
    documents with multiple signatures, 328
    examining hidden content in, 84
    Presenter, 163
    signing and certifying, 325
wrapping text, 149
writing quizzes, 178–181

X
X/Y coordinates, 133
XML (Extensible Markup Language) files, 88, 176
XMP (Extensible Metadata Platform), 318
XPDF file format, 88

Z
zooming
    magnifying layers with, 283
    reflow and magnification with, 114, 115